DISCARD

Third World
Literary Fortunes

Third World Literary Fortunes

Brazilian Culture and Its International Reception

Piers Armstrong

Lewisburg
Bucknell University Press
London: Associated University Presses

© 1999 by Associated University Presses, Inc.

All rights reserved. Authorization to photocopy items for internal or personal use, or the internal or personal use of specific clients, is granted by the copyright owner, provided that a base fee of $10.00, plus eight cents per page, per copy is paid directly to the Copyright Clearance Center, 222 Rosewood Drive, Danvers, Massachusetts 01923. [0-8387-5404-X/99 $10.00+8¢ pp, pc.]

Associated University Presses
440 Forsgate Drive
Cranbury, NJ 08512

Associated University Presses
16 Barter Street
London WC1A 2AH, England

Associated University Presses
P.O. Box 338, Port Credit
Mississauga, Ontario
Canada L5G 4L8

The paper used in this publication meets the requirements
of the American National Standard for Permanence of Paper
for Printed Library Materials Z39.48-1984.

Library of Congress Cataloging-in-Publication Data

Armstrong, Piers, 1962–
    Third World literary fortunes : Brazilian culture and its international reception / Piers Armstrong.
       p.   cm.
    Includes bibliographical references and index.
    ISBN 0-8387-5404-X (alk. paper)
    1. Brazilian literature—Appreciation—Foreign countries.
2. Brazilian literature—20th century—History and criticism.
3. Brazilian literature—19th century—History and criticism.
4. Brazil—Civilization. I. Title. II. Title: 3rd World literary fortunes.
PQ9555.A76   1999
869.09′981—dc21   98-43783
                                                                                CIP

PRINTED IN THE UNITED STATES OF AMERICA

Contents

Preface	7
Acknowledgments	9
Introduction	11

1. *Modernismos*: The Historical Character of Modern 21
   Brazilian Literature in the Context of Latin America
2. The Brazilian Writers and Their Work 45
   João Guimarães Rosa 45
   Machado de Assis, Mário de Andrade, Carlos Drummond
      de Andrade 71
   Jorge Amado 90
3. Domestic and International Reception 110
   João Guimarães Rosa 110
   Machado de Assis, Mário de Andrade, Carlos Drummond
      de Andrade 128
   Jorge Amado 133
   North American Critical Perspectives of Brazilian
      Literature 146
   Comparative International Reception of Brazilian and
      Spanish American Modernisms 150
4. Socioanthropology and Popular Culture 158
   Gilberto Freyre and Brazilian Popular Cultural
      Identity 159
   The Hegemony of Rio de Janeiro 172
   Carnaval and Social Theories 182
   Music as a National Cultural Forum 203
   Shifting Aesthetic Fault Lines and Cultural
      Fortunes 213
5. Third World Culture on the Market 221
   Brazilian Modernism versus Socioanthropological
      Populism 223
   Jorge Amado: Compatability of His Project and the
      Emerging Popular Cultural Ideology 229
   João Guimarães Rosa: The Interpretation of His
      Reception as a Paradigm for Brazilian Modernism 236

Notes	242
Bibliography	249
Index	257

Preface

The ideas in this book were gradually gestated during my studies in the Romance Linguistics and Literature Program at UCLA. I particularly thank the following professors: Carlos Quicoli, for conceiving and administering the program, which was highly flexible and afforded intellectual freedom; to Eric Gans for sheer intellectual acuity and admirably efficient academic direction of his many graduate students, including being in his office and available; to Claude Hulet, my chair, who let me cut my own course, and while exceptionally knowledgable about Brazilian literary history is also a humanist, sensitive to the cultural import of non-academic endeavors.

Outside UCLA, I thank Dr. Rowan Ireland, Australian Brazilianist and sociologist, a model of meaningful interaction between the academe and the world, who invited me to work with him and facilitated a long sojourn in Bahia; and Brazilian literary historian Massaud Moisés for his scholarship as a resource, his intellectual honesty as a guide, and his kindness in receiving me in São Paulo. I also wish to thank the librarians who diligently gather materials from afar, such as John Horacek at La Trobe and various UCLA librarians - your efforts really do make a big long term difference. Two Brazilian institutions were central to my research, the Arquivo João Guimarães Rosa at the Instituto de Estudos Brasileiros (U. S. P.), and the Fundação Casa Jorge Amado in Salvador; thanks to the founders for their determination.

If there is any literary sensibility in this study I originally owe it to my mother, Dr. Judith Armstrong, and further thank her for many instances of support with editing and everything else, as well my father, Greg Armstrong, for his vital long-distance organizational support through my continental meanderings.

Without a fixed list, I thank the many people who extended their generosity to me, and hope I reciprocate. Finally, I thank the authors discussed for the courage and labor of their solitary geniuses;

separately, I bow to the places in the world made beautiful by the love of beauty of a preponderant part of the populace at some point in the past, and I wave to the living communities engaged in the same process today. There is always a moral in the aesthetic, always a form to the moral.

Acknowledgments

I am grateful to the following for permission to reprint (from) the following items, and collectively register that they reserve all rights for all countries of the world for the respective items: Mangione, Filhos & CIA Ltda. for "Conversa de Botequim" (Noel Medeiros Rosa e Oswaldo Gogliano, 1936) and "João Ninguém" (Noel Medeiros Rosa, 1970); Gilherme Araújo Prod. Art. Ltda. for "Menino do Rio" (Caetano Veloso); Civilização Brasileira for *Guimarães Rosa* (Series: Coleção Fortuna Crítica 6) edited by Eduardo Coutinho; Editora Record for *Dona Flor e seus dois maridos, historia moral e de amor* by Jorge Amado; T.A. Queiroz, Editor, Ltda. for *História da Inteligência Brasileira*, Vol. VII, by Wilson Martins; Editora Cultrix and Massaud Moisés for *A Literatura Brasileira Através dos Textos* and *História da Literatura Brasileira* (Vol. II, Romantismo e Realismo) by Massaud Moisés.

Introduction

The Enigma

IF SPANISH AMERICA AND LATIN AMERICA ARE OFTEN USED AS synonymous terms, what is the position of Brazil? Why, amidst the jubilant success of Spanish American writers in the 1960s, were there no Brazilians in the ranks? What are the roles of non-Latin ethnocultural elements in the world's largest Latin nation? What do outsiders see in Brazil, who articulated the predominant images and why do they prevail? What cultural manifestations do no penetrate beyond the domestic realm? This book postulates a speculative answer to these questions.

The international reception of twentieth-century Brazilian literature can only be understood in the context of two contradictory cultural agencies: the literary canon as established by academic literary criticism, and the powerful extraliterary imagery of another Brazil, developed intellectually by humanist social scientists and popularly through a perspective which might be called either folk wisdom or international tourism. These last two terms concern the different perspectives of the popular classes within Brazil and of foreign visitors. The intersection of these viewpoints is represented by the experience of Rio's *carnaval*,[1] a uniquely Brazilian event attracting, on the one hand, the ordinary people, and, on the other, the foreign tourist. The mythology of this annual ritual functions very effectively for both audiences, as well as for the world which has never been to Brazil—to the extent that the ensemble virtually defines Brazilian civilization as a cultural phenomenon. From it, and its constituent symbolism, social scientists have extrapolated abstract theses of national identity concerning civic values, psychological identity, political attitudes, and religious beliefs. Although the event occupies only a few days of the year, it has become difficult to sustain any discourse about Brazilian national identity without reference to carnaval.

At the periphery of a world cultural economy which centers around Europe and the U.S., Brazil presents a disparity between socioeconomic underdevelopment and cultural development as registered in the dissemination of a European intellectual agenda. There is inevitably a sort of cultural schizophrenia caused by the disparity between Brazil's gross material poverty and the intellectual privilege of what is a conventional (Western-type) intelligentsia. This contradiction has its political correlate in an authoritarian civil society economically based on extreme disparity of income distribution. The continuity between political and cultural oligarchies would appear to be perfectly sustainable, were it not for an international audience which valorizes more the cultural expression of the disenfranchised Brazilian masses than it does the cultural production of the Brazilian elite. European taste savors the exotic in Brazil, and thus, socially speaking, the popular over the elite, and, ethnically speaking, the Afro-Brazilian and the Amerindian over the Euro-Brazilian. In this sense the European perspective contradicts the Brazilian social hierarchy, which holds the Euro-Brazilian elite as the natural leader of national society and as a class, or caste, surpassed only by the Europeans (and North Americans) themselves.

It is significant that Brazilian literature does not reflect the steady rise of carnaval as a cultural icon. The popular festivities dominated by the semiliterate masses are often avoided by the small upper echelon from which Brazil's intellectual and literary intelligentsia is drawn. This elite is not only white but also manifestly Eurocentric, whereas the amalgam of races in the popular mass is described as "coffee-colored" and thought of as culturally "other." "Otherness" is usually a negative term, invoked to indicate deviation from a European norm. However, in the case of Brazil, the reductive connotations of otherness go beyond the general signification of non-European. "The other" is recognized, and celebrated, as specifically Afrocentric. Carnaval foregrounds an ethnic axis which has its roots in the Recôncavo region of Bahia (that is, the coastal area around the Baía de Todos os Santos and the city of Salvador, the capital of Brazil through the greater part of the slavery era) but finds its most conspicuous expression in the Rio carnaval (a large part of the poor and dark-skinned element of the Rio population having ancestral ties to Bahia and the Brazilian *Nordeste*[2]). The Rio carnaval has little to do with other lines of the Afro-Brazilian cultural heritage, such as that of the state of Maranhão in the North, and even less with the non-Afro-Brazilian elements.

In this sense, commentary on extraliterary processes such as folklore and tourism become pertinent to the elucidation of a writer's work, even though they are not the themes of that work. Several distinct points must be made. The first concerns the constitution of the literary object. Both the gestation and the reception of the literary work contribute to the production of the cultural object, predicated on a dynamic relation between author and reader, and mediated by everything from publishers' marketing strategies to abstract elements of influence such as the cultural education, values, and expectations of the audience. The text itself merely occupies one position along an axis which might be perceived as a cultural argument to which a variety of persons will adhere or defer. The center of this axis is language, both in the horizontal or mechanical sense of a commonly interpretable code, and in the vertical sense of an ideological *communitas,* that is, a mutually recognized set and sense of cultural values and symbols. This axis, like a chain, is as strong as its weakest link: a masterpiece in an obscure language, or about a completely unfamiliar context, will remain unread. Curiously, however, the powerful and mysterious agency of human subjectivity makes this logic far from linear: a concentration of energy at one node along the axis can compensate for absence at another, or invent a substitute. Shakespearean criticism, which every year produces a vastly greater mass of text than the writer's own output, demonstrates the infinite possibilities for appropriation of the literary text. The *Popul-Vuh* cannot, *grosso modo,* be read on its own terms, that is, in the original. Its mythological and contextual frame or reference is largely unfamiliar. And yet the text is included in progressive anthologies of Spanish American literature, on the grounds that it is literature and comes from one of the lands represented in the anthology. This commendable gesture is ethically rather than aesthetically conceived, seeking belatedly to compensate for an initial denial of recognition of pre-Colombian indigenous literature. The mystery of the precise ethnicity of the ancient Egyptians, and the controversial retrospective association of their cultural prestige to various heritages, is a strong illustration of the creativity of appropriation, and the fact that absence within a node of the axis can incite compensatory energy in another node. Hitler's notorious "fiction," *Mein Kampf,* though read by very few people, remains a powerful negative talisman in the collective imagination because the general discourse on the Holocaust (developed beyond the context of the composition of Hitler's work) retroactively redefines or reassigns its meaning. The text as represented by its title has become one of the perverse poetic symbols associated with the evil of the subsequent historical experience.

Such examples illustrate the process of appropriation in an expansive, or "occupation of absence," manner. But the reconstitution of cultural arguments may, of course, take other directions, including simple decline into oblivion. Literary canons are arbitrary constructs, themselves subject to reinvention: Milton, once celebrated as the greatest English writer, is today little read, not because his work has somehow become any less perfect, but simply because of a decline in the pertinence of his worldview, the puritan vision. In the mutating twentieth-century canon of nineteenth-century American literature, Longfellow was replaced by the once-snubbed Poe, who is now ceding interest to previously obscure black women testimonial writers.

From such examples emerge three key issues: the complexity of the production process as it stretches along the axis reaching from writer to reader; the relation of the literary to the cultural whole, best conceived as an ongoing dialog; and the pertinence of extraliterary cultural discourse to the global situation of a literary text.

In the case of Brazilian literature the overview is crucial, given that the external perception of Brazilian culture is predominantly shaped by extraliterary concerns. Only through such a double exposure can a phenomenon which was previously a matter of mere curiosity be used to shed light on both the literary and the extraliterary in terms of the implicit conflict of ideas regarding cultural identity. The humanistic discourse of Brazilian social science has interacted with folk wisdom to sustain the belief that Brazil is blessedly free of the racial tensions of the United States (or anywhere that white meets other), and in the idea that Brazilian national identity is encapsulated in (Rio's) carnaval. The first idea has fascinated foreign social scientists, particularly Americans, and the second has been successfully marketed to the international audience, including tourists and readers or viewers outside Brazil. Within Brazil, however, this as it were "magical realist" identification is largely irrelevant to the Eurocentric elite, which tends to measure progress by the degree of approximation to Western prosperity and the conventions of rational discourse.

Brazilian literature adheres to the Western artistic tradition and by and large has reflected European developments throughout its history. But even more than the literary work itself, which at least draws directly on an immediate ethnic environment very different from the European, academic literary criticism faithfully reflects the European model. This is again understandable in that the European fascination with the other has lent it a certain prestige as the protagonist or subject of works of art, whereas, in the domain of criticism, the hegemony of Western rationalism is as powerful as ever, even in works whose intention is to denounce such a hegemony.

Why then does the discourse of Brazilian social science, whose speakers are drawn from the same elite, not find itself in the same Euro-mimetic situation as literature? Without attempting to explicate the ideological genesis of Brazilian social science, it seems that socioanthropology has successfully appropriated the internationally fetishized object, that is, Brazilian popular culture, while Brazilian literature has not. However, this does not mean that Brazilian socioanthropology is more free of deviation from European epistemological authority than is literature.[3] It is European anthropological fascination with the other which makes Brazilian society an exceptionally interesting case study for both Europeans and Brazilians. Brazilian anthropology could be surveyed as a reflection of European concerns, first with the inferiority of other races (an obsessive theme during the late nineteenth century) and later with the fear of the destructive power of eugenic theories of differentiation, and the search for harmony in multiethnic interaction. The Nazi experience on the one hand, and the transnational migration of the later twentieth century on the other, have become key issues in and motifs of contemporary civilization, and made Brazil, with its mythology of Utopian racial harmony, a vital point of reference.

In literature, however, the twentieth century has tended to turn against simplistic notions of national identity. The great Brazilian literature of the middle part of this century—represented notably by Guimarães Rosa but also exemplified in the work of Clarice Lispector—followed an individualist imperative at the expense of essentialism, that is, a formulaic definition of national identity. Yet it is precisely that lack of essentialism, of recognizable national representation, that has cost Brazilian writers so dearly in terms of penetration of the international market. Their impact has been tangentially different from that of the successful Spanish American writers of the *Boom,* who brought Latin America to the literary forefront precisely because they provided their audience with an ideological and historical panorama for the interpretation of world history in an age of ideological dissipation and significational dissolution. Hence our initial enigma of the dearth of Brazilians in the ranks of successful Latin-American writers during the period of the *Boom.*

The case of Guimarães Rosa is helpful, as a particular instance of the general framework in which two bodies of thought operate, but of which only one—Brazilian social science—is in successful dialog with the international audience. Rosa's receptive destiny is attributable to a paradigmatic logic rather than to particular circumstances—such as difficulty of translation, lack of publisher support, political opposition, and so on—which might prevent a writer from reaching a target audience. And while Rosa is the most extreme case in point, the same logic applies to other major Brazilian writers, such as Joaquim Machado de Assis, Mário de Andrade, and Carlos Drummond de Andrade, even though the extraordinary heterogeneity of these writers—itself proof of the maturity and modernity of Brazilian literature—precludes any attempt to confine the Brazilian literary tradition to a restricted pattern of form or content. Modern Brazilian literature presents a diversity comparable to that of European nations, the result of a Eurocentric education system.

There is however one significant counterexample to the reception phenomenon: Jorge Amado is the only Brazilian writer to have penetrated the world literary market in any substantial way. In terms of the argument of this book he is the exception that proves the rule. Amado's subject matter is compatible with that of the social anthropologists who locate Brazilian identity on the Bahia-Rio carnaval axis, a restrictive interpretation of the country's cultural heritage. To use the imagery of radio signals, one might say that the spectrum of ethnocultural diversity in Brazil is subject to blackout when it comes to international transmission, with the exception of a relatively narrow frequency band. The diversity of Brazilian literature is subject to a similar filtering process, which operates without regard to the putative artistic superiority of writers other than Amado, or to Amado's courage in presenting the masses, rather than the Eurocentric elite, as the narrative subject. But given his tremendous popularity both within and outside Brazil, it is important to recognize the divergence between the indulgent international and popular perspective, and Amado's domestic reception in academic literary circles, which has on the whole been very negative.

The first chapter of this book provides a context for the argument that Brazilian writers are much more difficult to unite in terms of a common project than most Spanish American writers, a situation which ultimately gives them less purchase on the international market. It includes a historical review of modern Brazilian literature, with emphasis on the difference between the development of Brazilian and Spanish American literatures; the relatively cosmopolitan maturity of nineteenth-century Brazilian literature; the lack of a Brazilian "anxiety of influence" in relation to European cultural domination and the lack of adherence to Pan-(Latin) Americanism; the Brazilian divergence from orthodox leftist ideologies and dissociation from the grand political adventures uniting the Hispanic world against perceived fascist, imperialist or otherwise evil forces (the Spanish-American War, the Spanish civil war, the political histories of Cuba and Nicaragua); and the absence of *engagement* in Brazilian writing. On most of these points Jorge Amado deviates significantly from his Brazilian counterparts, finding more in common with *Boom* writers such as Gabriel García Márquez.[4]

The second chapter details the background of the five major Brazilian writers under discussion: Guimarães Rosa, Machado de Assis, Mário de Andrade, Carlos Drummond de Andrade, and Jorge Amado. This exercise demonstrates the heterogeneity of the group, precluding any notion of a neat Brazilian rubric. Machado de Assis illustrates the precocious maturation of Victorian Brazilian literature, his work diverging thematically and ideologically from the international mythologizing of Brazil through its central motif of ambiguity. Mário de Andrade, who incarnated the spirit of *Modernismo*—the key nationalist moment in Brazilian literature—is essential to any understanding of the ideological and aesthetic vacillations of this movement; his chef d'oeuvre, *Macunaíma, o herói sem nenhum caráter,* is analyzed in terms of its ironic handling of the question of primitivist national mythology. Drummond is present because of his stature as a twentieth-century poet and his deviation from what might be called the Carmen Miranda syndrome, that is, the formulaic representation of Brazilian national culture in terms of a Rio carnaval with Bahian roots. Finally, the case of Jorge Amado presents a number of key issues: his orthodox Marxism, which implies an external perspective even in the treatment of regionalist subjects; the subsequent development of a Utopian vision resting on a highly essentialist account of Brazil's unique racial miscegenation; and his characteristically populist narrative mode, hailing back to eighteenth-and nineteenth-century narrative formulas, which makes Amado tremendously readable even for uneducated readers. The question of miscegenation is treated at some length because it demonstrates conclusively the continuity of cultural vision between Amado and the humanist socioanthropological line started by Gilberto Freyre. In Rosa's case the biographical data significantly illustrates the writer's Borgesian lack of concern with politics.[5]

The third chapter addresses the question of the domestic and international reception of all five writers, though focusing on the release of Guimarães Rosa's masterpiece, *Grande Sertão: Veredas*, in the English-speaking world. The general pattern decipherable from the various fortunes of these writers is one of domestic apotheosis complemented by international obscurity—with the signal exception of Jorge Amado. This pattern is then cast against a contrary one in the case of the Spanish American *Boom* writers. The North American market—in terms of both scholarship and commercial success—is the testing ground adopted.

The fourth chapter examines Brazilian humanist sociology and anthropology (socioanthropology). The development of this discipline is traced through a number of scholars, particularly Euclides da Cunha, Gilberto Freyre, Sérgio Buarque de Holanda, and Roberto da Matta. The cultural context which underlies the Utopian vision is also considered in popular artistic praxis: the aestheticization or mythologizing of Rio in the samba of the 1930s; the general history of the carnaval; the emergence of a privileged ethnoaesthetic space in Bahia, first through the musicians associated with the Tropicalista movement of the 1960s, and later in the re-Africanization of the carnaval of Salvador in the mid 1970s and its rivaling of the Rio carnaval from the late 1980s on. The substitution of Salvador for Rio as the Brazilian carnaval par excellence is conceived as a recuperation of the artistic roots of the Rio carnaval, but also as a sort of cultural rarefaction consistent with the preeminence of the Bahia-Rio axis as the privileged vein of cultural and spiritual identity.

The final chapter brings together the literary and cultural investigations of the previous chapters: the compatibility of Amado's project with the logic of "socio-musicultural intellectual populism," that is, the Utopian apologia of Brazilian Afrocentric multiculturalism; the irrelevance of Guimarães Rosa in this frame, and hence his international obscurity; and the embracing of Rosa by Eurocentric literary scholars at the expense of Jorge Amado.

Third World
Literary Fortunes

1
Modernismos: The Historical Character of Modern Brazilian Literature in the Context of Latin America

THE RECEPTION OF JOÃO GUIMARÃES ROSA AND JORGE AMADO can be interpreted, in a contrasting duality, as symptomatic of the aesthetic and ideological underpinnings of modern Brazilian literature generally. The positive domestic and negative international reception of Guimarães Rosa is merely the sharpest illustration of a global situation and is replicated in the case of the other leading domestically canonized writers studied here—Machado de Assis, Mário de Andrade, and Carlos Drummond de Andrade.

An inverse receptive pattern applies to Amado, a literary black sheep whose work displays ideological continuity with Brazilian humanist socioanthropology (see chapter 4) characterized by the celebration of popular culture privileging mulatto ethnicity.

The articulation of popular identity is predicated upon an essentialist logic, that is, a confident assertion of a unique cultural identity, relatively insensitive to individual subjectivity and eccentricity. In general, European modernism—and mature Brazilian modernism—can be inscribed within the spirit of subjective individualism. Spanish American literature, on the contrary, has displayed a strong tendency to essentialism. The work of Alejo Carpentier, Octavio Paz, and the *Boom* novelists has been characterized by cohesive group identity, concern with the specific regional psycho-cultural identity of Latin America and its contrasts to Europe, with particular attention to ethnic essence, by the obligation of political conscientization and its contingent logic of group identity analysis, and above all by the sense of an historic mission to rewrite history, expressed in the warping mimesis of the work of art but also in the nonobjective discourse of the critical sociohistorical essay.

All these characteristics are conspicuously absent from the Brazilian writers studied here, with the exception of Jorge Amado, whose ideological project and whose thematic interests, leaving aside his general disinclination from the essay and other nonfiction genres, are largely compatible with those of the *Boom* Spanish Americans. Part of Amado's international appeal, we would argue then, derives precisely from his essentialism: Amado offers an artistic celebration of an appealing formulaic notion of Brazilian identity, developed by the author and also within the Brazilian humanist socioanthropological tradition and focusing on the popular culture of the Bahia-Rio mulatto axis.

Given that the curiosity of the international obscurity of Brazilian literature derives largely from the contrasting conspicuous international prosperity of the *Boom,* it is important to explore the widely circulated fallacy of a monolithic "Latin American" literature.

The terms "Spanish" and "Latin" are used almost interchangeably in studies of the *Boom*. One must, however, contrast the two literary traditions, both to dispel erroneous assumptions about the overall character of Brazilian literature and to provide a portrait, albeit minimal and selective, of that other literary current which both makes the Brazilian case strange and affords a better contextual perspective for the situation of Amado.

Spanish American *modernismo*[1] was initiated just prior to the turn of the century largely by the Nicaraguan poet Rubén Darío. Although both the Spanish American and Brazilian literary traditions reflected nineteenth-century trends in Europe, the former was most solidly represented by regionalism and the attempt to portray through literature and give account to particular sociohistorical realities in a Eurocentric but isolated and ignored continent. Darío, who visited Paris and met Verlaine, used aesthetic techniques developed in French symbolism to recast Spanish American literature from its status as a locus of antiquated and provincial underachievement. The prodigious virtuosity of the poet made him a sort of continental inspiration, and he spent periods in the capitals of Chile, Argentina, and other Spanish American nations. Darío's professional career contributed symbolically to the cultural restitution of Spanish American integrity which had been undermined by the political fragmentation of the passage from Spanish colonial dominion to independence. For the Nicaraguan, these greater South American states provided legitimate satellite metropolises of Paris. But as a Central American, Darío was also keenly aware of the new global historical trauma faced by Spanish America in the form of the impending neocolonial hegemony of the United States, made tangible by the problematic late passage to independence from Spain by Cuba, United States interference and, finally, the Spanish-American War. Darío was the literary spearhead of two successive, paradoxically counterpointed psycho-cultural revolutions: the break from the artistic shadows of the Iberian peninsular to integration with Paris-centric cosmopolitan modernism, and the reassertion of an ideology of Latin-Hispanic communion in opposition to the specter of North American Anglo-Saxon philistinism (represented as a Caliban and set against the spiritually enlightened grace of Spanish America in *Ariel,* José Enrique Rodó's enormously influential essay of 1900).

During this period, which lasted roughly until World War I, Brazilians were largely indifferent to such a dramatic perception of alien menace. Neither was there the sense of a quantum leap associated with Spanish American *modernismo;* Brazilian literature had developed more organically through the nineteenth century in tandem with European currents, so that one cannot speak in the same way of a sudden, new aesthetic and ideological radicalism. The *carioca* (i.e., of Rio de Janeiro) elite had for some time considered themselves as transplanted but fully fledged Europeans—not just in the negative, racist sense of a white minority differentiating itself from the colored masses, but also in terms of indulging a cultural consumer lifestyle parallel to that of the European elite, enjoying the reliable importation, with a relatively small lag, of European cultural practices and fashion.

There is nothing in the Brazilian nineteenth-century tradition corresponding to either of the two seminal Argentinian literary works of the period, Sarmiento's *Facundo,* with its Manichaean denunciation of South American unenlightened barbarism, and Hernández's archetypal celebration of the cultural regionalism of the *gaucho* in *Martin Fierro.*

The major Brazilian writer of the pre-realist period, José de Alencar (1829–77), had grappled with the problem of cultural identity, developing an identificational mythology nominally privileging the Amerindian (*O guarani, Iracema*) and writing a series of regionalist frescoes (*O gaúcho, O sertanejo, As minas de prata*). In *Iracema* in particular, Alencar attempted a literary implementation of an authentically Brazilian Portuguese lexicon with substantial indigenous influence; indeed, the title, an anagram of "America" but defined by Alencar as deriving from Tupi-Guarani words for 'honey lips" is, despite its dubious etymological pedigree, a splendid example of his naïve but keen sense of a new civilization. Alencar's characters penetrated the popular psyche and achieved a popularity that continues today.

This sort of national cultural critical analysis was continued in a very different way by the notable naturalist writer, Aluízio de Azevedo (*O mulato, O caboclo*). Azevedo's one great work, *O Cortiço,* significantly locates the urb of Rio as the definitive Brazilian cultural locus. This Zola-inspired novel (there are clear reflections of *L'assomoir*) follows the fortunes of two Portuguese immigrants, one of whom utilizes astutely and cruelly his European "superiority" to ascend socially while the other, imbued with courage and virtue but not foresight, declines, in accordance with the ideas of contemporary pseudoscientific sociobiological laws, into tropical degeneration under the influence of the Delilah-esque mulatto[2] temptress Rita Baiana. Rather than pursuing the pure or original ethnic motif through regionalism, the novel presents Rio as a metropolitan ethnocultural crossroads and social laboratory (in a manner comparable to certain literary evocations of twentieth-century New York).

Brazil may be perceived here as a racial but not a cultural melting pot, for though blood may mix, particularly through transitory sexual attraction, the system preserves the discreet stratification of a hierarchy of cultural praxes with the European at the top (indeed, the upwardly mobile protagonist abandons his black concubine after extracting years of labor from her, marries a white woman, and sets out to acquire a peerage from the court, thus underlining the differentiation between sexual interaction and the social establishment of family). Azevedo presents a very concrete Darwinian perspective which assigns maximal social fitness to European whites. The writer does not go so far as to suggest the eventual demographic elimination of the darker element of the population. However, many Brazilian intellectuals of the decades around the turn of the century subscribed to quite literal positivist-influenced Darwinian notions whereby this would occur, and later government programs sponsoring European immigration did indeed partially realize this process (so that later Afro-Brazilian radicals speak of an alleged black ethnic genocide). It could be said also that Azevedo was merely giving a literary-(pseudo)scientific interpretation to the urban reality of Rio, where the white elite was for most of the nineteenth century greatly outnumbered by the pool of blacks and mulattos (a situation contrary to the American south and to all American centers of the nineteenth century except in the Caribbean).

It is important in this regard to grasp the peculiarity of Rio de Janeiro within the South American fold. The prodigious industrial and demographic expansion of Buenos Aires at the very end of the nineteenth century parallels that of São Paulo. Rio, however, had, through the historical debacle of Napoleon's Iberian incursions, become not just the capital of a newly independent nation but a seat of Empire. Pedro II was emperor from 1841 to 1889—thus roughly concomitant with Queen Victoria—and the only American monarch. He commanded fourteen languages and governed as a sort of enlightened despot in a society where a preindustrial economy was maintained through slavery (abolished in 1888). The emperor was not in fact a real despot; he maintained the political lead by deft management of the conservative and liberal camps in a somewhat tenuous system of constitutional fluidity. The two groups, which could not really be called parties, by agreement alternated in dominating the cabinet of ministers, an arrangement which contrasts, for example, with the ongoing violence between the two camps in Colombia which García Márquez has explored. With the exception of the long-winded and bloody Paraguayan War, which did not impact excessively on the court in a direct sense, this was a peaceful period of cultural stability and prosperity for Brazil.

Within this context, Brazilian literature developed considerable maturity in most of the successive literary genres dominant in the "capital of the nineteenth century," Paris. Brazilian literary historians are thus able to use the familiar rubrics of Romanticism (with the invented Amerindian mythology substituting for the continental fascination with the Middle Ages), Naturalism, Realism, Parnassianism, and Symbolism. All of these genres, at least as practiced in prose, were successively assimilated and partially integrated by Joaquim Maria Machado de Assis (1839–1908). This writer is still considered Brazil's greatest by most critics, a literary historiographical precocity absolutely divergent from the patterns of development in Spanish American nations. In relation to Rio's intellectually European character—irrespective of the arbitrary subjectivity of such a construction—the other crucial fact concerning the master is that he was himself mulatto (more exactly, quadroon) but left not a single conspicuous trace of this enormously important biographical detail in his literary testament.[3] Machado de Assis is simultaneously the incarnation of a impressive process of maturation of Brazilian letters, and of a psychological focus on the sociological experience of the white elite and not the colored masses.

There were virtually no significant novelists in Brazil early in the century. Dominating the mid-century, Alencar successfully cultivated regionalist themes and also "Indianism." The latter is from an antiracist perspective a condescending fetishization of indigenous protagonists, who by Alencar's time were sufficiently marginalized and rare as a real demographic element as to be appropriable and ennobled in literature. By the later years of Machado de Assis, the literary establishment was sufficiently substantial as to legitimize the establishment of a national academy, of which he was the first president, and also had the cultural self-confidence to turn its attention to its immediate metropolitan environs. Like Athens, with its universal suffrage—for free men—and virtually invisible slave population, the rarefied, white, and bourgeois ambient of Machado's work reminds us of the limits of access to Brazilian civil society. However, the shift from the exotic ethnic other, lost in history, to the local contemporary bourgeois is by itself an enormous psycho-cultural achievement; Brazilian literature had moved from the search for a sort of American para-medieval mythology of heroes to realism and even the modern antihero.

The transition in Brazilian literature between the major literary movements was inspired by external models as much as moments of internal dissent. Machado de Assis underwent an initial romantic phase, a realist phase, and eventually found his voice in an introspective and intensely interior disposition of characters which suggest symbolist withdrawal and even Proustian psycho-emotional analysis; further, he experimented with antirealist fantastic elements. With some notable exceptions, or rather adaptations to local conditions, a Eurocentric mentality prevailed in the developing Brazilian intelligentsia through to World War I, while Rio "café society" directly paralleled the felicitous bourgeois gentility of the *Belle Époque*. Given the socioracial context and consequent issues of identity, it would be problematic to speak of an untraumatized psyche or attitude. However, any such alienation was pragmatically balanced by both a confident sense of successful political transition to the new century in the form of the Republic which had replaced the Empire, and general economic prosperity. Just as there was no painful sense of needing to catch up with Europe by transcending regionalism, neither was there was the sentiment, so keenly felt in the Spanish American world, of forced sociocultural conscientization occasioned by North American imperialist encroachments.

Certain writers, notably Lima Barreto, adopted an *engagé* approach of social criticism. Barreto's *O triste fim de Policarpo*

Quaresma ridicules an idealist who strives to forward the indigenous Guarani language as a sort of Brazilian Esperanto, implicitly parodying the elite's lack of touch with the urban mulatto masses. But the overall pattern confirms the Machadian trajectory. The most poignant and probably the greatest symbolist poet, Cruz e Souza, was not mulatto but black; he adopts as major themes in his work the symbolist motifs of the swan and the color white. Overall, Brazilian letters from the 1880s, when the first really accomplished works with cosmopolitan spirit came out, through to World War I, existed comfortably in a satellite relation to the Parisian scene, with just enough autonomy and eccentricity to suggest a cultural confidence adequate to find a way between slavish imitation on the one hand, and on the other the embittering resentment or anxiety of being located at the margin. Despite its speed, Brazil's literary evolution was remarkably civil, smooth, and gradual. We simply do not encounter in the Brazilian context the sudden formal revolution of Darío, the geopolitical conscientization and the furious resentment of Rodó, and there is very little purchase on the notion that the New World was, painfully or gloriously, necessarily a different civilization from that of the continent.

A formal and ideological revolution in Brazilian letters did take place after World War I. The cumulative prestige of the avantgarde movement, taken as whole rather than in its various specific wings—some prewar, such as Cubism and the valorization of primitive art, others postwar, notably surrealism and the mass enthusiasm for jazz—made Paris in the immediate postwar years the center of formal innovation and ideological radicalism and a mecca to which rallied intellectuals from across the Americas. The literary innovations which would consequently sweep Spanish America and Brazil followed parallel paths—at least in the inaugural moment of the early 1920s—and are known respectively as *vanguardismo* and *Modernismo*. The heralds of these movements, the Chilean Vicente Huidobro and the Brazilian Oswald de Andrade, present strikingly similar profiles. Both enjoyed an advantageous social origin against which they rebelled with a degree of adolescent *épater le bourgeois* glee. Encountering the perfect *outré* antidote in Paris bohemia, they ignited formal revolutions at home— from the continent. Oswald de Andrade remained in Europe from 1922 to 1929 and it was from Paris that he launched his historic *Pau-Brasil* manifesto, just as Huidobro composed his masterpiece, the poem "Altazor" in Europe. Prior to this long sojourn, Oswald was one of the principal organizers of the *ur*-event of Brazilian *Modernismo,* the *Semana de Arte Moderna* held in 1922 in São

Paulo, a metropolis which by now had supplanted Rio as economic capital, and was also the center of intellectual and artistic innovation.

Through the course of the 1920s, various opposed movements emerged from the united revolutionary ranks of the *Semana*. Through a succession of radical discursive maneuvers (*Pau Brasil:* the celebration of Brazil's multiethnic and tellurian authenticity; *Antropofagia,* or cultural cannibalism) Oswald de Andrade articulated an intellectual reading of the uniquely Brazilian flexible ability to assimilate the alien, captured in the supreme historical metaphor of the Portuguese bishop made the supper of some Amerindian cannibals. Ever posturing at the forefront of internecine rivalry, he would later embrace Communism, for which cause Oswald theatrically rejected his earlier works (though he continued to publish them[4]). Oswald's rhetorical tropes and ideological movements are singular by both sheer audacity and as an unsurpassed christening act of original national identification, a euphoric apologia of Brazilian exoticism.

The formula of utilizing European radicalist aesthetic and political logics (the avant-garde and Marxism) to privilege a marginalized, exotic non-European community, and then to claim communion by osmosis (coincidence of nationality) with that community is nothing less than an archetypal procedure of twentieth-century Latin American intelligentsia, and it must be recognized that Oswald de Andrade gave an original and probably unsurpassed performance of this conceptual ballet.

But Brazilian modernism is perhaps made most singular in the Latin American context by the movements against which Oswald militated, notably the *Verde-Amarelo* group (green and yellow being the Brazilian national colors) of Cassiano Ricardo, Menotti del Picchia, and Plínio Salgado. These modernist writers participated in the initial celebration of the authentically Brazilian in theme and lexicon, but took the latent nationalism of this perspective in a completely different direction which lead to a politically conservative nationalism, the militant resurrection of Catholicism and, finally, fascism. Brazilian modernism is possibly unique in this deviation from Leftist political orthodoxy, and in this sense particularly at contrast with Spanish America. The Brazilian Literary Academy has continued to integrate surprisingly divergent political positions. The new generation of *Modernismo* in the 1930s was dominated by socially critical novelists from the *Nordeste* who were by in large Leftist, and whose two leading exemplars, Graciliano Ramos and Jorge Amado, were both communists. Brazilian letters through the twentieth century have, however, also been distinguished by a large number of writers who are more or less apolitical or not easily placed on the Left-Right spectrum, and whose ideological vocation is better described as spiritual rather than political. A very interesting example in this sense is the gifted poet Jorge de Lima, successively distinguished as a neo-Parnassian, a pasticher of Afro-Brazilian folklore, a social protest writer on the *Nordeste,* and, finally, as an eccentric Catholic mystic with surrealist influences.

The next, and final, identifiable generation of Brazilian modernism is known somewhat arbitrarily as the *geração de '45* (also: *Neo-Modernismo* [Tristão de Ataíde], or *Terceiro Movimento Modernista* [Massaud Moisés]).[5] This term does not refer to a cohesive movement; rather it indicates the closure within the interwar period of an evolving *Modernismo* materially documentable in its manifestos and/or identifiable group bondings. The writers of the *geração de '45* enjoyed the privilege of thematic and formal liberation established through early *Modernismo*'s nationalist subversion of what had been an extremely conventional, Eurocentric bourgeois artistic order, a dissension that gradually came to exercise a virtual hegemony within the creative intelligentsia. In this sense they were themselves conventionally rather than electively modernist.

The three most conspicuous writers of this generation, Guimarães Rosa, the feminist existentialist novelist Clarice Lispector (born 1925), and the engineer-poet, João Cabral de Melo Neto (born 1920), developed divergent, highly personal aesthetic philosophies which cannot easily be embraced within any school or group. The work of these writers can be seen as a sort of reaction against the pamphleteering of the first modernist period and the utilitarian social conscientization ethos of the second. In terms of their formal approach, these writers are united by an unstated credo of *l'art pour l'art,* a very deliberate, constructive aesthetic method. This implies a clear rejection of the puerile exuberance and spontaneity of the first moment of *Modernismo* and suggests a disinclination against the *engagé* stance of the second, as is expressed, for example, in this private declaration by Guimarães Rosa in 1947:

> All art, from now on, will have to be, more and more, literary construction. We are by now in a new era, we are already rehabilitating art after the long and unfortunate period of slackness, of a brutalization of the language, of loss of the prestige of style, of facile primitivism

and bad taste. . . . You will sense the "turn", the change of direction, in the best literature. In this, in fact, as with everything else, what happens here is a merely the reflection of what occurs in the really cultured countries. The order of the day is: construction, profundity, careful and painstaking elaboration of the "raw material" that inspiration provides, craftsmanship![6]

The fundamental subjective individualism of these writers would reveal original and mutually alien modes of creativity, each marked in their own way by a latent asociality in terms of conventional *engagé* mimetic obligations to a chosen *communitas,* that is, the expectation that the Brazilian writer articulate representative national types. Lispector's work is critical of gender relations rather than social hierarchies in the political sense, and phenomenally introspective and narcissistic. Cabral takes a tangentially opposite tack: developing his own version of Francis Ponge's "Parti Pris des Choses" doctrine, the master-image of *pedra* (stone) emerges as a totem in a style supposedly stripped of the subjective projection by a human poetic protagonist or voice onto its object ("Educação pela pedra," *Paisagens com Figuras*). If Lispector is a master articulator of psychic tropes, and Cabral an evoker of natural scenes (or human locations, such as a region or town apprehended in its own subjectivity rather than as the backdrop of a human protagonist), Guimarães Rosa is the quintessential virtuoso of the inherent poesy of language, comparable in this sense to Gerald Manley Hopkins. His subject matter is adapted from routine rustic scenes and folkloric reinterpretations of the same, recast so as to afford a masked colloquy on universal metaphysical questions, drawn from an eclectic reading of diverse literary and philosophical traditions.

Given this complete difference of artistic trajectory, if we leave aside the common focus on the literary craft itself, the *geração de '45,* in literary historiographical terms, can really only be defined negatively, that is, in terms of its rejection of previously privileged themes and consistent formal tendencies. The most fundamental common absence in these writers in relation to their modernist predecessors is the über-theme of Brazil itself. Guimarães Rosa notes the satellite relation of Brazil to Europe ("what happens here is a merely the reflection of what occurs in the really cultured countries"); this reality is not, however, cast as a traumatic but rather a natural circumstance, seamlessly inserted within his general exhortation to artistic excellence. By the time of these writers, it is as if the revolutionary nationalism of the inaugural Brazilian

Modernismo has revealed itself as a sterile iconoclasticism and imploded, as if the cathedral of Western High Art has reemerged at noon from the morning fog.

A genuine existentialist—and thus inherently at odds with any sort of national essence, Lispector's focus is so heavily interiorized, and psychic rather than social, that if a handful of place references were omitted the scenario could barely be recognized as Brazilian. Guimarães Rosa's regionalism exploits intensely the local natural animal and vegetable range and the linguistic repertoire of rural Minas. However, historical reference, even at the local level, is deliberately obfuscated, and there is almost no mention of a global picture of Brazil (this point is discussed further in the following chapter section). One of Cabral's key scenes is his native Recife in Pernambuco, but the sense is of a locale intimately known and felt in its own subjectivity and not as a microcosm or an illustrative insertion within a national context. His procedure is the opposite of the 1920s intellectual colonialism of the rest of the country by the *paulistano* (inhabitant of the city rather than the state of São Paulo), the confidence to wax fictionally, lyrically, and theoretically about the diverse corners of the vast nation state, exploiting the poetic impact of the exoticism of places usually unknown in truth to both writer and audience. Further, Cabral's philosophy of place is in a significant part of his opus applied to a secondary location outside Brazil—Seville, in Spain, where Cabral spent several years on a diplomatic post.

The second major negative attribute characterizing this generation—in contrast with both the politicization of the late 1920s *paulistanos* and, even more so, with the social testimony of the 1930s realist novelists of the *Nordeste*—concerns political perspective. Lispector is a counterhegemonic feminist thinker but offers no discussion of conventional political or ethnic questions; there is no evident problematization in her work of her own elite privilege as white and bourgeois (except in her last work, *A Hora da Estrela*). Cabral and Guimarães Rosa were both diplomats, an occupation in practical terms requiring an apolitical stance. Cabral was nominally Leftist and in 1952 was briefly ousted from the Foreign Service by Getúlio Vargas; his famous extended poem, *Morte e Vida Severina,* is a sort of mini-epic of the central social problem of the *Nordeste*—population movements spurred by drought—and thus can be inscribed within the literary discourse of conscientização or consciousness raising. The poem is, however, more exactly another evocation and disposition of scene, albeit human and hardpressed; there is not the sense of an historical protagonist and a program of action, of an exhortation to specific redemptive social action, but rather that of a meditation on the unfathomable resigned stoicism of the rural downtrodden, not dissimilar to the great nineteenth-century literary psychoanalyses of the Russian peasantry in Dostoyevsky and Tolstoy. Meanwhile, the bulk of Cabral's other work is deliberately desubjectified and even, theoretically, dehumanized, and thus apolitical. Guimarães Rosa is, however, the most singular incarnation of the complete political disengagement of the *geração de '45*. The novelist was posted in Hamburg from 1938 to 1942, and interned in Baden-Baden for four months. He attended the Paris Peace Conference in 1945 and the 9th Pan-American Conference in Bogotá in 1948. Not simply through his wide reading but in direct personal experience, then, circumstance created the optimum environment to inculcate an identification, if not with Brazilian domestic politics, then with the global drama and the clash of Left and Right. But there is simply no trace of political sentiment in Guimarães Rosa's work—not even the occasional glimpse of deprecation towards Nazism offered by Borges, the most conspicuously apolitical Latin American writer.[7]

The *geração de '45* declined the almost *de facto* obligation of Brazilian modernism to make affirmations of national identity, either in the manner of the first modernist generation's exoticist, fetishizing celebrations of a unique essence, or in the manner of the second generation's commitment to representative portrayals of a problematic contemporary social reality. The work of the second generation can very usefully be compared to Steinbeck. However, the Brazilian writers of the 1930s, reflecting an arbitrary and superstitious prestige of the country over the city and of the old over the new, favored the *Nordeste* as somehow more genuinely Brazilian than the rest of the country, particularly the southeast. This dismissal of the south, the industrial landscape, and, ethnically, the first-or second-generation Euro-Brazilian, suggests a subliminal cultural essentialism.

The *geração de '45* is fundamentally aestheticist, apolitical, and disinterested in the literary mission of national identification of Brazil as a transcendent thematic subject. The posture of this generation is, in a word, remarkably similar to that of Machado de Assis. Of course, the watershed of *Modernismo* stands between the old master and these writers, and their stylistic techniques are radically different. But I would argue that there are profound links between their respective perceptions of the role of the writer. We have already noted that there is minimal formal unification within the *geração de '45;* working with our negative logic of differentiation, however, we encounter a consistent motif: a curious detachment from all the ethnically exotic, and socially and politically problematic cultural aspects which Western audiences normally anticipate in literature from the Third World.

In order to understand this gradual process through the successive generations of *Modernismo,* from flamboyant revolution to subtle counterrevolution, it is informative to look more closely at the evolving intellectual position of the man who was both the principal artist and organizer and, after the event, the most important critic of the initial modernist phase, Mário de Andrade. Several of Mário's creative works of the 1920s, examined later in this chapter, are seminal texts of the first period of *Modernismo.* The writer's critical perspective, however, reveals an increasingly negative collective evaluation (that is, both in relation to his own work and that of others) of the literary qualities of the creative works of these early years, seen in retrospect as undisciplined and agitational rather than artistically profound. This judgment does not constitute a wholesale rejection of the movement. In fact, Mário maintained great authority as a commentator, through the 1930s until his death (1945). Though he balked on adhesion to the Communist cause, his political sentiments were progressive and distant from those of the *Verde-Amarelo* movement. With a pioneering participation in the 1930s in education projects for the popular classes, Mário remained socially *engagé* till his death, but rejected the political polarization of the 1930s. During this period the revolutionary tone dropped from his artistic vision, which actually became distinctly conservative, insisting on technique. His final critical position is a defense of the abstract value of *Modernismo,* particularly in the sense of championing the right to freedom in artistic projects, but, at the concrete level, a rejection of the artistic validity of many of the individual works actually produced; for Mário, the iconoclasticism of the movement was right in breaking the false barriers of bourgeois taste and Eurocentric focus, but deluded in its juvenile notion that the iconoclastic act in itself inferred the pedigree of the Parnassian muse. This is concisely stated in the following paragraphs of his essay, "O movimento modernista":

> What characterizes this reality imposed by the modernist movement is, in my view, the fusion of three fundamental principals: the permanent right to aesthetic inquiry, the modernization of the Brazilian artistic intelligentsia, and the establishing of a national creative consciousness. . . . The fundamental novelty was the conjunction

of these three standards in an organic whole in the collective consciousness. . . .

Though it incorporated figures and groups with a constructive sense, the modernist spirit which swept Brazil and determined the historic character of the national intelligentsia of the period was destructive. (1943, 242)

Mário's later fictional works were highlighted by disciplined attempts at classic genre formats, notably the orthodox short story. Indeed, Mário's main creative piece from the 1930s, a collection of short stories, was entitled *Belazarte*. Though his ongoing fame derives from his irreverent, iconoclastic work of the 1920s more than the later work, Mário's ultimate aesthetic perspective was surprisingly concomitant with that of the *geração de '45,* and this despite the gulf between his communitarian loyalty and political sense and their withdrawn individualism and political indifference.

Brazil's greatest poet, Carlos Drummond de Andrade, whose activity began in the later years of the first generation of *Modernismo* and continued, with growing prestige, through till the 1970s, followed an evolution of aesthetic philosophy largely parallel to that of his namesake Mário.

The fundamental differences between the developments of Brazilian *Modernismo* on the one hand, and on the other of Spanish American *modernismo, vanguardismo* and the *Boom* reveal quite divergent cosmovisions which for a brief moment—the Paris-centric, iconoclastic breakthrough of the post-World War I years—afforded some support to the assumption of a common reality between these two branches of Latin American civilization. The nineteenth century clearly presents qualitatively different paradigms in the two domains; another difference is observable in the master historical narratives of the twentieth century privileged by Spanish American and Brazilian writers as the civilizational frame to their work.

The stylistic culmination of Brazilian *Modernismo* in the *geração de '45* was characterized, according to our own account, by a negative response to the nationalist essentialism and sociopolitical criticism of the earlier generations of *Modernismo*. Further, though in 1945 Brazil emerged from fascist dictatorship and embarked on a twenty-year experiment with democracy unique in its history, the *geração de '45* was disengaged from the Leftist historico-materialist agenda dominant amongst European and consequently Brazilian intellectuals. Contrary to the Brazilian literary pattern, not only have Spanish American writers identified with—and in many ways come to lead—orthodox Leftist geopolitical thought, but also, from the 1890s on, they have encountered with chronological regularity crucial concrete historical dramas which fed their artistic vision with a necessary complement of social substance.

Though the prewar period spawned a fecund initial experimentation with modernist techniques in France, the impulse to social agitation which, in the Bretonian surrealist project managed to fuse Marxism with the implicit antihistorical character of Freudian thought, was largely due to the supremely disillusioning experience of the Great War—psychologically fratricidal, patricidal, and deicidal. The reactive iconoclasticism and antirationalist creative energy of the early postwar period was embraced and appropriated by both Spanish American and Brazilian writers.

In the Brazilian case, Oswald de Andrade (despite his tardy nominal adherence to Communism) seized on the vanguard's celebration of the primitive and developed a euphoric apologia of Brazilian history and *brasileiridade* (poetically renderable in English as "Braziliance"). Such essentialism is, of course, ultimately contradictory to dialectic materialism. The rapid emergence, of a very significant Right Wing nationalist faction in the Brazilian modernist camp is suggestive of the extent to which Oswald had imported the formal innovations of Western modernism without its conventional Leftist intellectual substrata.

The Spanish Americans, however, with the Spanish, embraced the surrealist program with a deeper sense of political conformity. The father of the *Boom,* Alejo Carpentier, was, while in Paris in the 1920s, a member of the Bretonian clique, and his crucial theoretical position on Latin America—that this continent, rather than Europe, is the natural home of the baroque—was really an insider's critique of Parisian surrealism. The same movement also holds a consciously articulated, seminal position in the thinking of Octavio Paz, reinforced by Breton's stays in Mexico, and Buñuel's residence there. But perhaps the most instructive case is that of Pablo Neruda, which brings us to the next great historical drama of the intellectual Pan-Hispanic imagination, the Spanish civil war. Neruda's great early work of the 1920s in *Residencia en la tierra,* much of it written in Burma, appears to present a fecund balance between his own originality, the influence of Parisian surrealism, and the imaginative estrangement afforded by the stimulatingly drastic cultural contrasts between rural Chile, various great cities, and the Orient. Through the politicization of the 1930s, and the personal experience of the Spanish civil war, Neruda came to adhere to socialist solidarity, and to embrace communism, the real ideological motor of his subsequent long and dominant career as a poet. The other great Spanish American poet of the era, the Peruvian César Vallejo, was also profoundly marked by the cause of the Republic. The war occupied a unique romantic political space in the mind of the entire Western artistic intelligentsia, and 1930s Barcelona has been vividly memorialized by writers from various countries. But it is Vallejo who offers the most radicalized apotheosis of this moment, with the haunting neoreligious imagery in his final work, *España, aparte de mi este cáliz*. Octavio Paz would eventually emerge as a political conservative, and has spoken of negative lessons drawn from the war regarding the Leftist project. Nevertheless, the sense of a moral cause and the cultural camaraderie were formative experiences for the great Mexicanist.

After World War II, the cold war provided the frame of reference for ideological positioning, and in the Latin world the reigning intellectual orthodoxy united Western-hemisphere Leftists against a perceived capitalist imperialism. The next great concrete historical drama, however, was the Cuban Revolution (with its sequels in Allende's Chile and Sandinista Nicaragua). The intolerance of Castro's regime eventually provoked discord amongst Leftists, represented in the figure of the Padilla affair in the late 1960s and early 1970s, and the notion of a Leftist hegemony in the Spanish American literary intelligentsia becomes, though not untenable, certainly more complex and problematic.[8] However, during the halcyon period of the *Boom* in the 1960s, Cuba provided not only an institutional base for radicals, but also the exciting prospect that Latin America had assumed center stage in the global war of liberation.

The demonization of the U.S. as the master of the capitalist system may have attenuated the trauma of the umbilical relation of Latin American intellectuals to Europe which was as strong in the 1960s as in the 1920s. Most of the masterpieces of the *Boom* were written in Barcelona, Paris, London, and elsewhere on the continent. For the *Boom* writers, who were sufficiently "incestuous" or bound by solidarity as to be cast, derisively or enviously, as a "Mafia," Paris was the natural capital, and the Hollywood and Alexandria of their historical and intellectual mythologies. The powerful charge of intellectual incest, fueled by the intimacy of the writers and the increasing tendency to insert self-referential metaliterary *clés* into their novels, provokes many questions beyond the scope of the present study: the problematic question of the real nature of the attachment to Europe; the portrayal of the Latin

American popular reality as alienated, in implicit opposition to the writers' own intellectual enlightenment, and so on.[9]

The crucial point, for our own purposes, is simply that the *Boom* writers worked together under a common umbrella. Despite their active involvement with European intellectuals in what might be called Sartrean Paris, they were united, despite diverse national origins, by their Pan-American status and existed as a collectivity to which non-(Latin) Americans would be welcome allies but cultural aliens. Their progressive politics were registered in a variety of arenas and formats, notably Cuba's official review and cultural association, *Casa de las Americas*. While García Márquez was literally a political ally of Castro, the cohesion with Cuba is perhaps best captured by the subtler political status of Carlos Fuentes. Without adhering to communist discipline, Fuentes as critic embraced the revolutionary posture, focusing on cultural imperialism and corrupt elites. These commentaries were complemented in Fuentes's creative work, which focused on the frustration of the Mexican Revolution, a historical perspective allowing ambivalence as regards his definitive political position in contemporary events.

All of the *Boom* writers are distinguished by fertile experimentation with formal innovation. The central masterwork of the *Boom* remains García Márquez' *Cien años de soledad*. Apart from its phenomenal popularity, and its status as a definitive exemplification of the formal procedures of magical realism, this novel is exemplary of the subjacent ideology of the *Boom* in that it integrates a number of progressive historical readings and political protests. The author has observed that the historical inspiration for the book comes from the nineteenth-century cycle of internecine violence between Liberals (or Federalists) and Conservatives in his native Colombia. The twentieth-century imperialism is represented by episodes such as the social upheaval occasioned by the arrival of the Banana Company, eventually leading to a massacre of striking workers and, in the end, to sudden economic collapse when the company decides to leave—a parable of the "boom and bust" pattern characteristic of capitalist exploitation of the margin by the center, exposed and denounced by political scientists of the dependency theory persuasion.[10]

If García Márquez is the master exemplar of the marriage of exoticism (magical realism) with orthodox Leftism, Julio Cortázar presents the keenest sense of the existential tension inherent in the Spanish American intellectual between adherence to the Western intellectual tradition—Paris-centrism—and identity as a Latin American. But Cortázar also presents another interesting duality, for while *Rayuela* is probably the most formally radical of the *Boom* masterpieces, it also presents the tightest psychological focus on a limited group of subjects within a frame of reference concerned with culture rather than class. Cortázar's creative aesthetic interests also lead to a large part of his work belonging to the fantasy category, again a generally apolitical format, disengaged from contemporary social problems. Cortázar, a committed and activist Leftist who contributed to *Casa de Las Américas*, was well aware of his susceptibility to the Marxist charge of alienation from the proletarian cause. He defended the autonomy of the artist, defining his work not as a political tool but as a complementary mode of human advancement ultimately compatible with the advances of socialism in the sociopolitical domain, and insisted that the writer must be *engagé* as a citizen of the world.

A final aspect of *Boom* solidarity, important in comparison with Brazilian modernism and crucial, as will be shown later, in comparison with the Brazilian humanist socioanthropological tradition, is the motif of solitude and, generally, the tendency to a polarized Utopian-dystopian duality in the perception of Latin America. All of the *Boom* writers, with the possible exception of Cortázar, explicitly celebrate Latin American cultural identity, but profoundly question the historical trajectory of the continent.

This is best captured in García Márquez' *Cien años de soledad*, which tends to be apprehended by the innocent reader as a magical space where the most excruciating misfortunes are somehow taken in stride by the protagonists and thrown off when the next impossible adventure occurs. The idea that the novel is contextually derived from historically authentic wars, and may be seen as a sort of Marxist farce, is strange for most readers, yet it is precisely this dystopian aspect which criticism tends to reveal. The notion of solitude, then, which superficially appears to respond to the chance isolation of the protagonists in the jungle and the eccentric tropical capers thence ensuing, is a double-edged sword. The writer himself, in his Nobel Prize speech, underlined the negative aspect of the term and its sociohistorical implications. But neither is it the case that the work is merely a fascinating, colorful mask for a horrible underlying reality, for the biographical context of the storytelling is García Márquez's memory of the endless, extraordinary stories told him by his grandmother—a circumstance counterpoised as a cultural icon in the creator's imagination to the numbing violence of the Colombian wars. The fertile paradox of the work lies, then, in the balance between the psychological identification of the narration, at a subconscious level, with the escapades of the protagonists, and the conscious external intellectual frame of reference of the writer.[11]

Again, the motif of solitude is posited in Paz's seminal essay, *El laberinto de la soledad*. Paz presents a subconscious mythology of Mexico featuring a tyrannical conquistador patriarch figure, and an indigenous Earth Mother figure, raped and prostituted. But Paz also affirms a certain Latin American prestige in the historical vanguard, for, within the development of Western culture, the *mestizo* continent is exempt from the "fatal provincialism" of individual European nations caught up in internecine squabbles.

The term "Utopia" (no place) already contains the suggestion of its own unreality even as it denotes a perfect place. The idea of a Utopian Latin America is taken to its radical consequence by both Paz and Fuentes. Paz's Nobel speech, "La búsqueda del presente" (In search of the present), presents the argument that, given that the history of Latin America has been a series of misreadings by self-justifying colonizers, the true course of the past must be rediscovered if a real sense of present identity is to be attained, and that without such an authentic identification of identity no appropriate future path can be defined. Fuentes elsewhere collapses these observations into the paradoxical—and fetishistically baroque—notion of seeking the future in the past. On a more pedestrian level, the point is that Latin American history is a gallery of falsehoods, the results of which are cruelty, abuse, waste, and destruction. Nevertheless, both writers also assert a differentiation for Latin America in a positive sense. While Paz argues for the margin's advantageous perspective on Western history, Fuentes, pointing to contrasting patterns of family unity, insists on the civilizational superiority in certain aspects of the Hispanic over the Anglo-Saxon. A rich, comparative world is thus presented, with hyperbolic highs and lows and an urgent sense of difference in relation to the Western mainstream.

This reads as a variation on Carpentier's essentialist argument of the inherent superiority of Latin America as the locale of the baroque, just as Fuentes's comparative civilizational assessments recall Rodó's turn-of-the-century Ariel/Caliban distinction between the Protestant and Latin Americas. Despite their major formal distinctions, the cultural continuity between Spanish American *modernismo* and *vanguardismo* is striking. The cultivation in a literary-historical duality of fiction and the essay, by virtually all the *Boom* writers, is concordant with Darío's insistence on artistic innovation and ideological program as complements. Another constant is that of psycho-cultural positioning in relation to significant others. Paris remains the capital of Latin American art, the fulcrum of modern Latin illumination, the United States the pole of the modern tyranny of the capitalist center against the victimized margins. The love-hate relationship with Spain intensifies. The father country figures as the tyrannical father-pillager and burner of innocent indigenous communities in the New World, as forever retrogressive within the Paris-centric Western European context. And yet, as the original fountain of *hispanidad,* it is the source of any alleged cultural cohesion between Spanish American nations.

The Spanish American literary discourse of Latin American identity is consistently one of trauma. The recent dramas from the Spanish-American War through to Cuba and Chile are set within a macrocosmic historic frame which begins with the initial destructive act against the Amerindian indigenes and then Cortéz's Mexican campaign which led to the razing of Tenochtitlan and the destruction of advanced civilizations. The other major historical event contributing to this ambiance of trauma was the fragmentation into separate states of the Spanish colonial dominion. While it is arguable whether a unified state was ever a possibility, the frustrations of Bolivarian idealism figure as a sort of Babelian myth, where the possibility of union under *hispanidad* is denied by the fates of history, leading to division, conflict, and anarchy.

The sense of American trauma and the imperative to nonfiction statements of sociopolitical positioning are conspicuously absent in the greater part of Brazilian writers, particularly in the *geração de '45,* and in this sense, the Brazilian model finds more parallels in the United States than in Spanish America.

At least two patterns emerge in the comparison of the development of modernist literary discourse in Spanish America and Brazil, one of internal continuity within each current, the other of consistent contrasts between them. Both traditions present surprising continuities between generations. The concerns and themes of Rodó and Darío are in many ways concordant with those of the *Boom* writers, with the major difference lying in the problematization of *hispanidad* in the light of the twentieth-century valorization of the Amerindian as both legitimately human and the victim of *hispanidad.* In Brazil, the nationalist spirit in the modernist revolution, while establishing the need for authentic language, dispenses with imperatives regarding thematic content, at least in relation to both essentialist representations of the national self and the obligation of a social critical posture. The Machadian option of distance from such concerns, which might be called the universalist or literary purist option, is gradually reasserted by Mário de Andrade and then by the *geração de '45*. This approach is strongly implicit even in the absence of abstract declarations in their own publications, which are restricted to creative works (and not manifestos, essays, or even literary criticism).

The second major point consists of the radical contrast between the two literary traditions in a number of specific aspects. The Spanish American writers are agents of extraliterary ideologies, and, increasingly, social and historical commentators in extrafictional formats, notably the essay. The dominant Spanish American literary ideology is inscribed within orthodox intellectual Leftism. And yet it sustains an essentialist Pan-(Latin or Spanish) American nationalism or continentalism, justifiable alternately on cultural or materialist grounds, that is, in terms of the specificities of Spanish and/or Latin American identity, or in terms of the global capitalist system and its attendant historical development. Brazilian *Modernismo* is singular in that it proved perfectly adaptable to Rightist as well as Leftist ideologies, and to the apolitical stance of Guimarães Rosa and others.

Brazilian *Modernismo* also differs significantly in its national and geopolitical sensibility. While nineteenth-century literary history presents a divergence of response in the two traditions to the question of regionalism—the dominant form in Spanish America, and a successfully cultivated but generally rejected genre in Brazil—the twentieth century actually presents a sort of mutual attitudinal inversion, whereby Spanish American regionalism is eclipsed in favor of national representations, while in Brazil regional locales are pursued with new vigor and originality. The one constant here is the distance between the two literary cultures. The rejection of regionalism in Carpentier's dismissal of *nativismo*[12] contrasts singularly with the status of socially critical regionalism as the central vehicle of the second generation of Brazilian *Modernismo* and, again, of Guimarães Rosa (further discussed in the following chapter). Finally, the Brazilians simply do not identify with the Spanish American call for continental consciousness and solidarity, so that, for Brazil at least, the casual synonymy of Spanish America and Latin America is quite inappropriate.

In relation to Paris-centrism we find a pattern analogous to the divergent relations of the two traditions to mainstream Leftist ideology. Paris (and by extension, non-Iberian Western Europe) exists as a necessary center for Paz, García Márquez, and Carlos Fuentes almost as it did for Darío. In Brazil, the importance of Paris for writers is less, and diminishes over time. While Oswald de Andrade's trajectory recalls that of Vicente Huidobro, it is telling that

Mário de Andrade, for whom São Paulo existed as a surrogate Manhattan, never left Brazil; indeed it would be tempting to integrate this biographical divergence into an analysis of the ideological and theoretical break which by the end of the 1920s divided the two writers. Similarly to Mário, Machado de Assis, for whom it may be said that Rio existed as a provincial "capital of the nineteenth century," never made the trip to Paris, a curious fact given that the Brazilian Literary Academy, of which Machado de Assis was not only an "immortal" but also the first president, was inspired by the Parisian institution. Finally, Guimarães Rosa, who lived in Europe during the trauma of World War II, had as little affinity with or need of Paris as did Faulkner. His reverence for the Western literary tradition was relatively conservative, concerned more with the canon than the vanguard. The pattern is repeated in relation to the Iberian font; whereas the Spanish civil war was a crucial event for most Spanish American writers of the period, no major Brazilians were present; further, Brazilian writers show minimal identification with the parallel struggle against fascist dictatorship in Salazar's Portugal.

Both the *métropole* (the continental home bases of the various Western European empires) and, if we may indulge a neologism, the apposite *Ameripole,* feature as fundamental motifs in Spanish American literary thinking. The Utopia-dystopia motif in the Spanish American tradition responds to a sense of historical trauma which contrasts with both the ultimately impotent Oswaldian euphoria and also the abnegation of historical commentary and social testimony in the Machadian—*geração de '45* line.[13]

This brings us to a final point which I prefer to consider separately, and which is no doubt a relatively subjective judgment. I would argue that there is a general contrast between a Spanish American tendency to moralize and Brazilian amorality. The latter is taken to the extreme with the bravado of Oswald, but is better represented by the Machadian stance as dry observer of human fortunes and the quirks of human nature rather than as a social witness with a historical message to be communicated in the parables of fiction. The Brazilian tradition is also characterized by a greater presence of narrative ambiguity.[14] Machado de Assis's masterpiece, *Dom Casmurro,* is a transposed Othello plot where it is never clear whether or not the female protagonist is actually guilty or innocent. In Azevedo's theoretically naturalist work, *O Cortiço,* the method of socioscientific observation is frequently subverted by imaginative lyrical tangents, of which the most salient is an extraordinarily comical moment when a prudish girl, after seeing a man who stirs her blood, has her first menstruation at the age of nineteen, in a scene bordering on the psychedelic. Da Cunha's *Os Sertões,* an account of the millenarian rebellion at Canudos in Bahia which in any Spanish American—Brazilian comparison must be contrasted with Sarmiento's *Facundo* and its archetypal opposition of civilization and barbarism, is singular in that while it sets out, as nonfiction, to explain eugenically the inferiority of the fanatical *sertanejos,* it becomes an apologia of this ethnic group, and, in the process, literature. The poetry of Carlos Drummond de Andrade presents an ongoing tension between a yearning for solidarity and ideology, and a more potent skepticism. Guimarães Rosa's main work, *Grande Sertão: Veredas,* presents the discursive spectacle of an endless monologue of existential self-interrogation without closure (in fact, the original edition was marked at the end with an infinity symbol). The critical and creative changes through the career of Mário de Andrade have already been mentioned. His main fictional work, *Macunaíma,* is apparently in the Oswaldian line, but is really problematic in its affirmation of a Brazilian type, as the subtitle, *o herói sem nenhum caráter,* suggests.

These literary works will be looked at in more detail in the following chapter. In relation to the current discussion, however, it can be said that this inclination to ambiguity is symptomatic of the antiessentialist character of Brazilian literature, which contrasts with the essentialist solidarity of Spanish American writers from Rodó and Darío through to the *Boom.* It is not the case, however, that Brazil lacks its own essentialist tradition. In literature this mentality is first represented by Oswald, but much more importantly and substantially developed by Jorge Amado, who remains an exception to the rule within literature. Amado's perspective finds solidarity outside of literature, within the socioanthropological tradition, which is radically essentialist, and which, in various moments, affirms under a series of terms the existence of a Brazilian type for which we will use the term *Homo brasiliensis.* In relation to the Spanish American literary tradition the vital difference, as will be seen, lies in the fact that while the Spanish American tradition has emerged as a denunciation of the false Utopian projections of Europeans (literally as well as figuratively, since More's *Utopia* is theoretically located somewhere in the Americas) and an exposé of a dystopian reality, the Brazilian socioanthropological tradition emerges as a Utopian projection onto the present, through the celebration of the ethnic reality of miscegenation and cultural fusion. This tradition, counter to the Brazilian literary tradition, is explored in chapter 4.

In relation to the various group characteristics outlined above, Jorge Amado is the exception in Brazilian literature. Amado, first by exile and then by choice, spent considerable periods in Europe, particularly in Paris. Amado had strong bonds with the Parisian Leftist intelligentsia, both French and Spanish American (notably Neruda). As for Lisbon, despite ongoing visa refusals by the Portuguese government, Amado maintained contact with the factions of Leftist resistance which finally brought down Salazar, and after 1974 often stayed in the country. Amado, like Neruda, served in Parliament as a Communist and enjoyed Soviet sponsorship (both won the Stalin Prize, and traveled extensively in the Eastern block; Amado resided for a period in Prague). Though gradually less and less inclined to express himself outside the space of his fiction, Amado was an orthodox and even an obedient Communist artist.[15] He is also a Brazilian essentialist whose collected works have been compared to Balzac's *Comédie Humaine,* that is, a social fresco with an overarching historical and political perspective. The paradox of cosmopolitan Leftism and cultural essentialism makes the intellectual trajectory of Amado exceptional within the Brazilian literary tradition—a contributing circumstance, in our view, in both his poor domestic critical reception and his international popularity—and an aspect compatible with the Spanish Americans, despite the fact that Amado would seem the most ardently and exclusively Brazilian, or rather Bahian, of the writers considered in this study.[16]

2
The Brazilian Writers and Their Work

Guimarães Rosa

Background and biographical notes.

JOÃO GUIMARÃES ROSA WAS BORN IN 1908 IN THE SMALL TOWN OF Cordisburgo, about 200 km from Belo Horizonte, the capital of the state of Minas Gerais, which is named for the gold and precious stone mines that brought it to economic prominence in the eighteenth century. This landlocked state occupies a singular position in the development of Brazil, for unlike other essentially frontier regions of the interior yet to attain a stable and recognizable identity, the socioethnic infrastructure and cultural practices of Minas Gerais are virtually as old as those anywhere else in Brazil. The colonial *mineiro* (i.e., of Minas Gerais) city of Ouro Preto was briefly the capital of Brazil, when the state was the center of the first attempts to establish independence from Portugal. The grand old river of Brazilian history—not the Amazon, but the São Francisco—which for hundreds of years was the central artery in the development of the interior, rises in the south of Minas and runs northward, dividing the state between the eastern sector, already a sprawling outback, and the western sector whence begins the awesome expanse of the larger share of Brazil, still drastically underdeveloped. At a certain point the river turns eastward to run towards the Atlantic, constituting a natural border for a series of states which are considered to belong to the geographic and cultural zone known as the northeast (*Nordeste*), the oldest area of social development in Brazil and the crucible of Brazil's ethnocultural heritage. Minas itself, however, with its capital in the southeast corner of the state, is normally included in the socioeconomic and cultural zone known as the southeast, along with the states of Rio de Janeiro and São Paulo. Its politicians have in this century been key instigators of alliances with these two latter states which successively dominated Brazil economically and politically. In this way, Minas occupies a central position in Brazil, both physically and culturally.

Since the gradual depletion of the mines the state has been developed largely through agriculture and cattle; the consequent social fabric is often similar to the archaic subsistence economy of the interior of the northeast. On the other hand, against the *nordestino* pattern, the state has participated in agricultural modernization, rationalization of the post-slave economy, and the entrepreneurial industrialization with which the powerhouse of São Paulo has led Brazil into the twentieth century.

The circumstance of Minas's isolation from the coast makes it very different from its neighboring seaboard states. The character and disposition of its inhabitants, known as *mineiros,* is considered to be an aberration from the usual image of Brazilians as expansive, gregarious, and sensual. *Mineiros* are seen as inordinately cautious, introspective, and shy.

Guimarães Rosa's father was a moderately prosperous shopkeeper; after ten years in the rustic isolation of Cordisburgo his son was sent to a private school in Belo Horizonte. He had already developed an interest and an extraordinary autodidactic capacity in foreign languages, reading in French at the age of six and as a teenager teaching himself to read Russian. Eventually Guimarães would be able to read fourteen languages, and converse in six. At seventeen Rosa entered medical school and by chance established a friendship with a doctor who would become president of the Republic and the founder of Brasília, Juscelino Kubitschek. In 1929, through financial necessity, he took up a public service job in the state Statistical Services Office. In this year he also published his first work, a short story, after winning a competition in a local newspaper. In 1930 he graduated as a medical practitioner and from 1931–33 ran a private practice in a small town. In 1932 he participated in the Constitutionalist Revolution, served as a voluntary medical officer in the Força Pública, and was subsequently appointed as its Staff Physician; in 1933 he won the position of Medical Officer for the 9th Infantry Battalion, at Barbacena, still in Minas Gerais. In the following year he entered the Foreign Service exams in Rio and was placed second. From this time until his death he served in the Foreign Service and related government ministries, winning a steady series of promotions up to ambassadorial rank. In 1937 a collection of verse he had compiled won the Brazilian Academy of Letters's poetry competition, but Guimarães Rosa declined to seek publication. Yet he gathered his major short stories to date in a thousand-page manuscript and submitted them to the Humberto de Campos Competition for prose fiction, established by the José Olímpio publishing house, the single most important editorial institution for Brazilian literature for a good part of this century. His manuscript, submitted under the pseudonym Viator and simply entitled *Contos,* was just edged out for first place in a close competition judged by several major authors. In 1938 Rosa was appointed vice-consul in Hamburg. In 1942, with other Brazilian diplomats, he was interned at Baden-Baden for four months, before returning to Rio. In 1945 he served in the Brazilian delegation at the Paris Peace Conference and in 1948 went to Bogotá with the delegation to the 9th Pan-American Conference, before spending three years in Paris. He finally established himself definitively in Rio in 1951. In 1945, as well as managing a return visit to his birthplace, he had worked intensively to pare down and improve the long manuscript entered in the Humberto de Campos Competition. In 1946 this collection of tales set in rural Minas Gerais came out under the neologistic title *Sagarana,* which draws on the Norse "saga." The book was a resounding success, exhausting two editions that same year, and winning a prestigious award, the Prêmio da Sociedade Felipe d'Oliveira. From this point on Guimarães Rosa's literary stature passed from careful obscurity to general recognition. Though José Olímpio had not acquired the rights for the first publication of *Sagarana,* the publishing house actually adopted this title for its landmark series of major modern Brazilian works. Nevertheless, Rosa did not join the ranks of the literati. He continued his Foreign Service career in orthodox fashion, merely taking advantage of the relatively light workload to indulge his eccentric and intensely private literary production. Just as the evolution from initial drafting to published product for *Sagarana* had taken place over a ten-year period, it would be another decade before he would release another literary work. His most important publication in the interim was an account, or report, "Com o Vaqueiro Mariano" ("With the Cowboy, Mariano"), published in newspapers in 1952, describing a long cattle drive in the distant Western state of Mato Grosso that he accompanied on horseback, scrupulously taking down notes on flora and fauna and folkloric traditions and terms, as he had always done while in the countryside. It is hard to know how and in what order Guimarães Rosa proceeded on each of his subsequent works. At any rate, in January of 1956 another collection of shorter works, this time of novella length, was launched in two volumes totaling 880 pages under the title *Corpo de Baile.* But in the same month a significantly emended fourth edition of *Sagarana* also appeared. Rosa seems to have had as much difficulty in accepting versions of his works even after they were published as he had in releasing them for initial publication. In June of the same year his major work, *Grande Sertão: Veredas* also appeared. The book quickly picked up three prizes, the Machado de Assis prize of the Instituto Nacional do Livro, São Paulo's Carmen Dolores Barbosa prize, and Rio's Paulo Brito award. It sold well, and amongst critics provoked reactions from stupor to unabated admiration; most importantly it left very few members of the literary intelligentsia indifferent. From the moment of its release the work was one of the sensations of the century in Brazilian letters.

Guimarães Rosa's literary output after the watershed year of 1956 was relatively restricted. In 1962 he released a disparate collection of short stories under the title *Primeiras Estórias (First Stories)*. In 1967 he published another collection with the alternate titles of *Terceiras Estórias (Third Stories)* and *Tutaméia* (a neologism difficult to translate, presumably drawing on the terms *tudo*—all—and *meio*—center or half; it has been rendered with the English word "trifle").

In 1957, the year following the release of *Grande Sertão: Veredas*, Guimarães Rosa was an unsuccessful candidate for the Brazilian Academy of Letters. But in 1961 he was awarded the academy's own Machado de Assis prize for the ensemble of his work, virtually guaranteeing admission to the pantheon should he stand again. He did so in 1963 and was elected unanimously. Apparently for superstitious reasons, Guimarães Rosa declined to formally assume his seat until late 1967; three days after going through the induction he died from heart failure, at the age of 59. His professional writing career thus barely exceeded twenty years. His rapid ascension to heavyweight status as an author was marked, apart from his admission to the academy, by his appointment as vice president of the first Latin American Writer's Conference in Mexico City in 1965.

Earlier works of Guimarães Rosa and the exploration of regionalism.

Given, on the one hand, Guimarães Rosa's method of retaining manuscripts for very long periods and including in any collection short stories which do not necessarily fall into neat chronological sectors as regards genesis and final composition, and, on the other hand, the fact that the great majority of his pieces share the same regional thematic context of rural Minas Gerais, it is difficult to precisely trace the evolution of his work. However, while the exact generation of any given story will be obscure, it is possible to describe the published works as stylistically and conceptually distinct projects.

We are forced to disregard the verse collection, *Magma,* since the author declined to publish it and did not produce any poetry in his maturity. However, the work did receive the academy's prize, at a time when poetry still retained a central status in Brazilian literary production; such an honor suggests that the author was already capable of exceptional achievement, and, despite his obscurity, of winning the admiration of the literary elite. But prose was to become the vehicle of Guimarães Rosa's poetry. Graciliano Ramos, the outstanding Brazilian writer who served on the jury of the Humberto de Campos competition in which Rosa's long prose manuscript (later known as *Sagarana*) was awarded second place, referred to poetic effects such as onomatopoeic verses inserted into longer sentences, alliterations, and phrases of fourteen pentasyllables (Ramos 1962, 267–70). The final, substantially reduced, version of *Sagarana* was itself to be subject to at least three revisions in subsequent editions, until the editors barred Guimarães Rosa from further meddling. The work contains nine rather long short stories (of an average length of forty pages), set in rural Minas Gerais in an imprecise time frame. For the most part the stories draw heavily, if not on local folklore, then on local wisdom and cosmovision; the narrative perspective is impersonal and consistent with the limited knowledge and discourse of the protagonists, rather than that of a more educated commentator. The main element distinguishing the narrative perspective is the richness of the references to flora and fauna which punctuate the otherwise regular rhythm of narrative action. The discursive register in these cases is more or less consistent with that of the protagonists, although the sheer quantity of references suggest an ornate centrifugal buzz around the main plot. Nevertheless, the overall tone is essentially even keeled, leaving *Sagarana* faithful to orthodox regionalism—comparable, for example to Verga's *Cavalleria Rusticana.*

The opening story, "O Burrinho Pedrês" (The Ash-gray Burro) is a minor masterpiece of the genre, sustaining over sixty pages the sort of technical control and methodical deliberation of Mérimée, though adding a subtle metaphysical overlay; the unexciting tone of the color mentioned in the title in fact effects a clever initial minimization of the protagonist, whose story moves along step-by-step with the inglorious persistence of the burro, his stoic heroism only slowly revealed. The closing story, "A Hora e a Vez de Augusto Matraga" (The Time and the Turn of Augusto Matraga) has become the most famous. It relates the demise of a brutish, bullying landowner who after many years of abuse and impunity gets what he deserves, realizes why he has been so thoroughly beaten, and achieves a sort of beatific acceptance and resolution of various deep-rooted conflicts before dying. This story also has become a classic version of a particular moral emblem or narrative figure, that of the law of karma (chickens coming home to roost). The juxtaposed aspects of the protagonist's fortune are suggested, again, in the title: Augusto connotes the lordly exercise of both power and stability, while Matraga (from *matraca*) suggests eloquence and mockery and also something which is slow in arriving (but also the French *matraque,* meaning truncheon or club). This is a good example of the lexical complexity and depth in Guimarães Rosa's work, though perhaps not typical in that it is relatively transparent. The stories in *Sagarana* are, by and large, far more straightforward than his later work, and his characteristic hermeticism is here tempered with ideas that bear a fundamental childlike appeal.

Only a couple of stories deviate from this orthodox regionalism. Of particular interest is the story "São Marcos," which relates the first person encounter of a skeptic with a voodoo fetishist; the skeptic undergoes intense intellectual disorientation, the effect reinforced by the close camera angle of the narrative. The story introduces the metaphysical emblem at the core of *Grande Sertão: Veredas*—the unresolved nature of both belief and disbelief, and the extraordinary arabesques that the adventurer will unwittingly perform either in pursuit of self-knowledge, or at least to achieve a resolution of intention and action.

Sagarana remains Rosa's most read work because of its accessibility. The poetic inclination, tending to deviate from orthodox realist narrative style and phrasal distribution, is compounded by other elements which include oral speech patterns such as repetition, and short phrases and clauses, linked freely. Of course, in real oral discourse intonation often specifies the relative hierarchization of each conceptual unit. The loss of this specification in written texts, combined with the relative dearth of devices of conventionally elegant prose, has a number of consequences. Most importantly, the reader is obliged to participate, reconstructing, as he reads, the appropriate interrelation of elements. Just as reading requires more of the imagination than does television, so does a written text which suppresses conventional syntax. Rosa's style is demanding. It requires of the reader a more substantial and interactive relation with the narration and with the characters, whose discourse and psychological perspective must be provided by the reader. Another effect of this suppression of syntactic hierarchy, and one of particular interest to the writer himself as well as to the sophisticated reader, is the implicit equity of the discursive elements. Minor prepositional or adverbial phrases, normally subordinate, are given a status approximate to that of a main clause. Whereas the ordinary reader tends to favor elements pertinent to plot development, plot-peripheral elements are the very substance of Rosean discourse; it is not so much the outcome of the story as the way it is told which identifies the writer. To illustrate this point through exaggeration: if there were a period after each grammatical phrase in a text, not only would there be an emphatic staccato effect, the logic of the arrangement would be equity between the various conceptual entities, major or minor, central or circumstantial, plot-essential or decorative; all elements would become fundamental. The consequent prose, moving against the usual logic of hierarchization, would bear a much closer relation to that of poetry, where each lexical unit has the status of an ideogram and is as essential as each of the tiles of a mosaic.

A further complication is the question of the derivation of such Rosean procedures from oral discourse. The impression of the mimesis of orality in literature is normally an illusion, that is, closer linguistic analysis typically reveals an essential distance between the discursive style developed by the writer and the actual speech patterns of the community nominally represented.[1] Though donning the mask of regionalism, it should not be thought that Rosa's stylistic eccentricity is that of the rural *mineiro* dialect spoken by old campfire storytellers. The arbitrary inclusion of references to a rich array of flora and fauna is a good example of something which might be attributed by the naïve city reader to rural discourse, but which in fact is virtually absent from real campfire stories, which relate human adventures and focus on the agents of narrative action. Of all Rosa's works, *Sagarana,* though not necessarily the best, is the one which mixes most felicitously his personal style with instances and motifs dear to regional folklore and experience. It is at once the perfect introduction to his work, and the terminal point for a large number of his readers.

Ten years passed before the appearance of *Corpo de Baile.* This work, published in 1956 in two volumes, comprises seven novellas, all sharing the familiar ground of rural Minas Gerais, or more accurately, the vast, dry high plains known as the *gerais.* This term, meaning something like prairie, is not derived from the state's name; the *gerais* extend well beyond state boundaries. Rosa's close exposure to the folklore and lifestyle of the region had come as much from his 1952 trip with cattle drivers in Mato Grosso state as from his rural upbringing in Minas. The novellas vary greatly in thematic context, psychological approach, and narrative structure. This variety, and the absolute perplexity it has produced, from the first critics through nonprofessional readers ever since, is partly related to the publishing history of the work. The 1956 edition offers two consecutively numbered volumes; the table of contents then divides the stories into two categories, novels (*romances*) and short stories (*contos*), a qualitatively rather than a quantitative distinction, since the longest *conto* is, at 109 pages, longer than the shortest *romance,* of 90 pages. The *romances* are grouped under the subtitle "I, '*Gerais,*'" and the *contos* under "II, 'Parábase.'" But the division into volumes does not coincide with this tabular division into item I, *romances,* and item II, *contos.* Rather, the sequence is one of intercalation of the two genres, so that the first physical volume includes a *romance,* a *conto* and another *romance* and the second a *conto,* a *romance,* a *conto* and a *romance.* The second edition (1960) managed with greater efficiency to include all the original 820 pages in a single volume. As of the third edition, however, the original structure of *Corpo de Baile* was effectively ruptured by a new distribution of the novellas into three more now autonomously conceived works bestowed with new titles: *Manuelzão e Miguilim, No Urubùquaquà, no Pinhém,* and *Noites do Sertão.*

In his admirable introductory work, *João Guimarães Rosa,* Jon S. Vincent investigates the question extensively, noting both the difficulty of precise transition from Brazilian-Portuguese literary terms to those employed in English such as novella, novelette, short novel, long short story, and so on, and examining, within the Portuguese, the particular question of the generic nature of the narrative units of *Corpo de Baile.* The conclusion is essentially that the sheer diversity, complexity, and unorthodoxy of the narratives render the question unresolvable in conventional terms. The issue is perhaps better illustrated than analyzed. The first and last stories (in the original order, and thus *romances*), "Campo Geral" and "Buriti" share a common protagonist, Miguilim. In the first he is a boy of eight, oppressed by a vicious father. Miguilim gains insight into the meaning of good and evil by talking with the cowhands with whom he lives. But the grand revelation is ultimately as much physical as metaphysical: it occurs when the boy is given glasses by a doctor who has grasped, unlike the boy himself, that he is so nearsighted as to be almost blind. The world at large is suddenly unenshrouded. The vagaries and meanderings of folkloric insight accessed through contact with the community are set against the sudden impact of this event, and also against developments of drastic import such as the death of his father. In this way a personal adventure is established against a background of metaphysical and moral perceptions framed by the rustic inhabitants of the *gerais*. But as if marking a deliberate transition toward a more evolved state of society and of personal maturation, the last story focuses on a more socioeconomically privileged group of individuals. Following the mode of bourgeois civilization rather than the disparate, nonindividualist *communitas* of folklore, the cast is limited to a handful of characters, each individual fleshed out as in a conventional psychological novel, with specific desires and eventual fulfillment or frustration. Miguilim is now a young man and a doctor. The first part of the story follows his slow approach towards a ranch; it has rained and the land has sprung with new life. Key moments in the anterior segments of the storyline are revealed in mental flashbacks. However, the dominant feature of this long initial section is the lengthy description of flora and fauna by a narrative voice which almost seems lost in a mystical pantheism, with an overabundance of local references and animal and vegetal names. The title of the story refers to an indigenous species of palm, recurrently evoked and personalized through a complex series of psychologically descriptive terms drawing on human comparatives.

Though Miguilim is the central protagonist, accompanied by an omniscient narrator for much of the text, he is in fact merely a peripheral agent in the slow, torrid drama lived out by a family on a country estate. Having, during a brief visit, fallen in love with Laura, one of the daughters of the house, Miguilim is drawn back irresistibly to the property, though much time passes between his visits and he doubts he will be considered an acceptable suitor either by the landowning patriarch or even by the daughter herself. At this point the sympathetic Miguilim appears to play the role of a wandering knight in a medieval romance. Despite his doubts, the intervals between his visits in fact serve to swell the daughter's reciprocal desire almost to the point of despair. The romance ambiance is in fact the narrative correlate of the psychological innocence and idealized desire of both Miguilim, and, to a lesser extent, Laura, marking their distance from confrontation with the crudity of real human interaction driven by sexuality and brutality. But

Laura's desperation swings the story into another perspective, that of the pervasive repression within the cloistered house, where the family members live in a limbo of frustration and noncomprehension of their deepest desires, tormented by strange, incestuous feelings which eventually erupt in violent action. The patriarch's son has been away for years, but his abandoned daughter-in-law lives on the property under the generous, and eventually covetous, protection of the patriarch. In the interims between Miguilim's visits, the hothouse flowers in this Freudian *Huis clos* ripen and rot. The two young females, both ardent to resolve the demands of incipient womanhood, develop an affinity suggesting a lesbian attraction. An apparently innocuous landowning neighbor, with whom Miguilim stays when in the area, and who is almost the only regular visitor on the porch in the evening, eventually assaults and rapes the daughter. This does not lead to retribution and resolution: the fetid atmosphere simply drags forward. When it is learned that the son has had a child by another woman, an unwritten primitive law allows the concubine to supplant the legitimate spouse; whether through spiteful frustration or acceptance of an unexpected sexual bonding, the daughter-in-law gives herself to the patriarch. At this point Miguilim arrives at last, and is united with Laura.

Under the circumstances his arrival seems at best belated and at worst a sign of impotence, his hero status undermined by the unavenged despoiling of his damsel. It seems an improbable and inappropriate dénouement to a drama reminiscent both of Greek tragedy, in its steady march toward transgression, and of certain fictional depictions of macabre, incestuous sexuality in the old south. In fact the author has, simply but ambitiously, pinned together apparently incongruous psycho-narratological genres and their attendant cosmovisions, such as romance, where sexuality is sublimated and diffused through imaginative metaphorical systems, and stark drama, where sexuality is an unmediated element in plot development. The pantheistic aura surrounding Miguilim's approach is both a testimony to his innocence and, in its evocation of the land sprung to life, a metaphorical edifice likening him to the force of Spring itself. In this context, and lending support to the basic cohesiveness underlying the collection, the first story of the younger Miguilim assumes significance for the present story, both in portraying the childhood of the adult Miguilim and also in the sense that both stories share the motif of Miguilim's transition from ignorance to knowledge. A deeper irony lies in the fact that in the earlier story, the plight of the vulnerable child is ameliorated by his new spectacles, whereas in the later story the strong and good young man, for whom the reader entertains hopes of heroic status, manages to fulfill only a questionable desire, since the prize won is not the prize imagined. Contrary to conventional romance, the hero's knowledge is fundamentally inadequate, his achievement compromised.

The novella sustains two plotlines: Miguilim's fulfilled romance, where the pantheistic meanderings of the narrator function in a similar way to the magic that enriches the psycho-mythological universe of the romance hero; and, back at the ranch, a psychologically and sexually searching drama in the vein of Tennessee Williams. The two stories are conjoined by two distinct agencies: on the one hand, Miguilim himself and the conscious psychological battle between the characters, and on the other, the persistent device of nature used as a metaphorical emblem. The latter argument is strengthened by various elements: the title of the *romance,* repeated in the title of the ranch (*Buriti Bom*); the faunic and flora ramblings which dominate the first section of the text; and by the physical character of the buriti palm itself, which gradually assumes more and more poetic potence in the second section. The property is in fact called Buriti Bom, though this explains little. The gigantic, oil-laden palm trees stand in a cluster, on the property but away from the house, always described in ominous, almost triffidlike terms, by night or by the falling light of dusk. One of their various metaphorical connotations is that of a colossal phallic collection, threatening and cryptic in its plurality. Because of the sheer weight of the reader's task, this story has remained relatively obscure for all its stylistic virtuosity and psychological depth. The success of "Buriti" as a fusion of heterogeneous genres is difficult to judge; however the earnest reader can only be awed by the sheer ambition of the attempt.

The discussion so far of the first and last stories of *Corpo de Baile* has emphasized the articulation of the story. Another story, the *conto* "Cara-de-Bronze," an open, experimental work, depends more on stylistic and narrative innovation than on plot. The text, which depicts the interaction of an array of country folk gathered for a cattle sale at the ranch of a mysterious landowner known only by the name which provides the story's title, is presented as a play, at times even as a cinematic script, with stage and lighting directions and slots to mark in footage and duration. It is normal in the context of a such a gathering in rural Brazil that the people provide their own entertainment, singing traditional folk songs and newly composed ballads relating the exploits of notorious personages, improvising in troubadour fashion eulogies and parodies of present company, and so on. In this way the text is simply an imaginative extension of the interaction which might occur on a given night in the country. It begins with a third-person introduction specifying the place where the play or social gathering, the performance event, will occur, while the folk arrive during the preceding daylight. As they gather, songs and verses appear spontaneously, representative of each person's social background. As in plays, a name indicates each speaker, but the tone is more that of a transcribed conversation: the characters greet each other, comment on things bovine, and are questioned by an outsider, Moimeichego, as to their own identity and particularly to that of their host, Cara-de-Bronze. This latter point occasions more disagreement and vagueness than clarification. The host is a mystery. Not only do people have differing views even about his physical characteristics, one character claims that Cara-de-Bronze's complexion, though dark, was once darker. The text now mutates to full screenplay format, with the title "ROTEIRO" (script, but also itinerary or road book) and specific stage directions. The characters are by now clearly orchestrated players. Eventually a full-fledged story is told by one of them, a cowhand called Grivo, who has just returned from a two-year journey in some way commissioned by Cara-de-Bronze. However, the narrative voice has returned just prior to this to give a resumé of the situation, informing the reader that the real story is not so much about Grivo's long travels as the girl he encountered along the way: "Sim, a que se casou com o Grivo, mas que também é a outra, a Muito Branca-de-todas-as-cores" ("Yes, the one who married Grivo, but who is also the other one, the Very White-of-all-colors"; 1956a, 586). Grivo is the main narrator of his own story, with the other characters acting as a sort of folkloric chorus. But the omniscient narrator also takes over at certain points. When the characters next interject it is in their original capacity as real people arriving at the ranch for the cattle sale; they note that Grivo is no longer among them, apparently summoned by Cara-de-Bronze to other quarters of the ranch house. The characters are left to speculate on how Grivo's story subsequently developed and on the occult commission by Cara-de-Bronze which occasioned Grivo's travels. When Grivo appears, he is unwilling to explain this, interested only in negotiating the blessing of a priest who has joined them. The others, now wondering as much about what has just occurred between Grivo and Cara-de-Bronze as about the travel tale, find that Grivo is in fact willing to discuss the recent interview. Cara-de-Bronze had asked a few questions about aspects of Grivo's story pertaining to the bride. And then, says Grivo, their host wept with joy and said he wanted to be blessed. The others interpret this as an excellent omen for Grivo, whom they expect to become Cara-de-Bronze's heir. The enigmatic circumstances and the conclusion drawn by the others are explicable by the hypothesis that the bride is actually the host's daughter.

"Cara-de-Bronze" presents a story-within-a-story with the most diaphanous of boundaries between the two; the mise-en-abîme is not just an analogical or allegorical reinforcement; the same characters move between the two stories, and it is impossible to determine which story is the real story. But there is also the complication of the omniscient narration. Storytelling requires not so much verisimilitude as consistency of genre, that is, consistency in narratological context and psychological perspective of the characters. This pact is here stretched by the license of the narrator, who at times relates the story to the reader, picking up from Grivo and the other characters, but who also gives a hyper-aestheticized, poetically burdened depiction of the setting which is quite alien to the stylistic register of the rest of the narration.

The story opens:

> No Urubùquaquá. Os campos do Urubùquaquá—urucùias montes, fundões e brejos. No Urubùquaquá, fazenda-de-gado: a maior—no meio—um estado de terra. A que fôra lugar, lugares, de mato-grosso, a mata escura, que é do valor do chão. Tal agora se fizera pastagens, a vacaria. O gadame. Êste mundo, que desmede os recantos. Mar a redor, fim a fora, iam-se os Gerais, os Gerais do ô e do ão: mesas quebradas e mesas planas, das chapadas, onde há areia; para o verde sujo de más árvores, o grameal e o *agreste*—um capim rude, que boca de burro ou de boi não quer; e água e alegre relva arrozã, só nos transvales das *veredas,* cada qual, que refletem, orlantes, o cheiroso sassafrás, a buritizana espinhosa, e os buritis, os ramilhetes dos buritizais, os buritizais, os b u r i t i z a i s, os buritis bebentes. Pelo andado do Chapadão, em ver o viajante é um cavaleiro pequenininho, pequenino, curvado sempre sobre o arção e o curto da crina do cavalo—o cavalinho alazão, sem nome, só chamado Quebra-Côco. Cavaleiro vai, manuseando miséria, escondidos seus olhos do à-frente, que é só o mesmo duma distanciação—e o céu uma poeira azul e papagaios no vôo. Os Gerais do trovão, os Gerais do vento.
> No Urubùquaquá, não. (. . .)

> [In the Urubùquaquá. The lands of the Urubùquaquá—urucu-red hills, hollows and bogs. In the Urubùquaquá, a cattle ranch: the biggest—in the middle—a land unto itself. The one which had been a place, places, of deep bush, dark bush, like the earth. By now it had

become pasture, a corral. The Brahman-cross bull. This world, which goes too far, to the corners of the earth. The sea around, the end beyond, the prairie went on, the prairie of o and ah: broken tablelands and flat tablelands, of the plateaus, where there is sand; toward the dirty green of scrubby trees, areas of light bush, and more barren parts—a tough grass which neither a donkey's nor a cow's mouth wants; and water and merry paddies of wild rice only in the gullies of the green stretches, each one reflecting a border of fragrant sassafras, the prickly buritizana palm, and the buriti palms, the fine branches of the buriti groves, the buriti groves, the thirsty buriti. Seen moving across the Prairie is the traveler a little, little horseman, always curved over the bow of the saddle and the small of the horse's mane—the sorrel pony, nameless, just called Coco-cracker. Goes the rider, managing his misery, hidden his eyes from the ahead, which is simply the same as distancing—and the sky all blue dust and parrots in flight.
The prairie of thunder, the prairie of wind.
Not in the Urubùquaquá.] (1956a II, 557)

Jon Vincent observes in the first and second paragraphs of the story,

> at least a dozen neologisms or obscure usages, several ellipses, a number of reverses in word order, and sundry examples of internal rhyme, alliteration, onomatopoeia, and repetition as well as a representative sample of Guimarães Rosa's own inimitable style of punctuation. The page contains in addition an example of typographical alteration, the purposeful double spacing of the word buritizais ('fields of buriti palms') as it occurs fifth in a series of six forms of buriti'. (1978, 43)

Vincent also notes the use of bound morphemes (a syllable normally occurring only within a word, as in a diminutive or augmentative suffix), in isolation as autonomous words: "os Gerais do ô e do ão." This autonomy is compounded by the circumstance of these morphemes not occurring in the lexical item evoked (here, *gerais;* the case might read differently if, for example, the item referred to was *sertão*). Interpretation of such neologistic onomatopoeia is pragmatically free, though it is to be presumed that there is a specific significational intention on the part of the author, in a way comparable to Carroll's "Jabberwocky." Another Rosean license is the grammatical recategorization of terms, that is, the use of an adjective as a noun and so on, with or without the indication of an appropriately altered morphological inflection, as in *arrozã* (ricey)—or *o andado* (the walked, or here perhaps suggesting "having walked [up the high plain] and looked down"). Brazilian Portuguese enjoys a much greater freedom than English in the

2: THE BRAZILIAN WRITERS AND THEIR WORK

adaptation of past participle as noun, so that Rosa's usage could be considered to draw on the syntactic flexibility of his native tongue; the liberties he takes are, nevertheless, extremely audacious, and the text reads strangely. The elliptical license is also stretched: "em ver o viajante é um cavaleiro," meaning "the traveler, seen, looks like a knight." The effect is sharply contrary to normal expression, and deliberately so; the same information could be rendered in more orthodox Portuguese with no loss of economy: "ao vê-lo, o viajante parece um cavaleiro." But the structure chosen by the author in fact goes beyond the sense imposed by my paraphrase, which presents the rider as an object perceived by an external subject and loses the polyvalence of subjectivity in Rosa's phrase (in which the *viajante* is the verbal subject according to a secondary semantic take). The Rosean phrase, by imposing an impersonal phrase, *em ver o viajante,* in the rhetorically strong position as grammatical subject, forces the cinematic sense of landscape, the vastness of which is then communicated not by formal syntactic links but rather by morphology (the diminutive) and repetition. The subject is also merely implicit in the previous syntactic unit, "pelo andado do Chapadão," once again jettisoning conventional syntactic structures of subject-verb-object. The effect is that of an awesomely rapid zoom, from the view from Chapadão on to the vast landscape and the *cavaleiro,* to a new, more subjective close-up (the subsequent details of the exact pose of the rider, the color of the horse and its name). Other important authorial devices illustrated in this passage include the ellipse of the (normally obligatory) verbal element in a phrase and the juxtaposition (or coordination) of nominal units: "e o céu uma poeira azul e papagaios no vôo"; "No Urubùquaquá, não." Again, Brazilian Portuguese is more tolerant than English (and even than other Romance languages) of this device, which is suggestive of oral speech. And yet Rosa still plays outside the rules, because he does not adopt regionalisms in order to effect a sort of local color. On the contrary, his innovations are jarringly poetic; their purpose is neither mimesis nor utilitarian economy but rather a hypersensualized *engagement* of language itself, often drawing on lost etymological roots—hence the use of arcane terms as well as neologisms.

Rosa's proemic aim is not simply, through strangeness, in the Russian formalist sense, to make the text stop the reader and the words suddenly stand up straight in giddy verticality. There is also in Rosa's prose a tremendous rhythmic imperative; syntactic structures attract other structures of like kind: "Os Gerais do trovão, os Gerais do vento"; "Mar a redor, fim a fora"; "A que fora lugar, lugares, de mato-grosso, a mata escura, que é do valor do chão." The form dictates its own rhythm in an endless syntagmatic flow—not so much a stream of consciousness as a swelling tide of linguistic-aesthetic adequacy. Meter and other traditional poetic devices are used to reinforce this uncannily intuitive rhythm: assonance (mesas quebradas e mesas planas, das chapadas, onde há areia); alliteration (cavaleiro . . . curvado sempre sobre o arção e o curto da crina do cavalo—o cavalinho alazão, sem nome, só chamado Quebra-Côco); repetition, and so on. No matter how much the reader pauses to grasp the difficult fragments, or flips past peripheral details and rewordings, as Rosa's communications with his translators show there remains an ideal reading of the text in which the intended rhythmic contours of the discourse are immanent.

In contrast to the architectonic aesthetic of the extended sentence in the elegant prose of James or Proust, Rosa minimizes the period as a significant parameter. Whether because so many periods are thrown in that they lose their impact, or because syntactic units divided only by commas run on almost indefinitely, the result is an extended series of clauses and phrases with little hierarchical relation between them, rather than a series of discreet sentences, each containing its own hierarchy of clauses and phrase. This horizontal syntagmatic prolixity is exemplified in "Cara-de-Bronze" in the most extraordinary and eccentric fashion. Apart from references to Goethe, Dante, and the Upanishads, there are footnotes composed of all the names of variants of items that have been mentioned in the text. There are a long string of cattlemen's calls, a list of animals, and, unforgettably, a single list of four hundred trees, shrubs, vines, and grasses (amongst which the buriti is distinguished by capitalization). At the end of this five-page footnote, asked by an interlocutor whether or not the list is complete, the speaker replies: "A lot is missing. Almost everything," and begins again with other species, until the matter is unwillingly laid to rest with three dots. The names were indeed gathered by Rosa on visits to the bush, and one has the sense that a verbose author is here intruding clumsily on the aesthetically disciplined voice of the omniscient narrator. At least one critic, Massaud Moisés, with the advantage of hindsight and undaunted by the Rosean aura, has succinctly conveyed the excesses of *Corpo de Baile* in particular, and of a what might be called a vice or abuse in Rosean art generally. He observes:

> Regionalism leaning toward folklore, built around anecdotes, whether drawn from experience or simply imagined—this is the charac-

ter of *Sagarana,* which, with modification, continues in other works. Coming ten years later, *Corpo de Baile* is tuned to the same scale, though it enhances certain aspects of this moment in the career of the writer: the taste for detail, the accumulation of descriptions at the expense of the plot. The warbler of tales, the stylist, becomes the accomplice of the observer, overcoming the fiction-writer. His design seems to be to set up a descriptive chart of Minas Gerais, whose meaning, if it exists, disappears in the jungle of details. But the poetic element does not counterbalance the realist tone (. . .) The emphasis on the art of language, which tends toward a rhetoric which is not always purposeful and a baroque extravagance, explains the author's error of judgment in drafting *Corpo de Baile.* (1989, 464)

In fairness to the intellectual concept behind the story in "Cara-de-Bronze," it should be pointed out that its structure, which puts together two levels of adventure with open doors on each other, and the somewhat clumsy notes of the lexically voracious savant, is really an attempt to suggest a *mise-en-abîme*: Grivo's tale is set into that of Cara-de-Bronze's evening gathering, to which the character Moimeichego adds the enjoyment of the urbane witness. The journalistic notes on cattle cries and so on then introduce the author's real, extratextual experience of exposure to cattlemen over a period of months, and by extension the ideological and aesthetic project of his work as a whole. Just as there are several narrative voices in this *conto,* some of them overlapping with the authorial voice, there are also distinct instances of the author appearing in the text—not necessarily as narrator. The key instance is the character Moimeichego, whose name juxtaposes the first person singular pronouns of various languages. The secretive Rosa, who generally avoided writing about people from his own privileged social caste, is not normally guilty of this sort of biographical indulgence. But if the story is in part an undisciplined response to the sheer excitement he apparently experienced in actual interaction with the sort of people about whom he wrote, it is also an experiment which confirms his own philosophy: human nature is universal, the greatest wisdom can be sought amongst inarticulate subjects, and there is no clear division between levels of discourses, between the experiences of the humble and the grace of the muses.

The aesthetic and metaphysical quest of *Grande Sertão: Veredas.*

Grande Sertão: Veredas is Guimarães Rosa's central opus, though for various reasons atypical of his work. It is the only piece which qualifies unequivocally as a novel and the only one to have appeared as such in a volume unaccompanied by other stories. At about five hundred pages, and formally antithetical to *Corpo de Baile,* it makes for a long, hard read. A single unbroken narrative thread deepens the solitary epic adventure; there are no chapter divisions or internal subsectional titles. Also absent are the conventional order and discipline imposed by an impersonal third-person narrator. The reliability of the narration is brought into question by presentation of the discourse as a dialog. An old man, Riobaldo, a landed man of means somewhere in the outback of Minas Gerais, addresses a silent interlocutor, a professional man of the city, whose worldliness, education, and access to finer minds the speaker envies, as he tries to decipher the real sense of his own experiences as a youth. Though the narrative voice is exclusively Riobaldo's, several comments alert the reader to the interlocutory situation. Occasionally Riobaldo will interrupt his flow and apparently answer an unrecorded interjection on the part of the other. The first words of the text are also cleverly intended to enhance the reader's awareness of the nature of the discourse: for example, Riobaldo tells the *doutor* (i.e., a man benefiting from a superior institutional and worldly education) not to be startled by the gunshots they can hear which are simply those of the rancher's men practicing shooting at a tin can on a fence. The implicit disquiet of the silent interlocutor is a very effective reminder of his presence, which is, after all, purely theoretical, deducible only from Riobaldo's sporadic inferences.

Riobaldo's rambling tale begins with a discussion of the nature of God and the Devil, and man's confusion between the two. Initially, Riobaldo speaks in abstract, general terms, before introducing events from the long and bloody conflict between various frontier cattle warlords, that he lived through as a young hired gunslinger (*jagunço*). Many of these insertions are exchanges with his one great friend, a handsome young man called Diadorim. Remembering a gentle observation of Diadorim's about the ways of mothers, Riobaldo begins to speak of his earliest years, fatherless and poverty stricken, in a tiny settlement by the banks of the river. This prompt allows the narrative to settle down and proceed in more or less chronological order. A few childhood incidents are related. On one occasion Riobaldo actually met the child Diadorim, though under another name. The proud boy had a certain nobility about him; he invited Riobaldo to join him in a canoe paddled by a lackey for a foray onto the wide waters of the great São Francisco river, which the humble Riobaldo had never essayed, despite living on its banks. They crossed the river and went for a wander around the uncultivated land. A young mulatto appeared, and, thinking they were seeking isolation in order to experiment sexually, declared that he too wanted to be a part of it. The boy coyly invited him into the bushes, pulled out a large knife at a strategic moment and stabbed the mulatto deep in the thigh. The whole episode naturally forms a deep impression on Riobaldo's mind, but the two do not see each other for many years. Riobaldo also relates his first real sexual adventures and shows an independent and meditative psychological disposition, with the ability to distinguish between different sentimental attachments and not to cast conventional judgments on the prostitutes that are his first consorts. Riobaldo's mother dies and he ends up in the household of a more prosperous man whom he eventually infers to be his biological father but with whom he cannot identify psychologically.

Though he is well enough treated and given a basic education, Riobaldo runs away as soon as he is old enough. He comes into the service of a curious, politically ambitious fellow named Zé Bebelo, whom Riobaldo teaches in very little time to read, write, and add. With a war between two rival groups imminent, Riobaldo at first falls in with Bebelo's forces, but then runs away. He encounters another of the great leaders, a universally admired man named Joca Ramiro. He also meets Diadorim again, now known as Reinaldo, and discovering him to be no less than the son of Joca Ramiro, joins this side definitively. From this point on the intense friendship with Diadorim—a secret name known only to his father and Riobaldo—becomes the emotional pivot at the center of the adventurous and often bloody action.

Zé Bebelo is defeated in battle and taken alive. After obtaining the right to speak to his assembled enemies in a fair trial, he convinces them of his just conduct in the war, in an oratorical scene recalling some of the debates of the Peloponnesian War described by Thucydides, and successfully proposes that he be exiled rather than murdered; he also wins the concession that his exile last only as long as Joca Ramiro lives.

The precise reasons for the struggle are still not clear to Riobaldo, but events overtake this question and precipitate an inversion of the original alliances. Joca Ramiro is murdered by his former ally, a sinister man called Hermogenes, who now becomes the vital enemy in the conflict and the particular obsession of Diadorim. Zé Bebelo, duly liberated from his exile, returns with a handful of men on a raft, makes an alliance with a chief from the Ramiro camp, which includes Riobaldo and Diadorim, and with characteristic flair manages to win the leadership of the group. Despite his energy, his Napoleonic strategies, and his plans to transform the *sertão* into a civilized land in partnership with the forces of the distant National Government, the man lacks the blessing of fortune, and his dreams are like seeds sown on bad land; eventually he too dies and his overreaching rhetoric, the only thread which might have tied this tale of the *sertão* back into any conventional relation to greater Brazil, subsides as tangential babble in the face of the unquenchable reserves of clan hatred. The various groups loyal to Joca Ramiro, impeded by the rumored movements of government troops in the area and by *os Hermogenes,* as the enemy is now known, are unable to join together and elect a new leader. The ensuing dead time gives Riobaldo time both to reflect and to develop the bond with Diadorim, disturbing to Riobaldo because friendship has grown into love and an undeniable sexual attraction. In the meantime Riobaldo has met a nice, socially advantaged girl named Otacília on a friendly ranch and made arrangements for marriage; but from the start the intensely private Diadorim displays antipathy towards the girl. In typical male fashion, Riobaldo deals with the disturbing feelings not by pursuing intimacy with Diadorim but, on the contrary, by establishing deliberate boundaries which both ward off the feared danger and create a veneer of manly strength suggesting independence and indifference.

Finally the forces allied against the evil Hermogenes gather in a single place for a meeting. The man with the first right to leadership has died from a chest infection. Riobaldo, who is seen as courageous, decisive, and an accurate marksman, becomes the leader. His focus on executive virility—an obsession generated by contrary elements within himself—culminates in a decision to muster invincible powers by making a pact with the devil at a dark crossroads, soliciting a favorable outcome to his conflicts at the expense of his soul. The pact seems to prove efficacious. The rest of the story relates the slow march to a final victory over *os Hermogenes,* a climax counterpointed by two important incidents. At a vital moment of leadership, holed up in a house and facing heavy enemy fire, Riobaldo more or less passes out; when he comes to, he finds that the battle has swung in his own favor. Diadorim, intent on killing Hermogenes himself, recklessly engages with him in hand-to-hand combat and is killed. The bloodied body is recovered and taken back to be washed and buried. At this moment it is finally revealed with biological certainty that Diadorim is, in fact, a woman. Almost nothing of Riobaldo's subsequent existence is told, apart from the few basic circumstances making sense of his current situation many years later as a prosperous farmer happily married to Otacília, suggesting his shrewd judgment.

As a monumental adventure involving the deployment of rural forces which are virtually armies, the work stands as an epic saga of heroes and villains in the brutal frontier lands of the New World. In the strict sense of the term, however, it does not qualify as an epic since there is no notion of a defining history of origins of a given people. The generic logic of the epic goes against the Heraclitean connotations of Riobaldo's speculations about the process of becoming, the uncertainties which constantly renew themselves, and doubts which undermine any assertion of identity:

> Compadre meu Quelemém nunca fala vazio, não subtrata. Só que isto a ele não vou expor. A gente nunca deve de declarar que aceita inteiro o alheio—essa é que é a regra do rei!
> 'O senhor . . . Mire veja: o mais importante e bonito, do mundo, é isto: que as pessoas não estão sempre iguais, ainda não foram terminadas—mas que elas vão sempre mudando. Afinam ou desafinam. Verdade maior. É o que a vida me ensinou. Isso que me alegra, montão. E, outra coisa: o diabo, é às brutas; mas Deus é traiçoeiro! Ah, uma beleza de traiçoeiro—dá gosto!
>
> [My friend Quelemém never speaks in vain, never slips from the point. But I won't tell him this. You never should openly declare that you accept completely someone else's notion—that's the rule a king follows!
> Sir . . . look, see: the most important, and the prettiest thing in the world is this: that people aren't always the same, they still haven't finished forming but rather go on changing always. They become more fine-tuned, or out of tune. The larger truth. It's what life taught me. That keeps me happy a heap. Another thing: the devil plays rough; but God is treacherous! So treacherous it's beautiful—you get a taste for it!] (21)[2]

On the other hand, critics have often compared the book to medieval romance. The sense of a long adventure whose purpose is only gradually revealed with the unveiling of an impossible mystery supports this, as do the feudal echoes of chivalry, leadership, vassalage and so on, while the impression of constant metaphysical deciphering is parallel to the presentation in medieval romance of the protagonist's encounters with allegorically significant magic phenomena. But though the work does draw on various structural devices found in romance, and even exploits reader expectation of the genre, it would be inappropriate to classify it as a romance.

There is no consistent allegorical system of reference, no ultimately reliable form of authority making for the childlike sweetness of the vassal-master relation, whether in terms of Christian values or pagan metaphysical hierarchies. There is too much sense of the wantonness of violence and too much fascination with evil for *Grande Sertão: Veredas* to be the spawn of any era prior to that of the European modernism beginning in the second half of the nineteenth century.

In fact, despite these various classical literary echoes in the storyline, in terms of intellectual themes the work has most in common with the twentieth century. The Heraclitean impulse and the constant renewability of doubt are informed, philosophically, by existentialism. The focus on a single personal perspective, and the sense of loss of any reliable truth system beyond that generated by personal experience is characteristic of modernism. Further, the dubious nature of the protagonist's courage, his strength as a survivor rather than as the incarnation of an ideal, though it is not used for comic irony and is only to be inferred by close reading, is consistent with other modernist works. Thematically, the confusion of nominal gender roles—Diadorim incarnating heroic courage and the Icarian impulse, Riobaldo buying his courage with an illusion and suffering disorientation of sexual attraction—is not traditional. Finally, the stylistic license indulged places the work alongside other great modernist works that demonstrate great artistic virtuosity while revolutionizing previously held formal standards.

Though the point has not been properly digested by Rosa's critics, the consistency of the narration in terms of psychological perspective places the work at methodological odds with *Corpo de Baile* and in particular with "Cara-de-Bronze." And yet certain links remain. The invisible *doutor* character begs a mask, assignable by the reader. The obvious candidate is Guimarães Rosa himself, who as a young country doctor fulfilled precisely this role, visiting ranches on horseback and sometimes staying for a day or two. Even if biographical references are ruled out, there remains an intertextual circumstance of perhaps greater importance: the *doutor*'s attitude is little different from that of the reader, be he an upper-class Brazilian or an international reader of translations. The author aspires to a metaphysical and aesthetic dialogue between the private, marginal universe of the *sertão* and the worldly world of letters. Managing to suppress the undisciplined extra-narration incursions of "Cara-de-Bronze," in *Grande Sertão: Veredas* he deftly imposes the implied interlocutor, who we must imagine as the transcriber who actually writes down the oral story. But this listener, worldly but alien to the locale, is effectively an extension or personification of the reader, who is also implicated within the fabric of the narration. Thus, not merely in terms of semantic reference but in pragmatic terms as well, the dialogical frame spirals upward and outwards from the local to the universal; or, in the reverse sense, the text achieves a discursive axis between the external reader's cosmovision, the characteristically literary grand adventure story, and a local cultural microcosm from which common phrases, fragments of perspective, wisdom and belief, are quoted and intercalated in the narrative.

If the literary metaphysics, centered in the exploration of a rural, subaltern culture, are the same in the two works, in the novel the method is completely different, a veritable reinvention of authorial approach. Instead of forcing the issue of educated authorial enrichment of local discourse, there are only a few unobtrusive markers of the narratological superstructure. The story reads consistently in a single voice, though with attendant sociogeographic stylistic eccentricities, devices, and limitations. Despite his presumed intellectual inferiority to his interlocutor, the first person narrator, Riobaldo, is genuinely the protagonist of the discourse and not merely of the plot. He leads the story where he will in his own peculiar measure and meter. Gone are the heterogeneous regional voices of "Cara-de-Bronze," orchestrated, compelled, and dismissed by a narrator who can extract himself at will from the matter in hand and proceed to quote from Vedic or European luminaries or give botanical lists. In fact, the text achieves its organic cohesion by a sort of submission on the part of the author towards a single culturally subaltern voice, sustained over five hundred pages—a voluntary abolition of a more eloquent authorial self, which proved a rewarding challenge for Guimarães Rosa, a way of seeing the sky through the prison bars of a self-imposed discipline.

Riobaldo is an incurable autodidact, yearning for greater wisdom and aware of his limitations. His practicality miraculously mixed with the intuition of a diviner, his purpose is executive rather than legislative; he seeks exegetic resolution of specific questions of particular relevance to his own needs, not abstract musings of mere theoretical interest. Convinced that religion is an effective tool, he solicits practitioners of diverse faiths in times of need—where one fails another may succeed. Without the courage to commit himself to one faith, he is superstitiously reverential before all, gladly paying tribute to each on appropriate occasions, just in case. He is a man who believes that intuition will be more beneficial in the long run than virtue, who proceeds strategically, rather than being guided by conviction, propelled by fear more than morality. He is slow to decide on action but shrewd, and on occasion able to make vital decisions; above all, in an incredibly violent land he is a survivor, both materially and spiritually. Taking nothing for granted, he inherits the fruit of the earth which has swallowed up most of his peers. This is shown right from the very start of the book: while shots are being fired, Riobaldo takes the opportunity to converse with the *doutor*. He insists that the learned city-dweller stay with him for a few days, openly acknowledging that his real hope is to extract some insight from the precious visitor. He will very deliberately tell his long story, apologizing when he loses the main point but insisting on the attention of his interlocutor. This urge to understand or interpret even in the midst of gunshots, to think while others act on violent passions, is the fundamental *modus operandi* of Riobaldo. The long-winded and winding story is actually an attempt at concision, for his explorations and expurgations of the past can really have no end nor a single beginning.

Significantly, the central axis of *Grande Sertão Veredas* is an entity of nature. The focus is the Rio São Francisco, to which Riobaldo relates his own life in a series of comparisons. The river moves slowly but steadily, its vast course inexorable. The river's fate is, of course, termination at the sea, but this is not mentioned; metaphysical speculation is restricted to the present rather than the absent, to the process rather than final resolution, to life rather than death. The writer has restricted himself to the landlocked discourse of an aging countryman; the *sertão* is the universe of life, a flat earth without precipice or sea. The monologue attempts with partial success to unravel a metaphysical Gorgian knot rather than to rend it asunder by recourse to theoretical resolutions or to the principles of a single guiding religion. Omniscient, impersonal narration is necessarily foregone, and replaced with the unfinished quality of spontaneous oral discourse, and thought itself.

Part of the compensation for the consequent scattering of order is a more organic hold on metaphysical issues. Rather than elaborate the metaphysical questions developed by the authoritarian wisdom of professionals, philosophers, alchemists and so on, or simply accumulate a baroque multitude of problems without any serious attempt to solve them, the narration sticks resolutely to a handful of fundamental issues. The central enigma posed by Riobaldo is that of the existence of the devil. The theme is introduced at the outset, almost anecdotally, with Riobaldo's casual mentioning of a newborn calf massacred because, having emerged into the world with a canine snout and apparently laughing, it was taken to be a devil. Within a page a dozen alternate names for the Devil have been mentioned and Riobaldo has tried to deny its existence by mocking the ignorance of the locals. But the Devil, or some demonic principle, is also a key player in the drama of the novel (giving Riobaldo courage and success in exchange for his soul) and a vital element in the complex dichotomy—male/female, courage/ cowardice, absolute conviction/endless speculation, life as mission/ life as survival—formed by Riobaldo and Diadorim. For Riobaldo, Diadorim is, like the Devil, a compelling but unknowable quantity. Moreover, Riobaldo's sexual desire for Diadorim is in his own eyes unspeakable and diabolic. Finally, Riobaldo's reason and moderation detects in Diadorim's subjugation to vengeance an element of evil. In some way he incarnates a demonlike courage—hence the name Diadorim, simultaneously *te adoro* and *diabo*. Diadorim is both angel and devil, impossible woman and impossible man. The narration closes with a declaration that the tale has been told, with the wishful affirmation that the Devil does not exist, that the interlocutors are friends:

> 'Cerro. O senhor vê. Contei tudo. Afora estou aqui, quase barranqueiro. Para a velhice vou, com ordem e trabalho. Sei de mim? Cumpro. O Rio de São Fransisco—que de tão grande se comparece—parece é um pau grosso, em pé, enorme . . . Amável, o senhor me ouviu, minha idéia confirmou: que o Diabo não existe. Pois não? O senhor é um homem soberano, circunspecto. Amigos somos. Nonada. O diabo não há! É o que eu digo, se for . . . Existe é homem humano. Travessia. ∞

> [I'll stop there. As you see. I've told everything. Here I am out here, living almost on the river. I'm heading toward old age with calm and hard work. Do I know myself? I carry on. The São Francisco River—so big to see—looks like a fat stick, standing up, enormous . . . You heard me out kindly, sir, and confirmed my view: that the Devil doesn't exist. Right? You are a self-assured and circumspect man. We are friends. It's nothing at all. There is no devil! That's what I say, even . . . What exists is man, the human. Passage. ∞]

The term, *nonada*, (i.e., "trifle," but by etymology a double negation, *não é nada*), a repeat of the first word of the book, marks the circularity of the text. The exclamation mark in the phrase denying the devil's existence ("O diabo não há!") is a negative invocation marking anxious desire, fear rather conviction. The dots concluding the following phrase, after the conjunction of hypothesis and future subjunctive ("o que eu digo, se for . . ."), mark the interminable nature of this supposed conclusion. The last words give the only certainties: the human condition—never resolved—and the fact of travel rather than arrival. Following them in the original edition is the infinity sign ∞. Between living human experience and the cipher of the cosmos no more substantial link than interrogative desire is posited.

And yet this desire is itself a part of the human condition, something which itself alters reality. The text does not prove utterly circular; telling the story is not without its own consequences.

The paragraphs prior to the one quoted recall another telling of the story, this time not to the *doutor,* but rather with a previous listener, a neighbor, the wise and philosophical man, Quelemém. Riobaldo, after telling the whole story to him, musters courage to ask him whether he considers that he (Riobaldo) did in fact make a pact with the devil and sell his soul. As Quelemém replies: "Tem cisma não. Pensa para diante. Comprar ou vender, ás vezes, são as ações que são as quase iguais" ("Don't be worrying about that. Think forwards. Sometimes buying or selling are almost the same thing.") The text thus infers that by a process of pragmatic action and not of jurisdiction, Riobaldo has made his own way and constructed a reality by means of an exchange with the external world and its inhabitants, the ultimate terms of which barely matter or are indeterminable. In this sense the narration has reached its teleological purpose, both in the immediate sense that the story has been told and an adequate if imperfect understanding achieved, and also in the broader sense of narration as a journey through life. The levels of reference are masterfully bound together: the river and the Devil, the journey through life and the problem of evil and the question of its true locus, the act of staring in the mirror while thinking to interrogate the universe. In short, the notion of life as a performance of subjective narration in the first person, disguised as a passive ride down the river, encountering some new force of the external world at each bend. Notwithstanding the vertiginous, tropical abundance of ideas and "mythemes," (basic semantic motifs) the number of themes is blessedly simplified by comparison with *Corpo de Baile,* and is proportionate with the experience and imagination of the central protagonist who, despite his sense of distance from the intellectual norms of any worldly interlocutor (or reader, or author), achieves an existential legitimacy which is incomplete but organic.

Grande Sertão: Veredas does not feature the conscious delight in stylistic rupture, or the intense consciousness of accelerating historicity which marks the modernist movement both in Europe prior to World War I and in the Brazil of the twenties. Though it is possible to chronologically place the adventure at a period from just prior to the turn of the century through the 1920s, the absence of references to known towns or to technology on the one hand, and on the other the careful descriptions of eccentric landscapes effectively locate the work in a dreamtime. Guimarães Rosa exploits ignorance of his urbane reading public, foreign or Brazilian, as to the regional historical and geographical details, to make the subject matter a purely imaginative phenomenon. The governing principle is rather the act of memory made by Riobaldo for the purpose of metaphysical speculation, his own deliberately subjective reconstruction of concrete events which are now psychologically orchestrated as aspects of a greater epistemological problem of particular fascination to himself. The descriptions of mountain ranges and plains, bushes and species, for example, are not designed to give an objective sense of the lay of the land but rather to communicate the impression made on Riobaldo as he moves steadily and often laboriously through it. The subject in *Grande Sertão: Veredas* is not a hero but a speaker; as in the most radical works of modernism, the final protagonists are the subjective filters of perception, memory and language.

Machado de Assis, Mário de Andrade, Carlos Drummond de Andrade

Machado de Assis: Victoriana in Rio.

Like Borges, the eccentric literary genius of Machado de Assis diverges from the careers of almost all noteworthy Latin American writers. The "Machado de Assis enigma" is put thus by Massaud Moisés:

> The sorcerer of Cosme Velho' [an old suburb of Rio], 'a subterranean man', 'Cyclops of lucidity', are some of the epithets the critics have used to designate the Machado de Assis enigma. Astonishment, irritation, surprise, bedazzlement, indifference, exaltation, somnolence—his work has provoked every type of reaction. And after the demise of the writer, literary styles have succeeded each other in accelerating rhythm, almost as substantial and numerous as all the styles which preceded him (. . .) after him came Proust, Joyce, Huxley, Gide and more (. . .); in our literary world real stars burst upon the scene, such

as Mário de Andrade, Graciliano Ramos, Guimarães Rosa, Clarice Lispector, Osman Lins, just to mention the prose writers. But even with this, his dusky light, the insipid glow of a horizon which abandons the day without yet entering the nocturnal obscurity, has not dimmed. On the contrary, as literary modes come and go, time weathers all the 'isms', while the star of Machado de Assis continues to shine and to emit the same light of a strange planet, progressively strengthened by the successive tests to which it has been put. (Moisés 1984, 391–2)

Living from 1839 to 1908, Machado de Assis grew to manhood amidst the conventional romantic literature of the midcentury period in Brazil, but his world view was much better suited to the realism which became predominant in the last decades of the century through French influence. Having written romantic poetry, dramas, short stories, criticism, and some fairly ordinary novels, from about 1880 Machado de Assis produced several highly unusual novels which are distinguished by literary prowess, artistic maturity, psychological depth, and originality of conception. *Memórias Póstumas de Brás Cubas* constitutes a deviation from realism in the direction of fantasy in that its narrator is dead, flitting around both in the nether world and in a series of autobiographical reminiscences of a staid life in bourgeois nineteenth-century Rio. The eponymous protagonist of *Quincas Borba,* (translated to English as *Philosopher or Dog*), is an eccentric provincial character fatally inclined to grandiose philosophical rumination, accompanied by a dog who acquires his name after his descent into destitution and eventual death. The confusion is accentuated by one of the novel's favorite devices, speculation on the mute dog's thoughts. Despite the misanthropy and heavy-handed satire created by this gloomy situation, the sadistic elements are held in check by Machado de Assis's characteristic subtlety and unpredictable meanderings of plot. Machado de Assis's works were initially published in episodes in the press. His method of stringing together separate and autonomous scenes produced a slightly disjointed effect, but this tendency is deliberate: the vagaries of circumstance in the wobbly intrigue reflect the fickleness of fortune and the absence of justice. Often there is such a dearth of action in Machado de Assis's stories that the main point becomes cerebral or sentimental reaction rather than action as such. Another consequence is that the Machadian novel is dominated by the central speculative intelligence of the narrator. The characters themselves are too psychologically capricious to be consistent social representations; they remind us of the creative mystery of human interaction, and of the enormous potential for disappointment, for deviation from any reassuring Providence.

In some sense Machado de Assis must be seen to have anticipated the importance in twentieth-century European literature of the figure of bourgeois withdrawal from social and political movement. And yet, this tendency is counterbalanced by general and apparently gentle references to historical events so that critics have read into his work profound social commentary.

The late work, *Memorial de Aires,* presents the memoirs of a retired diplomat, an archetypal Machadian narrator in that his vocation and habit is to observe and make astute comments on the workings of the world, and occasionally to facilitate the dramas of younger persons. Ostensibly the main interest of the narrator is the prospect of a sound marriage for a niece. Though written late in the first decade of this century, the dated events take place at the time of the bloodless revolution in which military officers of a positivist ideology deposed the aging emperor and brought in the era now known as the Old Republic. There are various references to these events and to the fear of violence and abuse within the general public. But the anticipations prove needless; the whole point is that everything remains more or less the same despite the rhetoric. Reminiscent of the refined nihilism of Flaubert's *L'Éducation sentimentale,* the text subtly suggests the irrelevance of the claims of historical dynamism to the individual's sentimental existence. With the lapse of several decades between the time of these events and the composition and release of the novel, the starkness of this juxtaposition is lessened. However, the narrative structure, in which the descriptions of historical events are dated by journal entry to the exact date of occurrence and the speaker is well informed, remains as a prompt for the reader's consideration of the unexplained significance of the inclusion of these events. On the other hand, the work can be read as an account of a relatively eventless and almost tensionless salon melodrama seen through the eyes of an urbane but tired gentleman retiree. The work is, then, on one level a subtle historical reflection and on another more superficial level a placid, limp comedy of manners duly bought to resolution with the realization of the desired marriage.

If *Memorial de Aires* is an enticing book for those interested in the sociopolitical perspective of Machado de Assis, his *Dom Casmurro* constitutes a *tour de force* on a purely literary level, again with the same resemblance to a lake whose serene and motionless surface veils mysterious and murky depths. Published in 1900 and generally considered his masterpiece, *Dom Casmurro*

(*Lord Taciturn*) offers the characteristic Machadian voice of an elderly gentleman of solid Rio bourgeois stock who tells the story of his marriage to the neighbor of his childhood years, the seed of which was sown at an early age and nurtured by his shrewd future spouse. The story unfolds: he believes, eventually, that she has committed adultery with an old friend and that he is not the father of her child. He cuts off his wife and son, and both die far away in Europe, leaving him alone and disillusioned. There is no decisive evidence, however, that his suspicions are justified, and the case has become one of the great literary enigmas of Brazil. Brilliantly constructed, it develops a plausible case for both belief or disbelief. The very long period of the action gives rise to a whole series of humorous tableaux, many set during the narrator's innocent childhood. The entire household of relatives and hangers-on offers a rich portrait of social prototypes, tempered by the unpredictable behavior characteristic of Machadian fiction.

The black humor which enlivens this tale of embitterment (Dom Casmurro's real name is Bento, "blessed") is developed on another level, the metaliterary. The narrator is obsessed with Shakespeare's Othello, frequently quotes it, and actually attends a performance which stimulates his sense of the right to be intolerant of his suspected rival. Of course, the Othello motif in fact suggests to the reader the possible innocence of the accused. Fascinatingly, although it is probably the most studied book in the history of Brazilian literature, critics used simply to argue for and against the innocence of the female protagonist, or, at best, acknowledged that the point of the book was precisely to leave this issue perfectly poised, irresolvable. It was not until 1984 that a shattering deconstructionist punch was added to the debate by an English Brazilianist, John Gledson (*The Deceptive Realism of Machado de Assis: A Dissenting Interpretation of Casmurro*), who argued that not only is the woman innocent but that the narrator is quite mad, needing to write (or talk) alone to convince himself, reworking his biographical history until he has painted his enemy into a corner at the expense of his own lucidity. His interpretation goes so far as to read into *Casmurro* an entire social psychology based on the premise of the incompatibility between two Rio social classes or castes—the patrician, formerly landed upper bourgeoisie and the emergent urban nouveau riche. If this historiographical complement is more tenuous than Gledson's basic psychological reading, it does suggest the presence of another Machadian instance of disguised social commentary. If this view is then reconsidered in the light of the actual substance of the text, a good part of which presents subtle but increasingly amusing exposés of child psychology, it becomes apparent that the various ironies in the work are of the most complex order, whether on the level of the perception of the world by the protagonist as child, the adults' interaction with this child and with each other, the mature narrator's references to the grandiose rhetoric of Othello and its juxtaposition with trivial occurrences in his small existence, or, finally, in what the text may be saying about the psycho-social dynamics of a particular historical context. Machado de Assis is without doubt one of the great masters of irony in world literature, and also one of the great pessimist voices. He is also unusual in the nineteenth-century Latin American context in that his narrative mode is highly subjective, pointing towards the unreliable and complex narrators of later European modernism, well into the twentieth century.

Finally, Machado de Assis stands out in the Latin American context of his time in that, although he was Anglophile in his reading and Francophile by education, there is no sense of the anxious, intellectually intimidated northwestward look across the Atlantic to Europe, for most Latin Americans the seat of true civilization and home to its trend-setting luminaries. Machado de Assis's stories are set in imperial Brazil. Rio, already unique in the Americas as the former capital of a European empire (at the time of the Napoleonic occupation of the Iberian peninsula, prior to Brazilian independence) had by then become the court site of a huge sovereign nation, and, while most of its South American neighbors emphasized their provincialism and barbarity by interminable interfratricidal violence, provided a stable site for nineteenth-century civilization. Paradoxically, this stability and psychological sovereignty were probably preconditions for the flourishing of Machado de Assis's profound pessimism and skepticism: the birth of nations often is marked by teleological ambitions and naïve rhetoric, whereas social stability and intractability tend to frustrate individualism while inducing a sense of inadequacy between thwarted personal ambition and preestablished national grandeur.

Alone amongst his Latin American contemporaries, Machado de Assis is one of the world's great Victorian writers and a reminder of the hegemonic pervasiveness of this psychological moment in the history of civilization. His stories, particularly the earlier novels, tell of an excruciatingly stable metropolis, where the street, graced by carriages and later tramways, but uncluttered by heavy traffic, presents no threat to the social order, and where the drawing room, as in Jane Austen, is a temple of conversation dedicated to unthreatening domestic events. While Machado de Assis is most commonly likened to Sterne because of the intrusive and literary self-consciousness of the narrative voice, a more useful comparison might well be with Chekhov. Coming from a provincial background and socioeconomic disadvantage, each achieved bourgeois prosperity and composed works which on the surface are neither revolutionary nor even shocking, but which contain a subtle social commentary and an eccentric subjectivity. Operating in a frame of deceptive banality, Machado's works are extraordinarily and disturbingly mature, preserving a sense of alienation without the slightest trace of romantic narcissism.

Mário de Andrade: A *paulistano*'s three weeks in the Amazon.

Mário de Andrade, sometimes referred to as the "pope" of *Modernismo,* is also of central importance to any study of that movement. It is important to note that despite the authoritarian centralism of the inaugurating event of Brazilian modernism, the *Semana de Arte Moderna* in São Paulo in 1922, the ecclesiastic metaphor is inappropriate to the divergence of energies, ideologies, and local bases of the various branches of *Modernismo.* Mário de Andrade's situation is not comparable, for example, to that of André Breton's position of authority in the surrealist movement. Nor is it the case that Mário's literary output was so outstanding as to dwarf the achievement of others, in the way that Mallarmé dominates any discussion of French symbolism. In fact a more appropriate metaphor for Mário's role in *Modernismo* is that of "Renaissance man," for he played an important part in almost all the domains of cultural activity impacted by the movement. He was one of the many organizers of the initial *Semana.* For the better part of the 1920s he dedicated himself to literature, producing seminal poetry, short stories, and longer prose works. His original profession, however, was as a professor of the history of music. His output in the musicological domain is also extraordinary, in terms of its volume, erudition, and pioneering aspect, with eleven major works on a range of topics including popular music in the United States, and featuring as the major work *A Música e a canção populares no Brasil,* an encyclopedic compilation of notes on regional music which still stands today as probably the richest text in this area. Mário was also the most important literary critic of his time, which in Brazil preceded the period of specialized university literary scholars. In the 1940s Andrade published a lengthy monograph, *O movimento modernista,* as well as a volume of critical essays, *Aspectos da literatura.* He had had a long time to prepare his definitive commentary, for he had corresponded intensively from the early 1920s on, with other major figures of modernism such as Oswald de Andrade and Carlos Drummond de Andrade, and with a wide range of luminaries from other disciplines. Given his status as creative participant, as critical commentator with evolving opinions, and also as central witness to many real events, this correspondence is a gold mine for literary scholars, greatly facilitating penetration of many questions about the productive context of a given modernist work. So much of the correspondence has since been published in a steady flow of unrelated volumes that one is tempted to include this epistolary ensemble, as one would in the case of a Dr. Johnson or Mme de Staèl, as a virtual literary genre.

Finally, Mário de Andrade's vocation was, like Sartre's, more that of an intellectual than of a writer. The modernist movement tended to consist of writers and artists who conceived their work in terms of an intellectual project but who were more creative artistically than they were ideologically consistent. This is not true in the case of Mário, who conceived creative projects in accordance with his stance on the problem of the development of an authentic national culture. He was able to bring to the nationalistic but Eurocentric literary elite an expansive knowledge of folklore, popular music, and musicology—that is, a real understanding of the Brazilian national popular culture which liberal bourgeois intellectuals agreed deserved recognition, celebration, and assimilation, but from which they were psychologically separated by differences of class or ethnicity. Just as his thinking penetrated the barriers between different categories of artistic expression, Mário de Andrade also perceived the need for activity beyond the conventional domain of the arts. From 1934 to 1937, in the context of a new era of state interventionism, he organized and directed the São Paulo (city) Department of Culture which tried to provide the popular classes with access to the arts. His efforts in this direction have recently earned comparison to the internationally renowned organizer of innovative literacy programs in Brazil, Paulo Freire, thus relating Mário's ideas to the activist cultural politics of the Brazilian left prior to the military takeover in 1964 (see Schelling 1988). In earlier years Mário had traveled around Brazil, including the Amazon, in search of local culture—in a word, the mythical *Brasil brasileiro.* Marrying this sweeping embrace of national roots to his own particular *paulista* passion and the enthusiasm for the imminent cultural achievements of a great new Brazil, Mário de Andrade then dedicated his eclectic energies to the question of national culture. He spent 1938 and 1939 in Rio as the director of the Instituto de Artes of the newly created Federal University. Given the cultural prejudices of the time, it is extraordinary and revealing that Mário de Andrade never left Brazil.

His collection of poems from 1922, *A Paulicéia Desvairada,* was the most important opus contemporaneous with the *Semana* and a seminal text of first generation *Modernismo*. Apart from assimilating and illustrating the new modernist aesthetic—the depiction of movement rather than stasis, formal experimentation, the iconoclastic demolition of conservative artistic mores, the celebration of the authentic and the vernacular rather than the lofty Parnassian ideal, above all the search for something more genuinely Brazilian—the volume deploys an energy distinct from that of the new artistic agenda, and which resides in the poet's profound and lifelong passion for this new metropolitan giant of the twentieth century, São Paulo. Like New York, viewed objectively as a physical ensemble, the city leans as much to ugliness as to elegance, and yet, like its Yankee corespondent it stands as a beacon of real hope for millions of European, Japanese, and other immigrants and as the place of opportunity for millions of Brazilians, a magnet of diverse energies, and a capital of the human achievements peculiar to the twentieth century.

Mário was himself emblematic of the new *Homo brasiliensis*—innovative, flexible, racially synthetic. Visibly of mulatto stock, a fact he seems to have simply ignored in his texts though it was not unimportant to him personally, the preferred ethnic subculture of much of his work is that of Italian *paulista* immigrants. But São Paulo stands as the crossroads of the modern, the melting pot of cultural fusion and reinvention, fired by prosperity:

> Garoa do meu São Paulo,
> -Timbre triste de martírios-
> Um negro vem vindo, é branco!
> Só bem perto fica negro,
> Passa e torna a ficar branco.
>
> Meu São Paulo da garoa,
> -Londres das neblinas finas-
> Um pobre vem vindo, é rico!
> Só bem perto fica pobre,
> Passa e torna a ficar rico.

> [Drizzle of my São Paulo,
> -the sad resonance of suffering-
> A black man comes along, he's white!
> Only close up is his blackness seen,
> He passes and becomes white again.
>
> My São Paulo of the drizzle
> -London of the fine fog-
> A poor man comes along, he's rich!
> Only close up is his poverty seen,
> He passes and becomes rich again.]
> ("Garoa do meu São Paulo" 1987, 353)

In 1927, a first attempt at longer prose was published, *Amar, Verbo Intransitivo,* which recounts the domestic adventure of a rich *paulista* family whose patriarch hires a German to sexually initiate his son. The book is still published and marketed as a novel, with a conventional linear story. Its main impact at the time was through the social scandal of the situation depicted, a deliberate affront to bourgeois sensibility, in line with the modernist ethic, and a challenge to the racism that assigned biological and moral superiority to Aryans. In retrospect the book is most interesting as an object of formal literary analysis, for structurally the work is severely flawed. Mário himself called it an "idyll" rather than a novel. Its tone of psychological verisimilitude is undermined by deviations in the consistency of the characters. The *Fräulein,* prostitute and lover, occasionally adopts the rhetoric of Aryan supremacy; the narrator also intrudes on his own storytelling voice with a sociological argument. In an excited letter to the poet Manuel Bandeira, Mário himself acknowledges the confusion:

> It's an investigation. Is it a crazy idea? I like my Fräulein very much. If I am a comic writer, the book is the best I can offer as comic commentary. But I'm afraid of being wrong. The book is an incredible mixture. Everything is in there. Criticism, theory, psychology and even romance: I am myself, and I am a researcher. (1958, 54)

It is doubtful that the book would have survived if it were not virtually the only readily readable novel by such a famous writer. The confusion of this productive context is illustrative, however, of a generalized structural tension in his fictional work. The complications of an excessively heterogeneous agenda were enticing for the intellectual but ultimately destructive for the artist. Mário de Andrade was at least as gifted as other writers of his era and had a global vision surpassing their scope, and yet his literary repertoire is as inadequate as it is eclectic. Admittedly he did produce a solid body of short stories which are still widely read today, a few of which are quite polished. But in the domain of longer fiction his output is disappointing. The Voltaire of Brazilian modernism, Mário de Andrade figures as an omnipresent critical intelligence, while the most important, or most successful, creative works are produced by others.

Nevertheless, the only other longer fictional piece by Mário, *Macunaíma, o heroí sem nenhum caráter,* is the single most emblematic work of *Modernismo*. The hero is an Amerindian, typically enough from the Amazon. His various amoral adventures in the forest with his own family members and some fantastic entities illustrate the indigenous cosmovision as premoral, naïve and playful, sexually opportunistic and unpredictable, and above all as extraordinary. A twist in the plot leads him into conflict with a giant who lives in São Paulo and has a non-Iberian, immigrant name—Venceslau Pietro Pietri. The arbitrary plot brings Macunaíma into contact not just with the mysterious machines of industrial modernity but also with various traditional folkloric regimes from around the country. In this way the work brings together elements from an original anthropological triangle: the Amazon wilderness, the post-Colombian but archaic colonial heritage and the impending twentieth-century progress of São Paulo. Macunaíma is a national hero. Within the Brazilian racial triangle of Africans, Europeans, and Amerindians, Macunaíma's indigenous racial aspect is an inevitable choice, both because of the convenient neutrality of the Amerindian in relation to the urban white/black complex, and in the light of the precedent of the indigene as nationalist symbol in the Indianist tradition of romantic Brazilian literature. But given the surreal background of the work there is nothing to prevent the author from meddling with the usual division of races—Macunaíma, we are told, is actually born black, and later becomes white.

The twist to his zany and colorful adventures is the *nenhum caráter* (morally characterless) argument in the title. The hero is wonderfully flexible and indeed enjoys magic as an everyday part of existence. But there really is no rhyme or reason, no end purpose to the endlessly improvised games he plays. He is a Peter Pan figure, a brilliant idiot condemned to eternal childhood. Unlike Peter Pan, however, Macunaíma does reach a conclusion; the hero gets to the end of his road and, spent and sick, seeing no further purpose in life gives it up, whereupon he is conveniently turned into a constellation and apotheosized.

The ending confirms the likely categorization of the book as an epic, a national adventure. But the subtitle undermines this argument by suggesting that national identity is not a quest but a colorful and extraordinary carnaval with no real order, a rotating carousel with no intelligent control at its center. This pessimistic perspective must be seen in the context of other roughly contemporaneous intellectual arguments of national identity, such as Prado's pessimistic *Retrato do Brasil,* or Freyre's optimistic *Casa Grande e Senzala.* In these works there is a polarized or even schizophrenic oscillation between euphoric evocation of an exuberant Brazilian identity and a sense of chronic national inferiority. Quite appropriately, one of the seminal films of the 1960s *Cinema Novo* movement, and the definitive artistic work in the broader cultural moment of the late 1960s known as *Tropicalismo,* was an adaptation of Mário's masterpiece.

Macunaíma presents the greatest cultural kaleidoscope ever assembled in a Brazilian work of art and simultaneously insists, by its subtitle as well as by its plot, on the problematic nature of this mosaic identity. In this sense it is both precocious and judicious, and thematically quite extraordinary. There is, however, a clear limitation to the portrait, for since it never goes beyond game-playing it actually leans more toward farce than epic. Its insistence on the ludic and the improvised present as opposed to a solid mythical past or an awaited future seems to preclude any real judgment from the author on this state of affairs.

The work is normally grouped with novels, but, with the author's usual categorical ambivalence, it was christened a rhapsody. This borrowing from musical terminology is felicitous in its suggestion of artistic synesthesia. The book is a sort of mining of folkloric musical, visual, and mythic elements. Further, the whole playful psychology of the protagonist, assimilated in turn by the narrative voice which is generally in *style indirect libre,* is more along the lines of musical improvisation than prose fiction. *Macunaíma* is also a linguistic *tour de force,* a parade of lexical curiosities and a revolutionary exercise in disregard for conventionally correct syntax. In a word, it is self-consciously, overarchingly, and splendidly Brazilian, rather than Portuguese. The importance of this point is emphasized by Andrade's central placement, between two sets of eight chapters, of the *"Carta Prás Icambiabas,"* where Macunaíma writes a letter back to his illiterate friends in the Amazon in an absurdly courtly, antiquated peninsular dialect. By its contextual absurdity the text serves to underline the distance between the modern Brazilian vernacular and classic continental Portuguese literary models.

The impact of *Macunaíma* was enormous. It is perhaps the one work of fiction which, along with the various manifestos of *Modernismo* is obligatory canonical reading for the student of literary history. On the other hand it was also Mário's last relatively long fictional project. Characteristically, it was conceived in terms of an agenda reaching beyond the internal laws of fiction itself, to the broader struggle to assert a Brazilian linguistic and thematic identity.

If Mário de Andrade was not, ultimately, a novelist or poet by vocation, his forays into these domains are amongst the most important works of modernism. This is suggestive both of his talent and of the literary limitations of the movement. In time, as we will see in the following chapter, Mário proved to be sharpest critic of *Modernismo*'s first generation, which he had led.

Carlos Drummond de Andrade: against essentialism.

Carlos Drummond de Andrade is considered a member of the modernist generation, even though he was born too late to participate in its inauguration at the *Semana de Arte Moderna* in 1922. He escaped involvement in the polarizing aesthetic and ideological debates which eventually divided the ranks of the first generation of *Modernismo* in São Paulo, but which have little to do with his own highly personal project. Born in 1902, Drummond was engaged in the modernist current in literature and the press from an early age, cofounding a literary journal, *A Revista,* in 1925, and in the following year returning from Rio to Minas Gerais to take up work at a Belo Horizonte paper. Though he eventually became editor-in-chief, he entered government service in 1929, and in 1934 moved back to Rio. From then on he spent most of his career working in government ministries and residing in Rio, constantly composing and steadily publishing volumes of poetry, while writing *crônicas* for the daily press (short fictional or speculative pieces). His first volume, *Alguma Poesia,* appeared in 1930 and immediately won him attention from Mário de Andrade and other intellectual literary leaders. In it, Drummond conforms to the modernist trend of the deliberately vernacular tone, the adolescent cultivation of iconoclastic banality, and the prosification of the poetic voice. But contrary to the puerile gusto of the overwhelming majority of his contemporaries, the poet revealed a critical perspicacity, penetrating philosophical judgment, and a profound sense of measure, both metrical and ideational. His rebellion against convention is the opposite of *Modernismo*'s complacent inversion of the conventional hierarchy of the aesthetic and moral high ground of traditional poetry. Drummond battles constantly to see through appearances and analyze the extraordinary contained in the ordinary. Many aspects have been listed by a series of commentators as fundamental elements in the Drummondian poetic universe, which is too rich to be encapsulated in a brief paragraph. A few observations or suggestions can, however, be made. Major themes in the work include the love for rural and small-town Minas Gerais, and, alternately, the wretched anonymity of the middle or lower-middle class *carioca*, not as graceful Epicurean residing in the *cidade maravilhosa*, the definitive tropical metropolis, but merely as a rather plain and mediocre being in just another urb on the coattails of history. From a more metaphysical point of view, Drummond frequently juxtaposes the inner-self and the broader workings of the world. There is frequently a sense of tension between the sweeping universal and the idiomatic particular. Finally, he has a strong sense of limitations, of the balance between the poetic and childlike sense of all things being possible and the crippling impossibility in a dubious world of sure achievement and meaning: "Tenho apenas duas mãos / e o sentimento do mundo, / mas estou cheio de escravos" (I have just two hands / and the feeling of the world / but I am full of slaves) ("Sentimento do mundo," 1977,[3] 102). The sense of limitation applies also to the poetic act itself. Skepticism regarding any presumption of adequate communication in poetry and the gap between the sentiment seeking expression and the capacity of the medium is a consistently reappearing theme in Drummond's work:

> A poesía é incomunicável.
> Fique torto no seu canto.
> Não ame.
>   . . . .
> Tudo é possível, só eu impossível
>   . . . .
> Suponha que um anjo de fogo
> varesse a face da terra
> e os homens sacrificados
> pedissem perdão'
> Não peça.

['Secret'
Poetry is incommunicable.
be twisted in its song.
Do not love.
. . . . .
Everything is possible, only I am impossible
. . . .
Suppose an angel of fire
swept the face of the earth
and the sacrificed men
begged for pardon
Do not beg.]

("Segredo," 1977, 94)

Drummond is enticed by silence and noncommunication, or at least by psychological privacy, as much as by the impulse to expression. But the imperatives suggest an endless dramatic tension between protagonists rather than a real conclusion. The poem does not resolve the identity of the protagonists, and the ambiguity embraces various possible subjects, including the poet or the poetic voice, Poetry itself, or even an unnamed third party. The line from the middle strophe (above) suggests a continuum of impotence applying not only to the poetic vocation but also to personal identity. In other poems psycho-sexual impotence, or, more generally, inadequacy, is a prominent concern. In common with most Brazilian literature Drummond not infrequently adopts a stance of benign celebration—the *crônica* in particular constituting an appropriate narrative space for light comic elements. But despite a humorous element lurking in the poetry, the most striking feature is its sharp self-deprecation. The yearning for an authentic identity formed in childhood or in his present status as poet is evoked, but cast in the sober shadow of knowledge of some degree of failure or unreality:

E agora, José?
A festa acabou,
a luz apagou,
o povo sumiu,
. . . . .
E agora, José,
sua doce palavra,
seu instante de febre,
sua gula e jejum,
sua biblioteca,
sua lavra de ouro,

> seu terno de vidro,
> sua incoerência,
> seu ódio—e agora?
>
> Com a chave na mão
> quer abrir a porta,
> não existe porta;
> quer morrer no mar,
> mas o mar secou;
> quer ir para Minas,
> Minas não há mais,
> José, e agora?
>
> [And now, José?
> The party ended,
> The light went out, the people vanished,
> . . . .
>
> And now José,
> your sweet tongue,
> your instant of fever,
> your feast and fasting,
> your library,
> your mining for gold,
> your suit of glass,
> your incoherence,
> your hate—and now?
>
> Key in hand
> you want to open the door,
> the door does not exist;
> you want to die at sea,
> but the sea dried up;
> you want to go to Minas,
> there is no more Minas,
> José, and now?]
>
> ("José," 130)

Drummond's poetic persona is a kindred spirit to the paradigmatic antiheroes of twentieth-century literature, from Eliot to Kafka to Joyce's Bloom or Sartre's hypocrites. Like so many sensitive literary intelligences in our age, confronted with the lacuna between theory and practice, prescribed reality and anarchic present, in short, with the ever-accelerating contradictions of progress, the Drummondian voice is more reactive than active, more descriptive than prescriptive. The single strongest thematic motif is irony. This is neither cynicism nor a radical argument for the impracticability of faith. Drummond is modernist rather than post-modernist. The sense of tension, while at times dabbling in self-denunciation, is still precisely that—a dramatic balance between the pessimism of the aging adult and a touching capacity for childlike joy, between the knowledge of the imperfection of relationships and the power of love discernible in various loci of affection—the provincial child home, sexual love, Platonic friendship, and the solidarity between men in a century of progress.

Confessional, fraternal, and always highly personal, Drummond's project is in one important way analogous to that of his fellow *mineiro*, Guimarães Rosa. His observation and aesthetic appropriation of the concrete world—whether in the subculture of the rural Minas Gerais of his childhood, or in the metropolis—is integrated into an ahistorical, metaphysical problematic, that of the conflictive balance and mutual dependence of the inner-self and the external world.

> A treva mais estrita já pousara
> sobre a estrada de Minas, pedregosa,
> e a máquina do mundo, repelida,
>
> se foi miudamente recompondo,
> enquanto eu, avaliando o que perdera,
> seguia vagaroso, de mãos pensas.
>
> [The most exact shadow had descended
> on the road in Minas, stony,
> and the machine of the world, repelled,
>
> went recomposing itself discreetly,
> while I, weighing up what I had lost,
> continued on languidly, with my hands hanging.]
> ("A máquina do mundo," 273)

Drummond found substantial intellectual nourishment in the dominant European metaphysic of the midcentury period, existentialism. In the important collection of 1962, *Lição de Coisas,* he separated the volume into sections dealing with the main themes in his work, including his childhood roots on the land in Minas, Rio, memory, friendship, love, poetry itself. There is not a section on Brazil, but there are two remaining sections, entitled simply, "Ser" and "Mundo" ("Being" and "World"), which can be directly related to the existential themes of being and time, as well as, in a less abstract sense, his constant concern with the balance between the individual and society. The existentialist insistence on the present rather than the past or the future appealed naturally to Drummond, as did the rejection of myths. The preference for subjective precision over subscription to an ideology, national or political, is a recurring motif in the various sections of the volume and elsewhere in his work.

> Onde é Brasil?
> Que verdura é amor?
> Quando te condensas, atingindo
> O ponto fora do tempo e da vida?
>
> Que importa este lugar
> se todo lugar
> é ponto de ver e não de ser?
> E esta hora, se toda hora
> já se completa longe de si mesma
> e te deixa mais longe da procura?
> E apenas resta
> um sistema de sons que vai guiando
> o gosto de dizer e de sentir
> a existência verbal
>   a electrônica
> e musical figuração das coisas?
>
> [Where is Brazil?
> What greenness is love?
> When do you condense, reaching
> The point outside time and life?
>
> What does this place matter if every place
> is a point from which to see and not to be?
> And this moment, if every moment
> already completes itself far from itself
> and leaves you further from the search?
> And all that is left
> is a system of sounds which guides
> the taste for speech and for feeling
> verbal existence
>   the electronic
> and musical figuration of things?]
>   ("A Palavra e a terra," 325)

It must be observed that Drummond is more genuinely fraternal than Rosa and more concerned with the problem of solidarity, more attentive to ideological and social details, more cognizant of his place as a Brazilian, and more naïve. In his poems "Minas," and occasionally even "Brasil," become talismans, magic words, aligning him with the concerns and stylistic patterns of his contemporaries in Brazilian letters. But ultimately, for all Drummond's status as unofficial poet laureate, he was not a nationalist poet, for he rejected the temptation to compose a saga or epic of Brazilian identity. What he did produce was an ironic poem entitled "Hino nacional" "National Anthem." After parroting the oratorical politician-speak: "Precisamos descobrir o Brasil! . . . Precisamos colonizar o Brazil . . . Precisamos educar o Brasil . . . E cuidaremos do Estado Técnico" (We must discover Brazil . . . We must colonize Brazil . . . We must educate Brazil . . . And we will take care of the Technical State), he rejects the very notion of the nation:

> Precisamos, precisamos esquecer o Brasil!
> Tão majestoso, tão sem limites, tão despropositado,
> ele quer repousar de nossos terríveis carinhos.
> O Brasil não nos quer! Está farto de nós!
> Nosso Brasil é no outro mundo. Este não é o Brasil.
> Nenhum Brasil existe. E acaso existirão os brasileiros?
>
> [We need to, we need to forget Brazil!
> So majestic so limitless, so preposterous,
> it wants a rest from our awful embraces.
> Brazil does not want us! It's sick of us!
> Our Brazil is in the other world. This isn't Brazil.
> No Brazil exists. And Brazilians—do they exist?]
>
> ("Hino Nacional," 89)

Brazil and Minas, the places it is his lot to know, are, in the end, merely clues to the universal puzzle, the latter more authentic because associated with the precious trove of childhood, the former more suspect because subject, as a concept, to political maneuvering. Given the nationalistic roots of his modernist contemporaries, this rejection of nationalism, which applies not only to Brazilianism but also to Pan-(Latin)Americanism, was a decision of profound consequence, even if by default. After the Spanish civil war and World War II, which inspired Drummond to write some mediocre Neruda-esque poetry of international socialist heroism, he prefaced his 1948–1951 collection, *Claro Enigma,* with a quote from Paul Valéry, "Les Evénements m' ennuient." But his work does not, in fact, bear out such radical indifference to the *siècle:* Drummond dabbled with the social idealism of the

2: THE BRAZILIAN WRITERS AND THEIR WORK 89

Brazilian Communist Party, though he later withdrew from activism. His atheism was arrived at through personal search rather than party doctrine. His ultimately pessimistic attitude to religious faith, despite the prominence of Catholicism in the *mineiro* world, helps explain the question of Drummond's attitude to the quasi-religious issue of national identity and patriotism.

> Eu não sou daqui,
> sou de outra nação,
> eu não sou brinquedo.
>
> [I am not from here
> I am from another country,
> I am not a toy.]
> ("Canção para ninar mulher," 93–94)

While Drummond was, in the long run, unable unequivocally to throw in his lot with the political militants and engagé writers, he could not really embrace any definitive ideology of national identity, because he valued the critical capacity to question and doubt, in the existentialist sense, all essentialist truths. While tempering his youthful impulse to iconoclasm from his first published volume on, he maintained through his maturation a touch of what might be thought of as a sort of Gaelic willfulness, a nonconformity to the conventional nonconformity. Drummond did not try to resolve but rather exploited the dramatic tension inherent in internal conflict:

> "Brasão"
> Duas serpentes enlaçadas
> no timbre espanhol de Andrade
> em vermelho e ouro decretam
> a guerra dentro de teu corpo
> sem vitória de qualquer lado.
> Ao ataque de duas línguas
> bífadas, todo te contrais
> e na dupla, ardente picada,
> a alegria te invade ao veres
> sobre a pele de teu destino
> que uma pulseira inquebrantável
> surge do abraço viperino.
>
> ["Coat of Arms"
> Two entwined snakes
> in the Spanish Andrade family crest

in red and gold decree
the war inside your body
without victory for either side.
At the attack of two slit tongues
you crumple inward
and in the double, ardent bite
joy invades you as you see
on the hide of your fate
that an unbreakable bracelet
rises from the viperine embrace.]
(389–390)

Jorge Amado

Background and earlier works: the "proletarian novel."

Amado was born in 1908. In 1931 he published the short novel, *O País do Carnaval*. 1933–1934 saw the release of the so-called *ciclo do cacau* depicting life for the workers on cocoa plantations in *Cacau* and *Suor*. Amado's first really popular novel, *Jubiabá*, came out the following year, the first work to focus on the poorer classes of Salvador. This vein continued with *Capitães da Areia*, about street urchins, in 1936. A biographical work dedicated to the nineteenth century poet and folk hero Castro Alves, *ABC de Castro Alves*, came out in 1941. Chronologically, Amado's second major recognized work was 1943's *Terras do sem fim* with a less appreciated sequel, *São Jorge dos Ilhéus*, the following year. In the 1946 novel, *Seara Vermelha* Amado strayed for once from his Bahian roots to São Paulo, with mixed results. The period from 1947 to 1954 saw the release of a voluminous engagé trilogy, *Os Subterrâneos da Liberdade* (Underground Liberty), again of limited success. But Amado also produced a biography of the Brazilian Communist leader, Luís Carlos Prestes (1945), a drama about Castro Alves (*O Amor de Castro Alves*, 1947), and a collection of travel notes from various communist nations, *O Mundo da Paz* (1951). In 1958 Amado published his south Bahian period masterpiece, *Gabriela, Cravo e Canela*, which was subsequently received with phenomenal success in the United States. By now Amado had explored his key thematic areas: the history of the cocoa zone in southern Bahia, and various social castes in Salvador, capital of Bahia, notably the petty bourgeoisie, the bohemians, and the marginalized poor. Later works covered these themes from different perspectives. Amado also wrote on other *nordestino* areas, such as a minuscule fishing village to the north of Salvador (Mangue Seco in *Tereza Batista Cansada de Guerra,* 1973) and the dryer inland zone, called the *agreste,* in *Tieta do Agreste* (1977). Other noted works include: *Os Velhos Marinheiros* (1961); *Tenda dos Milagres* (1969), *Farda Fardão Camisola de Dormir* (1979); *Tocaia Grande: A Face Obscura* (1984). Finally, he produced a large volume of disparate memoirs, *Navegação de Cabotagem,* in 1992.

Jorge Amado was born in the cocoa-growing region of the south of Bahia but educated in Salvador, though his schooling was interrupted several times during his preteen years, when his fierce independence of spirit at school and within his own family manifested itself. These two locales and their distinct subcultures provide the basis for much of his later work. Amado worked as journalist in Bahia and then in Rio. He traveled extensively, even reaching the West Coast of the U.S. in his mid-twenties, and has spent considerable periods in Europe. With a populist but innately lyrical sense of drama and color, Amado achieved considerable popularity before his mastery of structure really matured. This capacity grew steadily, however, and the literary quality of Amado's work rose extraordinarily over a period of decades. As a writer he gives the impression of venting a natural storytelling talent which is robust but unsophisticated. The reality of his working method is, in fact, quite different, at least in later years; Amado is a painstaking writer who, while maintaining a high volume of publications, has come to write fewer and fewer words in each draft and to rewrite each one repeatedly. As his knowledge of human psychology grew with age, so did the intellectual complexity and the metaphysical depth of his work.

O País do Carnaval was published in 1931, when the author was only nineteen. It shows a talent for drawing characters, but is barely a novel. What is interesting, however, is its ideological nature. A group of young, mostly bourgeois bohemian friends interact in Salvador, each presenting a different psychological prospect as they gradually sort out how they want to direct their lives. Assessments of what opportunities Brazilian society presents, and hence judgments of the national culture and how it contrasts with civilized Europe (whence the title) are central. The book is evidently a partial reproduction of Amado's own adventures as an educated but fun-loving youth in Salvador. But instead of promoting a hero-figure, Amado ultimately dismisses with varying severity each of a group of socially advantaged young men, all tainted with the subtle flaws of their bourgeois condition: lack of courage, conviction, and imagination, a Eurocentrism which alienates them from the poorer classes, and, finally, squalid materialistic conservatism. One of the characters takes his law degree and heads off to his fiancée's home territory deep in the barren interior because through his patriarchal *latifundiário* in-laws he can acquire a judgeship. This destination, contrasting with the vivid color and earthly delights of Salvador's red-light area, stands as a powerful metaphor for the bourgeoisie's self-condemnation to respectable and dusty oblivion.

Amado had already found his vein: a genuine solidarity with and affection for the socioeconomically and ethnically disenfranchised, a paganistic celebration of carnal pleasures and the sexual appeal of women and an admiration for the manly qualities lacking in middle-class society. All of this could be summed up as a thirst for the earth, both in his perceptions of existing culture and in ideological aspiration. The quest for social justice was intellectually resolved for Amado with his adherence to the Communist Party. He later represented the party in parliament until it was outlawed, was officially invited to various Warsaw Pact countries and was subsequently denied reentry to de Gaulle's France. He was even subjected to a form of martyrdom in having his books burned publicly in Salvador. Apparently blessed by the stars from birth, Amado's punishments in Brazil were ultimately inconsequential and were compensated by privileged treatment in visits to most of the countries in the Communist zone, including China and Mongolia (where he was honored with an official homage in the capital's airport), and respect in the Left-dominated intellectual circles of Western Europe. Amado was in contact with Sartre and other luminaries in Paris, met Picasso, and established innumerable prestigious continental friendships.

Though hardly a socialist realist, through the 1940s and 1950s Amado bowed to the aesthetic directives of Moscow regarding the role of the novel. In 1951 he was awarded the Stalin International Peace Prize, and in Poland began to write the very long, now relatively obscure work entitled *Os Subterrâneos da Liberdade*. This period of orthodoxy was ignominiously crowned in 1950 with the nonfictional *O mundo da Paz,* a sort of tourist piece about the frontier of hope in "liberated" nations with a multitude of anecdotes on various experiences of fraternal camaraderie. It had started in the early 1940s with another nonfictional work, *Vida de Luís Carlos Prestes,*[4] a hero-worshipping account of the Brazilian Communist Party leader who had conducted his own Long March in the Brazilian interior (which ended in truce and diplomatic defeat rather than revolution). This work is more authentic in that it deals with the local context. It presents another instance of the devout admiration Amado had earlier displayed for the nineteenth-century Bahian poet, Castro Alves, cast as the romantic champion of the slave emancipation movement.

In fact this whole period was, in literary terms, quite impoverished. In the mixed slew of works prior to this period there are several which have stood the test of time and remain tremendously popular, notably *Jubiabá* (1935), named after an elderly practicant of Candomblé (Saluador's Afro-Brazilian religion), but describing the adventures of a fugitive mulatto street fighter and womanizer. Surviving by tremendous courage but victimized by his own ignorance, the protagonist's quest is eventually resolved with enlightenment: the answer is solidarity, in the form of a strike by the workers. Significantly, the wise old man Jubiabá does not advocate the strike. This suggests that ultimately, for all its qualities, the ghettoization that accompanies folkloric preservation is not a long-term solution; rather the rational, materialist path of class confrontation dictated by Marxist theory is necessary.

Gabriela and the Utopian vision.

The literary output of the decade from 1958, the year of *Gabriela,* was the most extraordinary in Amado's opus. Much has been said about this book, which realized, at least within Brazil, the supreme achievement of literary apotheosis: the creation of a *persona* which has subsequently passed into the extraliterary repertoire of characteristic types familiar in the general culture. The protagonist is, in some ways like Macunaíma, innocently premoral. But unlike Macunaíma, Gabriela is believable even if ideal, very much flesh and blood. Her phenotype is a happy fusion of Brazil's racial triangle. Arriving first as a refugee from the rural blight of drought which has frequently devastated the most archaic of the post-Colombian socioeconomic and ethnic regions of Brazil, the dry interior of the northeast, through her innate grace Gabriela steadily achieves liberation from oppression of all sorts. Accompanying her is another newcomer of sorts, her employer, master, lover, and eventual husband, the Syrian-born, thoroughly Brazilianized merchant Nacib. Gabriela is, miraculously, unfaithful and yet innocent, or at least genuinely naïve. The miracle is completed by forgiveness and the curing of the wounded ego of the cuckold, Nacib. The lesson of his hard won tolerance and charity is mirrored in the book's depiction of societal evolution. The domestic drama is set against the extraordinarily violent saga of the conquest of the virgin forest frontier of southern Bahia after the discovery that the land was ideal for that most lucrative of crops, cocoa. The few years of the story, set in the 1920s, show the shift in the balance of power from an agriculturally-based warlordship and brutal patriarchy to a relatively gentle provincial bourgeoisie with aspirations to urban civilization and progress.

The price of Amado's idyllic indulgence was, from Leftists, the charge of accommodation, of deviation from Marxist political correctness, and later, from feminists, attacks on Amado's gender stereotypes. Recent scholarly work suggests that Amado had not abandoned the Marxist fold in this nostalgic evocation of nascent capitalism; in the late 1950s following Khrushchev's challenging of Stalinism, the aesthetic precepts emitted from Moscow were cautiously relaxed, freeing writers from the "boy meets tractor" syndrome. Amado's depiction was consistent with the revisionist Stalinist conception of gradual and separate evolution toward socialism in different states, a developmental line along which the transition from agrarian feudalism to urban preindustrial capitalism could legitimately be located and portrayed.

But if he escapes the censure of Marxists, Amado remains the target of feminists. The charge can be applied to the depiction of characters in virtually all his works. Gabriela, who is physically late adolescent, is available, and expects nothing in return, is a preeminent object of male sexual fantasy. Her main talent beyond the bed is in the kitchen. This feature has warranted a substantial critical protest. What almost all critics have failed to grasp about *Gabriela* is that the real import of the book is its teleological idealism. The name of the heroine suggests the archangel who announces a new age. Gabriela's appearance in a region of economic expansion is not stressed, but in fact represents the plight of millions of *nordestinos,* whose successive migrations to the southeast constitute the central demographic pattern in Brazilian development from the 1920s through to the present day.

Gabriela is, further, an ideal rather than a real human type. In an important nuance, she is said not to come from any particular town, or even from the *Nordeste,* but simply from the north. Given the significance in Portuguese of this term, which can convey both direction and destination (as in the verb *nortear*) the detail is important. Gabriela simultaneously represents the hardship of the past endured by marginalized socioethnic groups and, implicitly, their future. The association with the past is in terms of a generalized cultural heritage rather than any specific personal experience;

indeed, one has the impression that Gabriela herself has no clear conception of her point of origin. Speaking in a sort of child dialect which superficially resembles the inarticulate speech of peasants, she does not have their rigidly conservative social vision. Her naïve ignorance suggests the limitations faced by members of the disenfranchised social caste from which she comes, but Gabriela is not historically condemned, as the laws of naturalist realism would dictate. On the contrary, her ignorance is the secret to an ultimately greater freedom. The Gabriela figure has a lot in common with that of Macunaíma in that she is a sort of open vessel of human potential without the constraints and limitations facing real adults. But unlike in *Macunaíma,* the diagnosis is not ambivalent; Amado is a true Utopian idealist, but one who eventually found an efficacious symbol of redemption within the common people rather than in political theory.

Gabriela is not herself an agent of transformation but a catalyst; it is those around her, the more socially and psychologically conventional characters who come to appreciate her special grace, which stands for Brazil's cultural miracle of harmonious miscegenation. The real protagonist of the plot is in fact a man, Nacib, through whose eyes the story is told. He makes a number of decisions in relation to the woman to whom he is attracted which constitute an escalating series of recognitions: of her beauty and grace, of her productive capacity as a worker, and generally of her human qualities, eventually appreciated as more significant than her social shortcomings so that Gabriela is worthy of his forgiveness of her infidelity and his consideration of her as a prospective spouse.

The achievement of the book lies on various levels. The plot and characters are organized and balanced with exceptional technical competence. The romantic story is touching while the historical evocation of period and ambiance is absorbing and thoroughly entertaining. But the supreme accomplishment of the work is the creation of a mythical type, the unforgettable Gabriela. Like Nabokov's Lolita, this young female has acquired through the gaze of the other an earthliness which does not exist in the character itself, so that the innocent object inspiring cupidity in others becomes a symbol of this cupidity. The vertical component of the character—her significance as abstract symbol of a national identity, of potential cultural identity—is masterfully played down by the text. The vitality, playful sexuality and childlike aspect of Gabriela's nature dominate the imaginative space of the book, enticing the reader toward this tangible creature rather than to any intellectual notions she might represent. In the manner of real myth, the deeper significance is cloaked in an absorbing carnality, and the metaphorical and analogical relations between the two levels are obscured. The story can be enjoyed at its surface level in ignorance of the deeper meaning, and yet, through the subliminal process, it is the latter which gives the story its long-term power.

The mythical level of *Gabriela* is also rich. Over and above Gabriela's function as a symbol of the recognition and enfranchisement of the colored masses, the general notion of sociopolitical evolution from feudalism to early capitalism and beyond is represented with the depiction of the interactions and struggles between all the major leading figures of the town. Though not inconsistent with his past ideological loyalties Amado adds a uniquely Brazilian inflection in the conviction that Brazil's success as a modern society based on harmonious and fertile racial mixing gives it a special place in global evolution. Through the miracle of miscegenation, Brazil, for all its backwardness and racial inequity, has taken a leap toward the ideal Utopian society where all the peoples of the world live in harmony.

The emphasis on Brazil as cultural democracy of races is a generalized myth, not peculiar to Amado, and usually linked to Gilberto Freyre. But the probing of this idea in correlation to Marxist theory is a significant achievement, given the incompatibility of the two sets of ideas. The argument of racial harmony has been highly convenient to a series of abusive Right Wing authoritarian regimes. Marxists, in turn, have branded the widely circulated credo of racial harmony as an illusion resulting from alienation. In this sense, Amado's tropical marriage of Brazilian and Marxist theory is really an extraordinary act of subversion in relation to both conservative authoritarianism and Soviet orthodoxy. Ironically, in true magical realist spirit, the dream of the characters in the book was played out in real life years later: Amado was recognized as an honorary citizen in the port town of Ilhéus (where the story takes place), and referred to reverently when the port was finally dredged (as had been anticipated in the novel).

This rich ensemble of symbolism is also inferred by the book's full title: *Gabriela, Cravo e Canela*. The *canela* (cinnamon) suggests the racially blended color of Gabriela's skin as well as the spice in her cooking; and can even be a carnal reference—*canela* also means shin. *Cravo,* translated as clove in the English title, also means "carnation," referring to the floral adornment in Gabriela's hair, and hence to her beauty and grace, possibly with the Polynesian connotation of innocent sexuality. But it can even admit a further meaning, independent of Amado and acquired after composition of the text. This flower was the symbol of the Portuguese Communist Party, in which Amado had comrades. The 1974 socialist revolution in Portugal, which ended the last intact European colonial empire, is in fact known as the *Revolução dos Cravos*.

The feminist accusations against Amado, whose early works center on manly characters and present woman two-dimensionally (either as dedicated to the male sentimentally or as well-endowed sexually), are that he objectified and stereotyped women, and concocted a literary soft porn with commercial appeal. However, with the maturation of Amado's work the attention given to females increases steadily; later in his career they become the predominant protagonists of works such as *Gabriela, Dona Flor and Her Two Husbands* (1966) and *Tereza Batista Cansada de Guerra* (1973; translated as *Tereza Batista: home from the wars*). In the earlier works, despite great compassion for the figure of the prostitute these women remained satellite characters, but *Dona Flor* tells the story of a very proper lady who gradually learns to accept the simultaneous sexual attentions of two husbands (one of whom is a ghost); in *Tereza Batista,* Amado finally takes the step of casting a (retired) prostitute and brothel owner as undisputed protagonist.

Gabriela constitutes the first move forward in this process of liberation by a writer who remains a *machista* but ceases to be male-centric. Given that the main protagonist is not Gabriela but Nacib, it is even more significant that she is celebrated in the title. Amado, who had always cast his lot with the oppressed and against the oppressor, perhaps gradually accepted the idea that, in their relations with men, women had a status analogous to that of colored persons in relation to whites, or the poor to the rich.

Necessarily therefore, the legitimate figure of salvation must come from the oppressed. The liberation of woman, represented by Gabriela's escaping punishment for infidelity, is symbolic of the liberation of mankind. Her sexual indulgence and untaintable innocence is a form of immaculate sexuality representing true freedom in an ideal future society, in which, according to Marxist doctrine, laws of ownership and prohibition will not be necessary. There is therefore a remarkable though gradual integration of the female as protagonist, a passage from mere sympathy to the conferring of autonomy.

Amado clearly posits in *Gabriela* the notion that independent of the mechanics of economic development, cultural realities can function as an agent of social progress. *Gabriela* remains the touchstone of Amado's achievement, for in this work he fuses the proud portrayal of a local, cultural reality—the same descriptive impulse inspiring his earlier works—and the later concern with a fully fledged vision of future social development. The real consequence of Amado's vision is the special place held by Brazil in the global system. Miscegenation is the right path for future development globally. Brazil is, uniquely, the land where the central twentieth-century problematic of colliding ethnicities has already been resolved, and thus a beacon for other societies irrespective of their superior material development.

Tenda dos Milagres *and the ethics of miscegenation.*

Although *Gabriela* is the crucial text in the maturation of Amado's perspective, the articulation of his values remains largely between the lines. The theme of miscegenation is overtly examined and becomes the real protagonist of a later novel, *Tenda dos Milagres* (1969). This is the only one of Amado's novels which might be considered challenging reading. Susceptible to the epithet post-modern, the novel interweaves two narrative threads and within each story line presents a multiplicity of contradictory perspectives.

The first story, set in the first years of the century, recounts the life adventures of Pedro Archanjo, an autodidact mulatto from Salvador, who challenges the prevalent Eurocentric theories of racial differentiation expounded at the Faculty of Medicine, the central Bahian forum for scientific debate at that time. Just as Archanjo is biologically a product of racial miscegenation so is he, culturally, a syncretist. He is a devotee of the Afro-Brazilian of Bahia, Candomblé. His best friend has a *tenda* ([work]shop) where he fashions small statues and scenes representing the saints. The practice actually derives from Folk Catholicism—an archaic mode of Christianity colored with paganistic elements inherited from the Iberian peninsula. Typically, after the successful intercession of a patron saint, the craftsman is commissioned to execute an *ex–voto* acknowledging and/or depicting the saint or the affliction. These objects are, by metonymy, themselves called miracles (*milagres*). The *tenda*'s thematic work is extended to embrace the Candomblé deities, known simply as *santos* in syncretist terminology (i.e., in Brazil but not in Africa). The overlap is quite natural as the practice of soliciting material intercession is common to both traditions and specific *orixás* (the Yoruba-Brazilian word for *santos*) commonly hold dual identity with Catholic saints. Since all practicants of Candomblé are baptized and most claim to be Catholic as well, it is a normal act for all religious sectors of the Bahian population to commission *milagres*. The syncretist implications of the *tenda dos milagres* thus present an ideal image to evoke the notion of cultural miscegenation, with the further connotations of, on the one hand, work, religious practice and day-to-day life, and, on the other, a notion of something miraculous which ties into Amado's views on the broader significance of cultural interaction.

The story is set at the time when Candomblé was not only outlawed but also actively and vigorously repressed. The carnival of this era had witnessed a rejuvenation of Afrocentric themes which came under the increasing disapproval of the authorities. The theories of European racial superiority, which in the last decades of the nineteenth century were cast in a solid scientific nomenclature, were of crucial importance to Brazilian intellectuals and government policy—resulting in the solicitation of European immigrants to satisfy the labor needs of coffee production and nascent industry in São Paulo. On the other hand, the emancipation of the slaves in 1888, partly attributable to the economic decline of the plantation system, had left a large underemployed mass of Afro-Brazilians in the northeast with no foreseeable socioeconomic redemption. The story is set, then, at a particularly acrimonious juncture of race relations.

Pedro Archanjo's is a tempered voice, not so much urging rebellion as insisting upon the miscegenist nature of the whole color spectrum of Brazilian society, particularly in Bahia. Archanjo is a Renaissance man, blending an exceptional faculty for learning and reflection with an abundant capacity for life and passion. His daytime activities in the Medical Faculty where he works as a beadle are countered by a series of nocturnal adventures. These involve both religious devotion—which often results in dealings with the police—and an impressive set of sexual encounters with handsome females, two in particular. One is Afro-Brazilian, a woman Archanjo has long admired but avoided sexually because of the danger of a conflict between their respective *orixás;* eventually this occurs with the two deities clashing in a grand pastiche of the *Iliad,* as they use their human devotees as stand-ins. The other woman is a blond, blue-eyed Aryan from exotic Finland. Archanjo impregnates her, consciously inspired by the desire to have a son who will be a perfect prince of miscegenation.

Although the *mise-en-abîme* story plays up Archanjo's ideological principles, there is a heavy irony in the archangelic name as is revealed in the second, more tricky, story, which is cast around a central axis of narratorial unreliability. The protagonist of this second setting is Fausto Pena—Faustian scribe—a poet with a dubious muse but also a journalist with a solid critical intelligence. If Archanjo is idealized, his nemesis is all too human, as the name suggests. Fausto, whose vices do not include vanity, aspires to the truth and the good but is, for want of a crust, susceptible to pecuniary persuasion. The recollection of the long-buried Archanjo as an old mulatto drunkard is revived literally out of the blue: a relatively young but world-eminent anthropologist from Columbia University has come across some of the beadle's writings, and in a strident New York accent has declared Archanjo to be a visionary genius. He arrives in Bahia in search of more material and is welcomed with the pandemonious fanfare that only a country quite confident of its cultural inferiority can summon, but is amazed that Archanjo has become an object of vilification. The local cultural establishment is embarrassed, and a chase ensues for any solid evidence regarding the newly regilded goose. Seminars are scheduled, TV and press conferences held. The latter turn out to be a competition between the female journalists for the attention of the vigorous intellectual. The prize is won by a magnificent physical specimen of miscegenation, Ana Mercedes, sometime muse of the wan-faced Fausto Pena. The scribe is subsequently contracted and dispatched to research Archanjo. Ana, meanwhile, initiates the professor into the more sensual domains of what might be called performance research.

Fausto's investigations reveal the contradictions of the human side of Archanjo and above all the sheer impossibility of penetrating the truth of the past. His efforts and reflections—lubricated, like Archanjo's, with healthy doses of grog—are spliced with the direct authorial narration of Archanjo's life. As Fausto gathers his material into some semblance of a narrative order so as to be able to collect from his gringo employer, it emerges that the proprietor of the omniscient narrative voice may in fact be Fausto Pena. This is never clearly determined, indeed, the whole point is that there is no such thing as a reliable narrative of the past. Even within the present, the impossibility of a decisive truth is apparent in the tropical ambiance of corruption and hypocrisy in which Pena exists. The media lose interest in the Archanjo theme, the plans for a Pedro Archanjo Library are abandoned, and the seminars turn out to be a farce. Promises are broken, grandiose declarations dissolve, and Bahian and Brazilian life reverts to its usual corrupt but tolerant character—although not without claiming another trophy in the form of the seduced professor. His pronouncements now seem quite naïve. Nevertheless, even if they only make sense in a place far away from where Archanjo actually existed, there is more than a grain of truth in them. The scenes from Archanjo's life do consolidate the discourse he expounds, and he really is a heroic character. Though the text defuses the inclination to idealize the man, his message stands. On the other hand, the outrageous pseudoscientific racist discourse espoused by the establishment is unequivocally refuted. Archanjo is insistent that all Bahians, even those that consider themselves purely white and discuss the racial inferiority of the black masses, have African blood. His chief detractor is outraged, whereupon Archanjo researches the former's lineage and demonstrates that they actually have a common ancestral link and are, in fact, distantly related. Archanjo's nemesis is an oppressive bigot and scientific failure. Archanjo, the beadle, is the legitimate individual who by virtue of his color is denied access to the station occupied by the other which should by rights be his—to the detriment of society at large. But by the book's optimism the truth will out in the end.

Archanjo's insistence on the inherent miscegenation of Bahian society is justified by the interaction between Fausto Pena and Ana Mercedes and subsequently between the *mulata* and the professor. The fact that the society is ethnically and culturally a mutation, beyond its official European origins, is also evidenced by the discrepancy between the project as conceived by the professor from the U.S., and how it pans out for all concerned, himself included. The humorous and ironic aspects of this situation serve not so much to deride a sort of tropical corruption endemic to Brazil as to mark the vast psychological differences between the two cultures and the problematic nature of imposing a rational agenda from one society on the other. Because of its overriding irony, the book generally rises above the question of whether what is not Brazilian is bad; the professor is neither ridiculed nor championed. His objective message—the recognition of Archanjo's legitimacy—is upheld, while the cultural complexities of Bahian society are revealed as legitimate and wonderful. Like Fausto Pena or even Pedro Archanjo, Brazilian society is all too human, and yet it does constitute a new species, incomprehensible to the dry mentality—and the naïveté—of northern social thinking. The critical outside thinker is in a position to recognize the value of a visionary discourse, but not to actually understand the society concerned, since the Brazilian case is without precedent. Brazil is something more than just another society, it is a living cultural laboratory (or artistic workshop) for a new racial entity—*Homo brasiliensis*.

Tenda dos milagres is also an astute reflection on a reverse process of anthropophagy—the creative assignment of meaning to Brazilian culture by foreigners. Presumably inspired by some real occurrences(s) in Salvador, Amado weaves around the main story of Archanjo a meta-story of contemporary cultural reception(s). The structure emphasizes the contrast between the appreciation of Archanjo (the archangel of miscegenation) by the intellectual blue blood (Levenson, a New York Jewish Dr. Livingstone), and the local pseudo-intelligentsia's disdain. The foreigner validates the Brazilian miscegenist popular *imaginaire*. Though the Eurocentric elite assumes a privileged position as knowledgeable interpreter of local popular reality and ethnic alterity to the important but naive North Atlantic visitor, it is not grasped by them that as a perceptive filter they are not corrective but rather transparent and invisible. On the contrary, once the visitor, indifferent to local stigmas, culturally anoints Archanjo's miscegenation thesis, the elite parrot his admiration of the mestiço because of their own Eurocentric snobbery. The irony is not lost on Amado. *Tenda dos Milagres* presents an understanding of the international interpretive frame which intuits a large part of what the present study extrapolates mechanically.

The question of folklorism, or cultural essentialism, versus orthodox Marxist theory arises again with *Tenda dos Milagres*'s ardent celebration, through Archanjo, of the credo of miscegenation. If the teleological vision of gradual social evolution in *Gabriela* is compatible with revisionist Marxist theory (i.e., not bound by the need for immediate revolution), the amusing celebration of the imperfect state of the world in *Tenda,* with its postmodern unreliable narration and implicit discrediting of unilinear truths, and the explicit and unequivocal celebration of miscegenation, suggest that the totem of cultural fusion has supplanted that of worker solidarity and mobilization. In *Tenda* there really is no notion of solidarity, at least in the prostituted world of poor bourgeois individuals like Fausto Pena and Ana Mercedes, who feed off the crumbs of the rich and powerful. There is, however, a strong fraternal bond and a color-class consciousness amongst the protagonists of the Archanjo story. But even here the practical necessities of the individual may prevail. Archanjo's fiercest lover chooses to distance herself from the dissident beadle because she has a child who will be will cared for if she is a faithful mistress to a wealthy white man. On the other hand, Archanjo's ring of solidarity frequently extends beyond those whose ethno-socioeconomic position resembles his own. The main subplot of the Archanjo tale concerns a mulatto youth more or less adopted into a rich white family; after completing his education and becoming an engineer, he proposes to his old sweetheart, the daughter of the house. Racist outrage ensues, but due to the astute maneuvers of Archanjo and company, the marriage is brought to term. The band of allies includes a range of figures, even a rambunctious elderly Portuguese singer who, with her catch cry of "Rien que champagne!" brings to the table both Parisian sophistication and, implicitly, the social approval of those whites moved by artistic and moral sensibility rather than bigotry. The real bond is one of empathy rather than social or ethnic profile—a potential heresy against the Soviet doctrine of *klassovost*.[5]

This is a conflict to some extent inevitable in the logic of the transformations brought about by miscegenation. The U.S. provides the perfect case for the argument that racist and classist division are parallel and inevitable consequences of the capitalist system. But the miracle of miscegenation emerges in Brazil despite the hegemony of capitalism. Amado must have contemplated these issues but was certainly not ready, in *Tenda,* to reject his intellectual heritage and the cause of solidarity. The question is broached periodically through a character who, unusually for Amado, has nothing to do with the plot, an active communist and an old friend of Archanjo. The two sit and drink together, and the comrade lectures the mulatto on how all progress leads to Moscow. Archanjo listens sympathetically but insists on the importance of regional cultural realities and peculiarities, and his own pet theme of miscegenation. The two never resolve their argument, but neither do they leave the table at the grog shop. Their vertical divergences are resolved in the horizontal solidarity of drinking themselves under the table (though it is not insignificant that here again Archanjo can hold his alcohol better and keep a steadier foot). The dialog seems to acknowledge that there is no easy answer to the implications of miscegenation for orthodox Marxism, but that in any case these differences of perspective do not impede solidarity between fellow foot soldiers of progress.

Popular Populist, democratic demagogue.

This study of Jorge Amado has so far pursued the abstract intellectual concerns of a writer who has mostly communicated in a populist vein. *Tenda dos Milagres* is perhaps Amado's most rewarding work for thinkers, but is atypical in its sheer complexity. Amado's more usual vein gives the impression of existing within a cultural continuum which is located outside literature, in the conversations to be heard on the streets of the magical city of Salvador with its ever-colorful stories and characters. His more characteristic fiction is distinguished by its interaction with the popular rather than by its intellectual pedigree—whether in terms of the creative sources of the writer or the appeal of the work to readers.

Amado is inspired by figures drawn directly from Bahian life. The championing of the marginalized mulatto population of coastal Bahia, whether in Salvador, baroque capital of preindependence Brazil but a decadent economic backwater through the nineteenth and early twentieth centuries, or in the frontier zone of cocoa plantations in the south of the state, is itself an act of dissent and the mark of a new cultural confidence. But Amado's work cannot be classified as regionalism since it is of such universal appeal. The work is, naturally, of unique pertinence to its regional population, and equally interesting to other disenfranchised sectors of the Brazilian population which might identity with its subversion of the hierarchical system. But even within the elite class from which is drawn the sector of the reading public most resistant to his work, the Brazilian literary establishment, Amado is widely read. The extraordinarily high sales figures for his works in Portuguese demonstrate that Amado has penetrated the domestic book-buying market, whose real center of gravity is in the broader bourgeoisie of Rio, São Paulo, Belo Horizonte, and the southern states.

Amado's appeal cannot simply be explained in terms of its subject matter, but must be understood as a successful technique in literary terms. Much of the debate within Brazil about the vivacity or bad taste of the work, about whether Amado is championing the underdog or exploiting the exotic, about the status of the work as pornographic demagogy or lyrical sensuality and so on, has overlooked the crucial issue of Amado as a proponent of established literary models within the Western tradition. Even his defenders do not stress his relation to literary forebears but rather his politically correct social values. The presence of the popular element masks the fact that the real stylistic forte of Amado is derived largely through a continuity with traditional, popular Western narratological models and a sensibility to the artistry of popular culture.

In *Dona Flor and Her Two Husbands,* Amado indulges his enthusiasm for all sorts of texts, literary or otherwise. He also includes apocryphal notes giving the impression that the volume is a sort of natural issue from the bowels, stomachs, minds, and other organs of the local community. The first edition of the work features on the inside folds of the front and back covers a disclaimer by Amado, in a mischievous vein, first denying any correlation between the characters and any real persons in Bahia, then immediately noting that a novel is derived from and recreates reality (without any contradicting conjunction such as nevertheless, etc.), and finally concluding that if any similarity exists it is an act of quixotic impertinence on the part of the real person who should know better than to go about imitating characters of fiction. The whole piece is done in a waggish and irreverent tone:

> One constant and monotonous event repeats itself with the publication of each new novel by the author of this story of Dona Flor and her two husbands: there is always some self-important Mr. or Mrs. who puts themselves in the shoes of one of the characters and denounces the scandal with screams of outrage—paraded in newspaper columns, with publicity, gusto and threats to the novelist of slaps to the face, lawsuits or death. So that the same should not occur on this occasion, the author advises all parties (. . .)
> (. . .) Thus, any similitude between the reality of life and the reality of the book—the one deriving from and recreating the other—is the consequence of experience and research; but, if perchance any resemblance exist between living persons and the characters of the novel, it will have been a random and unintended coincidence, though possible amusing.
> And so, when in the pages concerning the matrimonial adventures of Dona Flor the reader should find a fellow (or lady) whose name, profession and aspect remind him (or her) of an acquaintance with the same name, the same profession and the same aspect, let it be known forthwith: the character in the novel is not a portrait of the fellow (or lady) known to him (or her), and any resemblance between the two is not the fault of the author but rather that of so and so who goes around resembling the characters of novel as if this was a respectable occupation. An illusion of grandeur on the part of certain persons, dying to show off in public. Now, with this note, everything is clarified and the matter closed for good. Just as well. (1966)

The passage goes on, in Amado's trademark meandering but lucid fluidity, to mention various real persons providing information on the various technical matters of the book—cooking, pharmaceutics, and so on. Thanks are given, the period of composition is indicated, deference is paid to Amado's two personal *orixás,* Oxóssi and Xangô, and the dice are cast for the telling of the story, ("so that Dona Flor could live out her little life in this magical city of Bahia") which by now—without the first page having been read—has been appropriately located in the star-charmed Bahian microuniverse.

The title of the book appears after a sketch depicting the writer at his typewriter. *Dona Flor e seus dois Maridos* is subtitled, *história moral e de amor* (a moral story and one of love), and then *Romance*. But over the page a new subtitle appears, along with further important details regarding the author's residence, the illustrator and his residence, and even the publisher and his possible future residence in a rustic bohemian and seaside neighborhood of Salvador, reputedly the residence of the fishermen's *orixá*, Iemanjá, all in an ornate italic font framed with much flourish:

> *The esoteric and stirring story lived out by Dona Flor, professor emeritus of the culinary art, and her two husbands, the first known as Vadinho, the second, a pharmacist, by name Dr. Teodoro Madureira*
>
> *or*
>
> *The shocking battle between Spirit and Matter*
> *Narrated by Jorge Amado, public scrivener, dwelling in the Rio Vermelho district, in the city of Salvador of the Bay of All Saints, close to Sant'Ana Square, where resides Iemanja, our lady of the waters. Illustrated by Floriano Teixeira, officer of brush and pencil, Bahian by option, and dwelling also in Rio Vermelho.*
> *Published by José de Barros Martins, publisher and character, who will, one day, also live in Rio Vermelho.*
> *MCMLXVI*

The dedications to spouse and family and then to various indispensable friends follow. After this, replete with more hand sketches, come four quotes, one from each of the text's three main characters—though merely a pregnant "Ai!" by Dona Flor—and one quote from the cosmonaut Gagarin confirming that "The World is Blue." After this comes a letter ostensibly from Dona Flor to Jorge Amado, verifying a recipe and sending as proof a cake or two. The next page features a new sketch and a subtitle for Chapter I, on the death of Vadinho, first husband of Dona Flor, with mention of a couple of the major episodes, but also, in parentheses, a note that the local musician Carlinhos Mascarenhos will be accompanying on cavaquinho (ukelele). The next page brings a new sketch, this time of the male carnaval revelers in drag who inhabit the first scene, and a didactic note by Dona Flor. On the next page the narration begins. The reader by this stage has turned the page eleven times. The point at which the extrafictional has ceded the stage to the fable is untraceable. And in fact the counterimplication—just as was suggested in the first note on the jacket—is that reality is preserved in the fiction. Amado is sensitive to the lyrical element in popular cultural praxis. He imagines his story as an extension of a ballad which might be sung (by thematic empathy rather than form, since his own text is still over five hundred pages of conventional prose); he integrates suggestive sketches such as are usually found in children's literature, and, most importantly for the narrative structure, has an ear for the metadramaturgical devices common in European prose prior to the rise of the realist novel of the nineteenth century. The florid italics outlining the story, author, and so on, evidently are a literary pastiche of the scroll of the herald or town crier. Amado's sense of social landscape is very much compatible with what might be grouped as the prepsychological prose genres: the Spanish picaresque; the eighteenth-century English novel of outdoor and indoor adventure, notably Fielding; alternately, the stage melodrama with typical characters popular on the English stage in the nineteenth century and, in one form or another, around the world throughout early modern society. Gradually undergoing a transformation from his early work which he had described as being written "com um mínimo de literatura" ("minimally literary," asserted in the preface of his second novel, *Cacau,* 1934), Amado slowly increased this metaliterary element in the narrative structure to a level of systematic indulgence. For example *Tieta do Agreste* ("Tieta of the Scrubland," 1977) assumes various characteristics of these genres, particularly the vulgar pathos of the exhortations at the beginnings of chapter for reader identification with the heroine. *Tieta* is actually officially subtitled, "Tieta do Agreste, shepherdess of goats, or, The return of the prodigal daughter, a melodramatic serial in five sensational episodes: emotion and suspense!" The text begins with an account in italics of a childhood experience by the protagonist where she looses her virginity by rape. The experience is not so traumatic in fact, but certainly harsh. The text then gives the heading, FIRST EPISODE, the succinct subtitle, THE DEATH AND RESURRECTION OF TIETA OR THE PRODIGAL DAUGHTER, and then proceeds in deliberately sensationalistic tone:

CONTAINING AN INTRODUCTION AND HINTS FROM THE AUTHOR, UNFORGETTABLE DIALOGS, FINELY NUANCED PSYCHOLOGICAL DETAILS, LANDSCAPE TOUCHES, SECRETS, GUESSES, IN ADDITION TO THE PRESENTATION OF CERTAIN PERSONAGES WHO WILL PLAY A SIGNAL ROLE IN

THE EVENTS RECOUNTED IN THIS INSPIRATIONAL SERIAL—WITH DOUBT, MYSTERY, VILE BETRAYAL, SUBLIME DEVOTION, LOVE AND HATRED IN EVERY PAGE.

These tongue-in-cheek commentaries adopt the hyperbolic vein of circuses, or B-grade radio dramas from the 1930s. Despite the accusations of gutter literature, it is really just an ironic extension of the chapter preludes found in *Tom Jones* or even the syntactically rambling scenarios that precede each of the tales of the *Decamerone*. It seems unlikely that Amado was simply trying to increase sales—in fact his biggest selling titles remain principally *Gabriela* and the works immediately following it, which do not indulge this deliberate verbose sensationalism to the same extent. To give the writer the benefit of the doubt—something his long activist career surely warrants—the phenomenon is better explained as the culmination of Amado's search for a narrative form which speaks more and more to the imagination and habits of a mass audience, almost to the exclusion of the erudite. Even where Amado draws on canonical literature such as the work of Fielding or Boccaccio, the purchase on this material is in terms of its popularity rather than its respectability.

This must also be seen in terms of Amado's own ideological aesthetics: the promiscuous engagement of melodramatic formulas constitutes the antithesis of the early Amadian manifesto in the preface of *Cacau* to write "com um mínimo de literatura." Amado concluded that declaration with the question, "Será um romance proletário?" ("Is it a proletarian novel?"). Regardless of whether his mature works qualify as such according to party doctrine, they are dedicated to the masses, "of the people and for the people." Amado's intention was not to satisfy intellectual audiences but, on the contrary, to demonstrate the inexhaustible value of popular culture and to make it the protagonist of the work. The populist formula of *Tieta* and other late works represents the realization of a narrative form which not only draws on suitable themes, but also feeds back into mass audience consumption. This surely constitutes the most ambitious of literary projects in a nation of such compromised literacy as Brazil—to simply write something which can and will be read by a large audience, and in so doing to compete with the North American best-sellers which otherwise dominate the literary audience throughout Latin America. Contrary to the notion that with his later works Amado somehow disowned his own heritage, it can very well be argued that he became more true to himself with time, working his way through broader ideological imperatives in an organic manner, and finally shedding these external skins to celebrate unabashedly his own reading of Brazil and Bahia. And against the notion that Amado was not already, at the beginning of his career a memorable, swashbuckling populist, the following appreciation by none less than Albert Camus shows how much Amado could appeal to sympathetic European audiences for whom Amado was in not an embarrassment, but an ambassador:

> It is not a question of ideology in a novel in which life itself is the crucial thing—that is, an ensemble of gestures and cries—along with a certain ordering of urges and desires, a balancing of positive and negative, a passionate movement which is unaccompanied by commentary. One does not discuss the nature of love here. It is enough to love, and with all one's ardor. One does encounter the term, "fraternity", but rather black hands shaking white hands (not many). And the whole book is written as a series of cries or chants, of forward movements and retreats. But nothing here is indifferent. Everything is moving.[6]

3
Domestic and International Reception

João Guimarães Rosa

Domestic apotheosis after the release of *Grande Sertão: Veredas*

GUIMARÃES ROSA'S WORK WAS RECOGNIZED AT EVERY STEP OF the way: the unpublished manuscript, Magma, was awarded the prize for poetry in 1936; Sagarana was awarded another notable prize and quickly exhausted two editions in 1946, and *Grande Sertão: Veredas* collected three major prizes after its release in 1956. Although Rosa himself accepted nomination for but lost the election to the Brazilian Academy of Letters in the following year, he was compensated in 1961 with the Academy's supreme Prêmio Machado de Assis. In 1963, he was elected unanimously to the Academy.

Admiration extended throughout the Brazilian literary world in a way even more convincing than the victory of the prizes themselves. An extraordinarily high proportion of respected critics and a large number of leading writers wrote articles extolling *Grande Sertão: Veredas*. Wilson Martins, one of the most influential critics of the century, but quite unfamiliar with the new author, wrote in 1946 an extraordinarily long press article, "Radiografia de *Sagarana*" (Radiography of *Sagarana*) which is worth quoting at some length in order to communicate both his reaction and the attitudes of literary criticism at the time:

> An author who in his first book presents exception qualities as a fiction writer, who was able to create an original style of composition and narrative . . . endowed with a rare expressive power, and a capacity to transmit emotion which attains the highest level, who effected a real revolution in the Brazilian short story without adopting any of the literary tricks which are at the base of most such revolutions—I know few names in Brazilian literature of the past or present which unite

such an ensemble of literary qualities as those which distinguish Mr. J. Guimarães Rosa . . .

I believe that Mr. Guimarães Rosa, like Maupassant, would fail in the novel . . .

[It is] a book in which one does not encounter the typical and normal flaws of a first work. On the contrary; if there is any mature and complete work in contemporary Brazilian fiction, it is *Sagarana*.

A point of praise of Cervantes by Flaubert which I always remember in dealing with fiction occurs to me now in studying the book of Mr. Guimarães Rosa: he also shows us his paths without describing them, even though the temptation to describe is one of the deepest flaws in *Sagarana*, while at the same time one of its most brilliant qualities. More explicitly, the wealth of knowledge that Mr. Guimarães Rosa commands regarding the setting of his stories is simply overwhelming. He knows everything there is to be known: the names of the trees, the birds, the animals, the creatures of the sea and the land; he knows the marks used on cows and horses and gives an exact description of each one . . . he is not at peace unless multiplying, to the bedazzlement of the reader, the names of a quantity of unknown things . . .

A first book is always an enigma; but . . . he possesses strengths as a fiction writer which place him forthwith alongside our greatest practitioners of the genre. (1978b, 247–250)[1]

The enthusiasm for the book and the sense that, surprisingly, a patently regionalist work had such significance on the national scene was partly due to the prevailing context of exhaustion of much of the initial impulse of modernism. João Guimarães Rosa had developed a conscious ideological position rejecting the sloppy stylistic license perceived in much contemporary work, and the hyper-aestheticism of his work reacted against this in a way satisfying to many critics. In relation to *Grande Sertão: Veredas*, Martins observes in retrospect an additional circumstance favoring its reception, in the aggressive governmental and intellectual nationalism of the period:

> The regionalism of *Sagarana*, if extemporaneous in 1946, seemed, on the contrary, contemporary in its stylistic virtuosity; ten years later, *Grande Sertão: Veredas* would impose itself in that ultra-contemporary stream which constitutes the literary and artistic vanguard precisely because it was, simultaneously, aestheticist and regionalist (i.e., nationalist). (1978b, 373)

Grande Sertão: Veredas simply took the cultural elite by storm. The universal awe it aroused was expressed in euphoric tones, though some confusion admitted by many readers in private. To give an example, a now famous journalist, Paulo Dantas, wrote an article assessing Guimarães Rosa's position towards the end of 1956 in relation to the January release of *Corpo de Baile* and the midyear release of *Grande Sertão: Veredas*. The article begins:

> Legendary writer, a sort of magical realist of the mineiro backlands, João Guimarães Rosa in the space of a year took by storm an enviable position in the national literary scene achieving in half a year what many couldn't in decades.
> At the time of *Sagarana* Álvaro Lins displayed the appropriate exaltation, but now many more voices sing the praises of his enormous talent and, above all, his extraordinary creative process, based on a perfect identification with the regional dialect of the area his books are set in. ("Posição de Guimarães Rosa," [I.E.B. / U.S.P.])[2]

The presumption that the fount of Rosa's stylistic virtuosity was simply the raw oral discourse of a neglected region of the back lands reflects an ignorance of regional dialects and an ideological notion that *le Brésil profond* conserved cultural treasures awaiting liberation after centuries of disregard by a hollow metropolitan elitism. Later studies combining sociolinguistics and literary criticism would reveal the distance between the Rosean style and the oral storytelling style of the back lands of Minas. But the confidence of the presumption, the euphoric note, is more important as a cultural fact than an accurate attribution of literary quality. The nature of the triumph is best noted in an astute article, interestingly entitled, "The Discovery of a masterpiece that only Brazilians will be able to read," by an Italian journalist stationed in Brazil at the time:

> The discovery of a masterpiece is, naturally, a rare thing, but when it does occur here it is immediate, without mental restrictions, a joyous occasion. The critics seem not to fear to commit themselves or to be mistaken or to exaggerate; the day after finishing reading the book, they announce the miracle to you openly. And it should be understood that this applies not only to critics of lesser importance, but also to men with a solid preparation, men of letters of the first order and authentic artists.
> To us Europeans, it makes quite an impression to read in the paper a story with a title like this: "A masterpiece has been published: *Grande Sertão Veredas* by João Guimarães Rosa." In ten newspapers and in ten or twenty magazines I have come across the same sort of titles and texts. In the second half of 1956 the Brazilian critics have come across a *chef d'oeuvre* and have shouted the news from the moun-

tain tops with a genuine joy which appears to me typical and worthy of the New World.

Those critics who read this shouldn't hold it against me for suggesting it, but among us, in Europe, such unanimity of consensus and of glorification is unimaginable . . . In Brazil, on the other hand, I've seen everyone applauding at the same time and so far I haven't happened to find in the dailies or the literary press a single voice of discord. But the present writer for one does have the sense that the Brazilian critics have, in fact, inferred correctly, and that we can legitimately celebrate the appearance of a powerful and revolutionary narrative work: something like Joyce's *Ulysses*. (Grego 1956)

This adulation explains Guimarães Rosa's premature candidacy to the Brazilian Academy of Letters in 1957. As in France there is a fixed number of "immortals," and accession to the body is not simply a matter of winning national acclaim; an election is held only to replace a deceased member, and an aspirant's campaign may begin years before there is such a death. Votes are promised and consigned, allegiances prevail over literary worth. Elected members are usually advanced in years, whereas Rosa had only been publishing for a decade. The literary community seemed consistently in awe of him. The best testimony of this are the writer's own archives, whose 2,140 press clippings represent merely a part of the total coverage. Guimarães Rosa had the habit of keeping the items which displeased him upside-down, but even amongst these there is little negative criticism—it seems the problem was at most faulty interpretation.

The admiration for Rosa's work came, significantly, from both poles of literary ideology prevalent at the time: the orthodox Academy, representing the living but established tradition, and the new avant-garde radicals of São Paulo, who developed the Concretist movement of antisyntactic *calligrams* or "iconograms." The leader of the group, Augusto de Campos—a longtime literary sparring partner of Wilson Martins as it happens—in 1959 dedicated a very long article, "Um Lance de "Dês" do Grande Sertão," which has since been republished in several important critical compendia.[3] The "dês" is none other than the die of Mallarmé's "Un coup de dés." In the theoretical perspective of Campos, a truly extraordinary connoisseur of world literature in the tradition of Ezra Pound, the "great tradition" of the literary avant-garde, while including figures such as Blake and Rimbaud, consists above all of Mallarmé and "Joyce, the Mallarmé of prose." His perspective on Guimarães Rosa is, first, to insist on the Joycean influence (*Finnegan's Wake* rather than *Ulysses*), and, secondly, to cast him as a champion of the Brazilian avant-garde of the twentieth century along with Oswald de Andrade and Mário de Andrade of *Macunaíma*.

As Jon Vincent has noted, almost all Brazilian critics of note have at one time or another dedicated major studies to Guimarães Rosa. Analysis of Rosa's works dominates all domestic literary studies with the exception of Machado de Assis, still by far the most studied Brazilian writer. However, Guimarães Rosa's centrality in institutional Brazilian literary studies is not complemented by the reading habits of the broader public. Jorge Amado, on the contrary, is a writer with an exceptionally wide readership but receiving little attention from within the institutional domain.[4]

Guimarães Rosa, Brazilian literature and the perspective from foreign universities

Guimarães Rosa is widely studied in North American and European universities by specialists of Brazilian, Latin American, or Comparative Literature. This can generally be interpreted as a mirroring of Brazilian institutional patterns. In the case of the writers concerned here, two significant observations are made: first, there is greater scholarly interest in Amado outside Brazil than inside; second, the paradoxical pattern of institutional consecration of Rosa coupled with limited interest from the broader reading public becomes much more extreme. On the international scene João Guimarães Rosa is virtually unheard of outside academia.

Given that Brazilian culture is generally placed under the rubrique of Latin American culture, one might expect Hispanic scholarship to take an interest in Brazilian literature. Whether or not Spanish America and Latin America are synonymous terms is a complicated matter, and the two are frequently confused in the perception of most people. But there is also a genuine overlap in scholarly denomination; in some of his essays on Brazilian identity, the famous Brazilian anthropologist Gilberto Freyre, drawing on the Latin, calls the Portuguese settlers of Brazil "*hispani.*" The Mexican novelist and cultural theorist of Latin America, Carlos Fuentes, has invoked a more politically sensitive term, "Ibero-America," in an attempt to include Brazil within a Latin America usually denominated as *Hispanoamérica* by the Spanish-speaking intellectual community. Institutionally, outside the Iberian peninsula the two mother nations and respective languages are usually incorporated into departments of Spanish and Portuguese—if Portuguese is included at all. Within these departments, however, it is unusual to find Spanish scholars who have any expertise in Brazilian literature; irrespective of the question of cultural barriers, the language barrier effectively separates the two literary traditions as much as it would any other two national traditions.

Of course, there has always been a significant continuity amongst all Romance traditions; since the eighteenth century Paris has been the fulcrum of literary evolution for Portuguese, Spanish, Italian, Spanish American, and Brazilian writers. With the fear of an Anglo-Saxon cultural hegemony in this century, there was even an attempt to formally establish a front of Latin writers to preserve the tradition; conferences were held in Paris with the help of the French government and attracted great interest from Latin American writers, many of whom were resident in France. For them, such events were nothing less than a tactical re-ordering of the former metropolitan-dominated hierarchy and a promotion of the newly virile cultural forces of the New World. The differences and tensions between the European Métropole and the New World have proved an evolving source of literary inspiration, from the Eldorado myth and the Romantic speculations of Chateaubriand through to the demonizing of Spain as imperial tyrant by Fuentes, Cortázar's psycho-cultural axis joining Paris and Buenos Aires, all crowned by García Márquez's Nobel Prize Acceptance Speech on the solitude of Latin America and its relations with Europe. The patriarchal obsession apparently obscures fraternal dissension between different zones of Spanish American culture (the Rio de la Plata zone versus Mexico, for example) and between Brazil and its sister states. Separately, the domination of South America by the north propagates further resentment of the Anglo-Saxon alien.

Consequently, for all the rhetoric of solidarity, there has been very little scholarly consideration of exactly what are the differences between Brazil and the rest of Latin America. Within the social sciences this has not been an issue; the contiguity of the two, plus the economic domination of the margins by the industrial and political center, facilitates the notion of Brazil as simply one more Latin American nation. Literary discourse, by contrast, reveals two separately evolving traditions, further distanced by linguistic difference. Yet the psychological gulf between the continental partners is little recognized, understood, or invoked.

Such is the context of the international reception of Guimarães Rosa. If he were to become better known, the obvious path would be through inclusion in the much publicized *Boom* around the 1960s which brought Latin American literature to the front of the literary stage in Europe and the United States. But the *Boom* was largely fostered by Hispanicist intellectuals and those sympathetic to their interests. In academic institutions, the breach was manifested in the ignorance of things Brazilian by Hispanicists; consequently, very few of these intellectuals were familiar with Guimarães Rosa. Interest in his work was relegated to the numerically insignificant Luso-Brazilian fringe of departments of Spanish and Portuguese.

Periodically, eminent Hispanicist literary critics sympathetic to Brazilian culture have become enthusiastically aware of Rosa, and have urged their peers to read *Grande Sertão: Veredas*. A noteworthy example is Yale's Emir Rodrigues Monegal, who wrote various pieces dedicated to Guimarães Rosa. This extract was composed after the author's death:

> If it is easy to not be aware of him—and there are many who are not, inside and outside Brazil, it is very difficult, once one has caught a glimpse of the magical world of Guimarães Rosa, not to become an addict. It is like with Kafka or Borges: once a single phrase of theirs has entered into our blodstream, we are lost." (Coutinho 1991, 48)

Bella Jozef, an outstanding Spanish American literary historian, dedicates the greater part of an essay, "O Romance Brasileiro e o Ibero-Americano na Atualidade" (Today's Brazilian and Ibero-American novels; in Coutinho 1991, 187–97) to celebrating Guimarães Rosa and relating aspects of his work to particular narratological innovations in Spanish American writers such as Cortázar, Gallegos, Asturias, Rulfo Borges, and Rulfo. The last of these writers, Juan Rulfo, author of the extraordinarily esteemed novel, *Pedro Páramo,* and the least given of all Spanish American writers to public statement, in a rare interview conceded in 1971 simply commented, referring to Guimarães Rosa, that "the *Ulysses* of Latin Americans is Brazilian." (Rulfo, 1971)

The pattern, it seems, is that Guimarães Rosa is discovered and briefly celebrated as a diamond in the rough, then re-discovered some time later by someone else—as if by some mysterious process he had in the interim returned to the shadows of the mine shaft.

General reception in North America of Guimarães Rosa's translated works

The translation into English of *Grande Sertão: Veredas* (*The Devil to Pay in the Backlands,* 1963) was a significant literary event. It was commissioned personally by the eminent publisher Alfred Knopf, it was the first translation of the text into any language, and it was perceived by its diplomat-author as a vital step into the international mainstream. In 1958 the story, "A hora e a vez de Augusto Matraga," the first of his works to be translated, had two renditions, one into Spanish in an Argentinian journal, and one into French. As for English, translations of Brazilian literature were at that point extraordinarily few; academic surveys in the 1950s revealed that there were scarcely twenty novels available in translation. The number was doubled in the 1960s, largely through the efforts of Alfred Knopf's publishing house (bought out by Random House during this period) and the leading Latin American translator, Harriet de Onís, whose collection of titles over a forty-year career is truly remarkable, given that the authors translated were not just completely unknown in the United States but also often no more than emerging figures in Latin America; the list includes Carpentier, Güiraldes, Guzmán, Sábato, Uslar-Pietri, Reyes, Alegría, and an extraordinary triumvirate of Brazilians—Jorge Amado, Gilberto Freyre, and Guimarães Rosa. Having read and admired the Spanish translation of "Augusto Matraga," from *Sagarana,* Onís procured and read the entire book in the original, and then found a U.S. publisher, the journal *New World Writing,* for another story, "Duelo." She consequently engaged Guimarães Rosa in a substantial correspondence, itself the subject of a Masters thesis (Verlangieri), which continued till her death. In 1959, Guimarães Rosa and Knopf established a contract for the publication of *Grande Sertão: Veredas.* Ms. Onís undertook the gargantuan task despite severe health problems. After a year, overwork precipitated a transfer of the task to a Brazilian lexicologist and Stanford professor, James L. Taylor, who completed the first draft which was then reworked by Onís, and finally published in 1963 with the title *The Devil to Pay in the Backlands.*

The book was reviewed in the press around the country. Several academically minded critics complained of the translation, almost universally without a suggestion of how the task might better have been achieved. This sentiment was to give rise to a certain folkloric wisdom that the subsequent commercial fiasco, and the failure of history to anoint Guimarães Rosa as a *Boom* writer, was the fault of the translators. Closer study of the reviews reveals something else in fact. Though the reviews of course varied, the first and certainly the single most influential, that by Orville Prescott in the *New York Times* of 17 April 1963, is not unrepresentative. After indicating the context of the story, noting that the appearance of *The Devil to Pay in the Backlands* follows upon that of *Gabriela, Cinnamon and Clove,* and that Jorge Amado had provided the preface for the English translation, Prescott takes up the issue of Amado's eulogy of Guimarães Rosa:

> Mr. Amado calls Mr. Guimarães Rosa a master novelist and his book great. These verdicts may be a trifle over-generous but there can be no doubt that Mr. Guimarães Rosa is greatly gifted and that his book is an astonishing performance.
> It takes time, effort and patience to sink into this enormous novel, to adjust oneself to the strange rhythms of its colloquial and yet poetic prose, to become aware of the complexities and richness of meaning which is beneath its foaming melodrama. (1963)

Prescott goes on to describe Riobaldo's mode of reflecting, and to quote some these reflections. He concludes with the simple remark, "The translation by James L. Taylor and Harriet de Onís is superb." The bulk of other reviews acknowledge *The Devil to Pay in the Backlands* as a great work, with article titles such as: "Brazilian Novel Reflects Greatness in Awe, Terror" (Waterman 1963); "Notable Brazilian Novel" (anon., I.E.B. / U.S.P.); "A Sweeping New Wave from Brazil" (Wheildon 1963). Whether from academics or professional journalists, the tone is so consistent that it is more interesting to single out the odd negative piece. Theodore O'Leary's "Ruffians May Have a Certain Majesty" seems deliberately belligerent:

> The attitude of many American intellectuals toward foreign novels consists of a sort of reverse chauvinism (. . .). If it has enough bulk and is difficult enough to follow, almost any novel from Iceland or Estonia that gets published over here is likely to be called great or a masterpiece by at least one American critic even if in reality it is something of a bore or a puzzle (. . .). Now we have a big novel from Brazil, *"The Devil to Pay in the Backlands"*, which, we are told by its publisher and by another Brazilian novelist, Jorge Amado in a foreword, is a great novel. Inevitably some American reviewers will agree, but not this one, who thinks that while João Rosa's [sic] book possesses a certain majesty, it is too long, too repetitious and as a result sometimes tedious (. . .) Nor are there any other ultimate answers in this novel to the many questions it raises." (1963)

But even this article is quite substantial, describing narrative technique and the protagonist's perspective, and concluding,

> *The Devil to Pay in the Backlands* (. . .) preserves completely and vividly a savagely picturesque period in the history of one part of Brazil as certain American novels have preserved little known aspects

3: DOMESTIC AND INTERNATIONAL RECEPTION   119

of our history. Rosa's depiction of the natural background against which his *jagunços* move is superb. He insists upon and gets a response from all the reader's senses. But as an adventure story this novel lacks variety and sometimes moves ponderously, while as a novel of ideas it fails to progress beyond the obvious.

The review is interesting in two ways; first, in that the cantankerous country critic praises the novel strongly despite his declared intention and, second, in that he touches on the issue of the gulf between the broader reading public and the intellectual enthusiasts of foreign, "high" literature.

This question proved a real problems for the publisher. Knopf's correspondence with Guimarães Rosa[5] includes six-monthly royalty statements, the first of which, for "30-9-63," lists sales in a run of 5,000 or 10,000, of 2,640 domestic and 122 international. The figure really refers to books distributed to retail sellers, who could then return them. From this time on, the royalty statements are incredible and almost comically low: 410 returns and no new sales for the period to 30-9-64; 69 returns for the next period; sales of 22, 74, 38, 57, and 86 for the periods up to the death of Guimarães Rosa. The sales of the English translation of *Sagarana*, from its publication in 1966 till Rosa's death late the following year, reveal a similar pattern: 2,147 for the first six-month period followed by no further sales and 24 returns in the next period. Neither work has since had a further edition. Excluding library acquisition the number of North American readers was and is negligible; given that Rosa's archives alone contain copies of 27 1963 reviews by American journals and newspapers[6] the reality is that the reviewers and the small body of academics with a special interest in Brazilian literature must have constituted a substantial proportion of the initial readership.

Rosa's obscurity outside Brazil provokes several hypothetical explanations, the first of which concerns the quality of the translation. Perfect rendering of the idiosyncratic, colloquial, poetic prose in another language is impossible. The path chosen by the translators, Harriet de Onís and Prof. James L. Taylor, was that of communicability, of adapting the rural social context of the novel to a corresponding, but qualitatively distinct, deep continental North American rural context. As one academic reviewer observed:

> Taylor and Onís here use a conventional style, which reads well but fails to preserve the tone of the original language with its colorful imagery, although, admittedly, it would be an almost superhuman task

to render the exact flavor of the idiomatic expressions, proverbs, archaisms, and words coined by the author. (Johnson)

Guimarães Rosa himself was greatly concerned with the loss of poetic elements; in subsequent correspondence with his German translator he regrets various errors and refers to the Los Angeles Times review of 28 April 1963 by Professor Claude Hulet of the University of California at Los Angeles, "Brazilian's Recent Novel Loses Poetic Power in Translation." Certain phrases were unhappily translated, and in order to facilitate the flow of the rambling work various paragraphs or phrases were simply omitted. The ensuing problem was twofold. The rich semantic clusters were impoverished, as Rosa painfully and painstakingly noted; and while a parallel vernacular successfully evoked the vastness, desolation, and beauty of the remote rural clime, it distracted from the appropriate reading mood.

The vernacular of *The Devil to Pay in the Backlands* is not inconsistent with that of other (American) Western literature, and does not compare to the original Portuguese. *Grande Sertão: Veredas* has something in common with the meandering, slowly evolving structure of medieval romance: both are predicated on a rich and complex ensemble of symbols or "mythemes" and both resist the clarification and resolution characteristic of modern adventure stories. The sustained interrogatorial tone of the narrator has nothing in common with the pragmatism of the typical Backlands hero. Finally, *Grande Sertão: Veredas* gives a highly introspective, impressionistic portrait of place and time. It is remarkable, and clearly deliberate, to what extent the work avoids identifiable historical events and verifiable social contexts. It exploits the resource of local culture at an abstract, semantic level but avoids recognizable dates and events. The narrator of *Grande Sertão: Veredas* is not providing testimony of a bygone moment in the story of the world; on the contrary, the world he has known is simply an accumulation of testimony, his own mind and memory, which he uses to reflect on universal issues—good and evil, love, and fate versus circumstance. In sum, the rural setting, together with the folksy dialect, propel the work into a conventional genre to which it is a complete stranger.

The perception of *The Devil to Pay in the Backlands* as a literary Western was far greater than for other translations of *Grande Sertão: Veredas,* as is suggested by American review titles from 1963 such as "Cowboys and Gangsters in Brazil's Badlands" (Bergin), "Brazil's Wild West" (Holmberg), "The Evil One Led the Bands"

(Johnson), "Outlaw and the Devil in Brazil's Backlands" (Conroy), and "Brazilian Bandit Reminisces" (Schlesinger). The problematic distance between the reception of a text based on popular appeal and one assessed by academics was further compounded. The work fell into the void between two identities, one as Western adventure literature, another as an academically accredited classic, as obligatory reading. It fell to earth between two markets, one more numerous and popular, the other more privileged, this latter drawing on a minuscule contingent of readers representing the Brazilianist intelligentsia and Brazilian elite culture as an export item.

In Germany the work received a more satisfactory response. Curt Meyer-Clason's translation focused on the metaphysical richness of the text and did not shy away from neologisms in rendering Rosa's poetic prose; the facility and tolerance of the German language for new compound words was presumably a significant advantage. It was also possible, however, to promote Rosa's work in a different manner; not only the translation but the approach taken to presenting the book to the literary public emphasized its intellectual richness as a challenge and reward to the cultured reader: A relatively short article appearing in the *Kolner Kulturspiegel,* "In Köln und Rio gibt es mehr Mystiker, als man ahnt," makes a comparison between Rosa and American literature, (Emerson rather than Twain). It also mentions Goethe's comments on world literature and outlines the history of modern Brazilian literature. Finally, it grasps the vital point that the *sertão* is a stage, a metaphor for the universe:

> Yesterday, I did not know anything about him. And today I feel as if he had always belonged to me, as if, since my childhood, his works had been among the literary "Gods" that I grew up with and that are still worth living for. I must think of R. W. Emerson . . .
> I am talking about J. G. Rosa . . . He is from Brazil.
> Brazil . . . When Goethe coined the term "world literature" the imitative literature of this country could not yet be included . . . "The native idiom" Jorge Amado says, is now supposed to be transformed into a "language tool fit for literature" . . .
> (. . .). Grande Sertão, the spacious Brazilian back country, becomes the mirror of world events.[7]

In a letter to Meyer-Clason[8], Rosa himself made the following observation:

> As it seems to me, in terms of such a work the German reader is distinct from the North American in at least three points: 1) in relation

to metaphysical thought; 2) the more careful and detailed vision of landscapes and of nature; 3) the implicit poetry. I would tend to think that, as concerns these three issues, the German (and likewise the Scandinavians, etc.) reacts in a positive fashion, whereas the North Americans tend to react somewhat negatively. Am I right?

The article quoted above, alongside the contrary piece from Kansas, show up well the two extremes in attitude, one welcoming the work as World Literature, the other blinkered by hostility to the provincial exotic. Interestingly, however, the enthusiasm of German critics was not matched by the readership, so that while initial sales of the book were reasonable, Guimarães Rosa remains relatively unknown. In this way, though the German and the United States critical receptions reflect sharply divergent cultural paradigms and prejudices, the broad pattern is consistent: euphoric acknowledgment in closely focused scholarly circles, and general public ignorance; a gradual subsiding into obscurity, with the occasional rediscovery by a critical reader proving powerless to affect public indifference.

In America, other factors make the lack of public response even more remarkable. Firstly, Guimarães Rosa was in fact exceptionally fortunate to have Ms. de Onís as his translator; to judge by titles she was probably the century's most distinguished translator from Spanish and Portuguese into English. Ms. de Onís also worked harder on Guimarães Rosa than on any other project. Although for health reasons she could not complete *The Devil to Pay in the Backlands,* she took up the task of translating *Sagarana* in June of 1963. The two exchanged almost eighty long letters. Two years later, informing Knopf that she had finished the last story, Onís observed, "I have never worked so hard, but I hope or would like to think that perhaps I have never done such a good translation." Guimarães Rosa had come to refer to Onís as *minha madrinha.* The reviews of *Sagarana—A Cycle of Stories,* as for *The Devil to Pay in the Backlands* were generally positive. The work was included in the *New York Times Book Review* "Selection of Books for Summer Reading." There were the same grumblings as for *The Devil to Pay in the Backlands* from a few scholarly reviewers about the inadequacy or, more fairly, the impossibility of the right translation. However, in 1967 Ms. de Onís received the Pen Club's Prize for Best Translation in recognition of her achievement with *Sagarana.*

It is worth transcribing one of the earlier letters[9] from Guimarães Rosa to Onís to illustrate the extraordinary thoroughness of their communication, the hyper-sensitive stylistic virtuosity of the author, and the difficulty facing the translator—a factor illuminated, interestingly, by Rosa's difficulty in attempting incursions into English, despite his industrious accessing of the best dictionaries. The following examples do not concern the many Rosean Brazilian Portuguese words which quite simply are absent from the English lexicon, but rather relatively easy words.

"THE RIVER WAS A PROLONGED, MOANING TONE" (pag. 12, linha 15). No original: ["]O rio era um longo tom, lamentoso["]. Aqui, devo confessar-lhe um capricho de autor. Esta, em todo o conto, é talvez a frase a que me apego mais. Eu acho mesmo nela, em português—talvez pela aliteração, teor curto, e assonâncias,—algo de inusitado, de "traduzido", de estranho, de força encantatória. Por isso foi que, para passagem aparentemente tão simples, tão sem importância para o leitor comum, e que no seu primeiro *draft* estava perfeitamente traduzida quanto ao significado exerno das palavras, apresentei duas sugestões, no n° 111 das "NOTAS". Não me satisfaz o PROLONGED. E lhe peço: não seria possível deixarmos a forma:
THE RIVER WAS A LONG MOANING TONE—? (sem vírgula separando o LONG do MOANING). Sinto, nela, qualquer coisa de curto, forte, concreto, inteiro, animal, primitivo, elemental, escuro e dinâmico, intenso, menos comum, mais vivo. O "prolonged" eu acho diluído, abstrato, previsível na frase, não fere, não choca o leitor. E, a ausência da vírgula, que proponho, *con amore,* tira o LONG do TONE e prende-o irremediavelmente ao MOANING: como se decorresse de um TO MOAN LONG . . . Sei que, com isso violentar-se-ia um pouco o "repouso" idiomático do inglês. Mas . . . Sei que a Amiga compreenderá. São coisas e sensações difíceis de exprimir e de transmitir.

["THE RIVER WAS A PROLONGED, MOANING TONE" (pag. 12, line 15). In the original: ["] O rio era um longo tom, lamentoso["]. Here, I must confess an writer's caprice. This is possibly the phrase that I'm most concerned with in the whole story. I myself find in it in Portuguese—perhaps because of the alliteration, the brevity, the assonances—something unusual, something "translated", strange, like a spell. It was for this reason that, even for a such a small passage of little importance to the average reader and which was translated perfectly as to the external sense of the words in your first draft, that I made two suggestions, in No. 111 in the "NOTES". the PROLONGED does not satisfy me. So I ask of you: couldn't we leave the form:
THE RIVER WAS A LONG MOANING TONE—? (without a comma separating the LONG from the MOANING). I feel in this form something curt, strong, concrete, hole, animal, primitive, elemental, dark and dynamic, intense, less common, more alive. I find the "prolonged" diluted, abstract, predictable in the phrase; it doesn't hit or

shock the reader. And the absence of the comma, which I propose, *con amore,* takes the LONG from the TONE and joins it ineluctably to the MOANING: as if derived from a TO MOAN LONG . . . I realize that with this the idiomatic sense of English is a little wounded. But . . . I know that my great Friend will understand. These things and sensations are difficult to express and transmit.] (Unpublished letter, 2 May 1959).

Later in the same letter Guimarães Rosa takes to task the phrase, "The locusts were unbearably sad." He quite rightly observes that the Portuguese "cigarra" should be translated "cicada," and proposes, "The landscape was sad, with plenty of mostly sad cicadas, in the afternoon."[10] His next point concerns the translation of "esdrúxulo estradeiro," referring to a man with elephantiasis met on the road, carrying an image of a [patron] saint. Unhappy with "sorry wanderer," Rosa comes up with a series of possible alternates, of which the first is interesting, but the others, to the native English ear, simply foolish.

A nota que o autor quis dar não foi a de "triste" ou de "infeliz", mas a de : pitoresco, humour-negro, estranhez e fé absurda. Proponho:
extravagant wanderer
or:
sad-absurd wanderer
sad-singular wanderer
merry-sorry wanderer
sorry-merry wanderer
sorry-queer wanderer, etc.

[The sense that the author intended to suggest was not that of "sad" or "unhappy" but rather of the picturesque, black humour, strangeness and absurd faith. I propose: . . .]

Rosa's extensive correspondence with his translators has become the object of theses, and already a volume of letters to his Italian colleague has been published in both Italy and Brazil. The Brazilian critic Paulo Ronai observed,

I never know a more conscientious creator . . . the voluminous correspondence of the author with each of his translators, . . . [constitutes] a unique exegesis . . . a monument without analogy in any literary tradition. (Guimarães Rosa, 1973, xx)

Remarkably, a close examination of the correspondence tends to confirm this assessment. The last few years of Guimarães Rosa's life were largely consumed with this task.

3: DOMESTIC AND INTERNATIONAL RECEPTION 125

The second piece of fortune for Guimarães Rosa was the strong support of Alfred Knopf, whose publishing house had already established a reputation for introducing significant new foreign works. Mr. Knopf maintained a personal correspondence with Guimarães Rosa, whose work he had read and admired. Apart from the successful distribution to newspapers across the country for reviews of *The Devil to Pay in the Backlands,* Knopf advertised in two places in the same edition of the *New York Times*[11]. One four-inch block ad reads simply:

Note well this name:

João Guimarães

Rosa

—for he is a

literary figure of the

first importance

ALFRED A. KNOPF

(see advertisement on page 33)

The perspective of the publisher on behalf of this author, as distinct from the task of enthusing the reading public is perhaps best suggested by the counterpoint of this ad and another, immediately below it on the page and slightly smaller, which includes a picture of a cherub holding a heart playfully in the air (not reproduced here). This ad reads:

> A novel of pregnant possibilities—and vice versa
>
> GROUCHO MARX says: "I had no idea a book about aspirin could be so sexy."
>
> NATHANIEL BENCHLEY says: "I think it is an enchanting little ballad in praise of fertility."
>
> PHYLLIS DILLER says: "I *loved* the book"
>
> **PRUDENCE and THE PILL**
>
> A novel by Hugh Mills $2.59

A final circumstance which played into Guimarães Rosa's hands, and one perhaps not unrelated to what is implied by the second ad, was that the first and only ever Brazilian bestseller in the United States, Jorge Amado's *Gabriela, Cinnamon and Clove* had been released the previous year with spectacular success, amidst the general wave of enthusiasm for things Brazilian inspired by the impact of *Bossa Nova* music. Amado's special preface for *The Devil to Pay in the Backlands* gave Guimarães Rosa the most elevated eulogy possible, and the recommendation could not have come from a better source.

Whatever the shortcomings of the translation, the management of the translations of Guimarães Rosa's two major works was thoroughly professional; the writer was not an obscure regionalist but a consummate diplomat with the best connections and, apparently, with the blessing of fortune. *Grande Sertão: Veredas* had only been out in Brazil for seven years and already it was released in the United States, with all the resources of a respected and sympathetic publisher, and the unanimous support of Brazilianist intellectual circles. In the decade between the release of *Grande Sertão: Veredas* and Guimarães Rosa's death he had had published at least two works in English, German, French, Italian, and Spanish translations developed with a scrupulous attention to detail, a phenomenal effort of labor and the greatest possible cooperation between author and translator. The situation of the writer in his last years

3: DOMESTIC AND INTERNATIONAL RECEPTION 127

is suggested in the following testimony by Emir Rodríguez Monegal, an eminent Latin American literary critic at Yale:

> When I visited him, Guimarães Rosa had published very little: the tales of *Sagarana,* his first book; two volumes of novelettes . . . the novel which won him international fame . . . and *Primeiras Histórias.* These four titles made him famous inside Brazil and were beginning to disseminate his work abroad. On the day I visited him, July 13, 1963, it was impossible to find a copy of his early works in Rio. A book dealer, specializing in Brazilian literature and a publisher . . . told me that by now he had requests for a hundred copies of *Grande Sertão: Veredas.* Guimarães Rosa himself apologized for not having been able to send a copy of the novel to the European publishers who were interested in it and having to get copies from the private libraries of his friends. To better document these difficulties he referred to the translations under way, to the letters from Alfred A. Knopf (his North American publisher and personal friend), to the letters of his German publishers, to the "Éditions du Seuil" in Paris, who would send him letters written with fine French elegance: they hailed him as a master and acknowledged with enthusiasm the irrational condition of his stories and the almost mythical nature of his imagination. (Coutinho 1991, 50)

Monegal also speaks of his encounters with Guimarães Rosa in Geneva, together with Neruda in Manhattan at the PEN Club, of receiving packets of new copies of Rosa's works in Paris and of reading of his death in *Le Monde,* which in 1965 had singled out the writer as the greatest Brazilian novelist. Guimarães Rosa remains an enigmatic literary figure; having lived in Germany during World War II and worked to help Jews, having participated, with the highest honors, in Latin American literary conferences in Mexico and Bogota, and making the journey to Manhattan, his work nevertheless continued to focus on the rural Minas Gerais of past years. He had, however, the best possible connections, and, like Neruda, an enriching exposure to different cultures. There were ongoing rumors in the early and mid 1960s, eagerly devoured and reproduced in the Brazilian and Spanish American presses, that Guimarães Rosa was on the shortlist for the Nobel Prize. The question of Nobel status had actually been raised in 1962, on the Belgian radio program "Lectures pour tous," with the title "Un candidat au Nobel,"[12] after the publication of *Nuits du sertão,* which consisted of one long story, "Buriti," from *Corpo de Baile.* This relatively minor work, the second volume launched in France,[13] was thus appraised:

> This vision of the Brazilian world bears that mysterious quality through which one recognizes a universal work of literature. *Les Nuits*

du Sertão will take its place in that edifice of fiction which, from century to century, from Cervantes to Tolstoy, magnifies the entirety of humanity, torn from the immutable progression of History.[14]

The French case presents the same general pattern as in other languages, that is, an initial euphoric celebration by a small circle of cognoscenti, followed by a gradual decline, rather than increase, in exposure, with the disposition of the intellectuals unable to impose itself on the consciousness of the broader reading public.

Whatever it may lose in translation, a great book can stand the loss; indeed, many of the classic texts were written in dialects considered to be conceptually and aesthetically idiosyncratic and unreproducible—from the Homeric Greek to Dante to Shakespeare and finally to Joyce. The task of translating *Grande Sertão: Veredas* might well be compared to that of *Ulysses,* and yet the latter has had a profound influence outside as well as within the English-speaking world—and nowhere more than in Brazil, where Joyce was promoted by the avant-garde Concretists.

Consequently, despite the enormous difficulty of translating Guimarães Rosa, there is no solid evidence that this caused its poor international reception. Nor did Rosa lack contacts with commercial publishers. In Spanish, for example, *Grande Sertão: Veredas* was published in Barcelona by Seix Barral, the central editorial house for most of the Spanish American *Boom* writers.

How is it, then, that Guimarães Rosa remains in the intellectual underground? Is his situation as a Brazilian writer in the international domain generally illustrative or simply exceptional? What reception greeted the other writers?

Machado de Assis, Mário de Andrade, Carlos Drummond de Andrade

Machado de Assis. The Brazilian laureate lost in the crowd of the World Fair: the modest fate of his translated works

The most important comparative case is certainly that of Machado de Assis, bearer of the most royal mantle in Brazilian letters. His literary genius developed gradually. His earlier work was influenced by the romanticism dominant in the midcentury period and is not considered outstanding. His later work coincides with the influence of realism in the last decades of the century, as Brazilian letters followed European developments but with a lag of at least a generation. A handful of other writers wrote memorable works, notably Aluízio de Azevedo, who emulated French naturalism in *O Cortiço*. Machado de Assis's eccentric realism could never be conceived as typically Brazilian, but throughout his career he was a presence in the world of letters. He was active in the press for decades and wrote plays which were produced and volumes of poetry which were published; in short, he prospered in the *carioca* literary salon. As his successive works appeared, particularly in the full-length format of the novel, they gradually revealed a growing originality and extraordinary quality in relation to the output of his peers. Slowly but steadily, and independently of Eurocentric literary vogues, his literary genius imposed itself within Brazilian society and Machado de Assis acquired an ever greater stature which culminated with his uncontested leadership and inaugural presidency of the newly created Brazilian Academy of Letters around the turn of the century.

After his death Machado de Assis's work entered both the literary canon and the school syllabus, and was widely circulated in paperback editions for popular consumption. His dominance of Brazilian letters is so universal that it scarcely warrants scrutiny. He is, if not the Brazilian Shakespeare, at least its Pushkin—the core of the national literary heritage, possibly surpassed by certain works of later writers but unequivocally central to literary consumption from the classroom to the bus stop to the university and the literary review.

In the United States, the pattern of Machado de Assis's domination of the expatriate and Brazilianist literary scholarly circle obtains again. To what extent, though, has his work influenced the broader reading market of North America? The answer can be inferred from the publication history of his works. Until the 1950s there were no translations apart from the occasional version of a story in a journal or an anthology. In 1952 a translation of *Brás Cubas,* entitled *Epitaph of a Small Winner,* was launched by Farrar and Straus in New York, with a corelease in Britain by W. H. Allen and in Canada by Longmans. This could be seen as a belated but commercially respectable distribution. Impact was minimal, however, and another version was commissioned in Rio by the Brazilian government's Ministry of Education and Culture and published through the official government organ, the Instituto Nacional do Livro under the title *Posthumous reminiscences of Brás Cubas.* Still, there was a reprint in New York in 1956 by Noonday and another in Britain in 1968 by Penguin. This last must be seen as Machado de Assis's supreme publishing venture in English, even though it did not become available in the United States. Noonday, a minor but significant player in the world of commercial publishing, did pursue the potential Machado de Assis market and in 1956 commissioned and published the work which is considered central in the opus, *Dom Casmurro*, in a translation by a UCLA based scholar of classics and champion of Machado de Assis, Helen Caldwell. As with *Epitaph of a Small Winner* the version was coreleased in Britain and Canada by Allen and Longmans. Noonday subsequently reprinted the work in paperback in 1960. Significantly, however, the same translation was only reprinted later, in 1966, by the University of California Press, a launching which must be attributed to Ms. Caldwell's professional association rather than any commercial imperative. Finally, more than three decades after the paperback version of 1960, a different translation of *Dom Casmurro*, entitled *Lord Taciturn*, by R. Scott-Buccleuch, was released in hardback in Britain and the United States by Owen. The same translator and British publisher had already brought a minor novel, *Iaiá García*, to press in 1976, and would later continue with *Memorial de Aires* in 1990, the latter in corelease by the commercially insignificant Californian publisher, Magpie Press, which had had an earlier minor association with Ms. Caldwell and Machado de Assis, *What went on at the baroness's; a tale with a point* (1963b). The remaining commercial publication of note was of *Quincas Borba*, released by Farrar, Straus and Giroux in New York in 1954, and much later picked up by a major American publisher of quality titles in budget paperback format, Avon, in 1982. This launching was probably stimulated by the outstanding success Avon had enjoyed with many of Jorge Amado's works, though it failed to generate a similar number of re-editions. These commercial experiments with Machado de Assis suggest that because of his status in Brazil and, more importantly, in scholarly circles outside Brazil, important publishing houses were occasionally prepared to experiment with his work. Whether they made money or not is unclear, but Machado de Assis does by now have a respectable portfolio in translation at a series of levels—major commercial operations, minor independent publishing houses, and finally University presses. It is the last of the three which has been the most important. In commercial translation Machado de Assis's work has tended to slip into "out of print" mode. His work has been salvaged only through the efforts of Brazilianist scholars anxious to bring this outstanding work to the non-Portuguese speaking public, and perhaps keen to develop their own publishing record. After Ms. Caldwell's first translation of Machado de Assis was passed on to the University of California Press, thus outlet continued to publish other works throughout the 1960s, 1970s and 1980s, beginning with a collection of stories from *Papéis Avulsos* entitled *The psychiatrist and other Stories,* followed by the relatively obscure *Esau and Jacob* in 1965, *Counselor Ayres' Memorial* in 1972, and another early minor novel, *Helena,* in 1984. Ms. Caldwell also wrote the introduction to the translation of *A Mão e a Luva* (*The Hand and the Glove*) by a scholarly colleague, Albert Bagby Jr., released in 1970 through the University of Kentucky. Bagby put out a translation of *Iaiá García* through the same press in 1977. In Britain there was an almost simultaneous release of the same novel by a third aficionado of Machado de Assis, Robert Scott Buccleuch. Between them these scholars have extended the repertoire of the Machadian opus in translation to include items which even in Brazil are of limited appeal.

Although the situation is certainly not as spectacular as that of Guimarães Rosa, the pattern is similar: the writer who stands as a literary giant within Brazil cannot get more than a toehold in the external market, cannot penetrate the arena of the international reading public; the immortal champion of the Brazilian Academy cannot gain admission to the pantheon of Western consciousness. Again, though, as with Guimarães Rosa, a situation of diverging esteem emerges in the international context: in the scholarly domain the domestic literary canon is carried over from the Brazilian academy to the outside. On the other hand, the overlap within Brazil of the literary institution and the broader reading public becomes dysfunctional at the international level. Although Brazil occupies a significant place in the world imagination, this image is not located in its literary heritage. There is no correspondence between what Brazil constitutes, represents or is represented as, in the international cultural market on the one hand and in the domestic literary market on the other.

Mário de Andrade. The definitive *paulista*. The international perspective: limited scholarly interest, commercial obscurity

The spirit of Mário de Andrade lives on in São Paulo, the industrial and intellectual capital of Brazil. The rich municipal library bears his name. His archives are kept at U.S.P. and have provided an endless source of thesis material. Mário de Andrade had not been translated into English till the 1980s, with the exception of a forgotten version of *Amar, Verbo Intransitivo* of 1933, entitled *Fräulein,* and a handy bilingual edition of *A Paulicéia Desvairada*

(*Hallucinated City*) brought out by J. Tomlins in 1968. Finally in 1984 *Macunaíma* was released simultaneously by a major commercial publisher in the United States and in Britain. But the work has not been included in general literature courses in these countries. The writer remains virtually invisible in the English-speaking world. Nevertheless, in North America Mário de Andrade has attracted a certain amount of scholarly attention, attracting at least fifteen Ph.D. theses. A third of these are nonliterary in focus, referring to Andrade in a relatively minor way as a commentator on regional cultural practices. Of the literary theses, several are similarly tangential, with one, for example, on stereotypes of the Amazon by Brazilian writers, another on female sexuality in a range of Latin American novels, and another on human to animal metamorphosis. Mário's inclusion in these theses is essentially due to the colorful exploitation of myth in *Macunaíma,* which is not really representative of his fiction or his poetry. Two of the theses are concerned with Andrade's intellectual role in the modernist movement; two others alone focus on representative fictional works, in both cases the short stories. One traces the development of São Paulo through solid material evidence such as census data, then considering Mário's fictional evocation of this urban context.

The eclectic genius of Mário de Andrade continues to attract the interest of scholars, but his literary efforts simply do not lift him to the ranks of the international canon. This contrasts with the situation in Brazil, where, because of his intellectual leadership in the modernist movement, his literary output is canonized, so that when, for example, an unpublished short story is discovered amongst his papers it is released with fanfare in the Brazilian press. Mário was an intellectual innovator in relation to a series of distinct themes which have, with time, become more important. However, Brazilian literary modernism, the area he is most importantly associated with in his own country, does not attract a great deal of attention. Theses mentioning Mário on stereotypes of the Amazon and Amerindian music, and the prominence of the tropical adventure of *Macunaíma*—an exception within Mário's opus—illustrate the extent to which the agenda of recent international scholarship on Brazil diverges from the agenda of traditional Brazilian literary scholarship.

Carlos Drummond de Andrade: Domestic reverence and international ignominy

Drummond constitutes an essential case in this sort of analysis because he occupies a comparable, though lesser, position in the canon of Brazilian poetry to that of Machado de Assis in prose. Since he died only in the last decade, it is telling that Drummond is already quite universally regarded as the greatest Brazilian poet of the century and presumably of all time. How lustrous, then, was the international reflection of the medals of domestic glory so steadily accumulated on the modest breast of Carlos Drummond de Andrade? Upon his death in 1987, homage was duly paid in Octavio Paz's *Vuelta* in Mexico, a review of international renown, in a series of articles by a collection of eminent writers and critics from Brazil and Spanish America, including Severo Sarduy, a Cuban writer on the cutting edge of the aestheticist avant-garde of the Post-*Boom* period. It is difficult to interpret Drummond's real impact in the Hispanic world however, as all semi–institutional journals, such as *Vuelta,* a voice-piece set up by a former diplomat who has become the unofficial chief cultural ambassador of Mexico, or the Cuban *Casa de las Americas,* are politically obliged to pay obituary respects in concordance with the official cultural hierarchies of allied states. On the other hand, in the mass of non-fictional writings of the Spanish American giants of the *Boom,* younger than Drummond, there is very little reference to the Brazilian poet. He has been translated into Spanish more than into any other language, but not distributed in large numbers.

In the North American domain, here used as the testing ground for international reception, Drummond has remained in obscurity. As is typical for the scholarly publication of Brazilianist, a short volume of Drummond first appeared in a bilingual translation of sixty-three poems in 1965 (*In The Middle of the Road*). Nothing more was produced in the following ten years. However, Drummond was later paid the honor of translation by the distinguished team of the noted poet Elizabeth Bishop, who has a strong knowledge of Brazilian poetry, and the professional translator Gregory Rabassa, the doyen of English language versions of *Boom* novels from Spanish America (see *Traveling in the family: selected poems*). The book is still in print, through Random House, though it did not have much impact at its initial release, and was not even widely distributed to libraries.

In terms of scholarly commentary, Drummond has received minimal attention in the English-speaking world.

Jorge Amado

The universal popularity of Jorge Amado

The most important example of the international reception of Brazilian literature is Jorge Amado. Phenomenally successful both inside Brazil and abroad, Amado is virtually the only Brazilian writer to have had any international impact beyond academic circles. Whereas the marketological untranslatability of Machado de Assis, Drummond, and Mário de Andrade, confirms the pattern outlined for Guimarães Rosa, Jorge Amado is the conspicuous exception, a crucial counterexample showing that it is perfectly possible for a Brazilian writer to communicate with international audiences. The literary work of Jorge Amado is uniquely compatible with international curiosity about Brazil; his books respond to and satisfy the appetite of international readers, which is shaped largely by perceptions of Brazil drawn from extraliterary sources.

Jorge Amado is widely read, both within Brazil and externally. In Portuguese his most famous novel, *Gabriela,* had no less than sixty-seven editions from 1958 to 1984. Still more remarkable, some of the least popular of his enormous collection (twenty-five novels and various other pieces) have a distribution record which would surpass that of all the works of the other authors. *São Jorge dos Ilhéus,* the relatively obscure volume which sequels the better known *Terras do Sem Fim,* went into its fiftieth edition in 1987. Perhaps his least popular novel, *Seara Vermelha,* from what can be termed the Stalinist era of his career, was in its forty-seventh edition in the same year. Amado's nonfictional account of the Communist leader of the 1930s and 1940s, Luis Carlos Prestes, *O Cavaleiro da Esperança,* was in its thirty-seventh edition in that year, although it was eclipsed by Amado's other work. New releases by Jorge Amado, even his memoirs (*Navegação de Cabotagem*), come out in print runs of one hundred thousand. This is exceptional in Brazil, where the reading or book-buying public is highly restricted (the purchase price of a five hundred-page paperback currently stands at around a quarter of the minimum wage, earned by the majority of the population). A typical print run is often five or ten thousand. Internationally, in terms of raw sales, Amado challenges the most famous of *Boom* writers, García Márquez. By the late 1980s Amado was estimated by the Fundação Casa Jorge Amado in Salvador to have sold about thirty million volumes around the world. Initially aided by his contacts and support in the communist block and subsequently by sheer market economics, Amado has been translated into fifty languages.

This last fact must be seen in a dual context—Amado's initial political privilege in the Eastern block and the steady acquisition of recognition and popularity in the open market of the West. This peculiarly Amadian phenomenon of contacts with European Marxists, politicians, literary luminaries, and figures of popular culture are reflected in the Fundação's photos of the author with Georges Lukacs, Henry Belafonte, Sartre, Leopold Senghor, François Mitterand, Mãe Menininha do Gantois (the most loved, feared, and venerated priestess of Bahian Candomblé and the confidant of Brazil's artistic elite and Bahia's most powerful politician, Antonio Carlos Magalhães), Grande Otello (a Chaplinesque buffoon and *bête sacrée* of Brazilian stage and cinema), and Picasso. It would be difficult to nominate a single individual with the twentieth century more at his fingertips than Jorge Amado.

Meanwhile, in Brazil Amado was, from an early stage, one of the handful of writers who could more or less live by the pen. His position in this respect was discredited within the elite by the allegation that he was really sustained by his privileged contacts with International Communism—an entity perceived grossly by the Brazilian upper class in a way comparable to prewar German perceptions of the machinations of International Jewry. But Amado's outstanding journalistic writing—a sort of intellectual social column full of amusing and peppery accounts of the latest events, or, often enough, simply giving vent to his muse[15]—gained him his first employment. He traveled, was able to observe firsthand the national political machine, and, living in Rio and occasionally São Paulo, mix with the intellectual elite. He was always able to live by his pen one way or another. Notwithstanding official actions such as a 1938 bookburning in Bahia (complete with *auto-da-fé*), Amado revealed himself precociously as that rarest of animals in Brazilian letters: a best-seller.

This exceptionally rich mix of biographical threads—extraordinary international acquaintances and alliances, from Parisian intellectuals to the Washington-Moscow axis of the Cold War; rich friendships and interaction within Brazil with the emerging literary elite based in Rio and known later as the generation of 1930; close ties with the Bahian folkloric underworld which inspired many of his fictional characters; full involvement with the São Paulo centered Brazilian Communist Party and periodic State retribution including imprisonment and house arrest; steadily growing domestic and foreign sales, which eventually reached extraordinary heights for a Brazilian writer—is complemented by a strange phenomenon: an ongoing, frequently open disdain on the part of dominant sectors of the elite. Exactly how and why Amado rubbed the establishment the wrong way is far more complex than the simple issue of radical political sympathies would normally suggest. It is probably more due to the regionalist and racial overtones in his work, the championing of Afro-Bahians. Yet his critical reception in the literary world was not unequivocal.

Immortal pariah. Controversy and neglect in Brazilian criticism

The polemical nature of Amadian criticism is neatly encapsulated in a 1991 article on the question by Eduardo Assis Duarte,[16] "Do rodapé à crítica universitária, Jorge Amado, um caso polêmico" (From the footnote to university criticism: Jorge Amado, a controversial case), which groups this analytic literature into two main categories: *Crítica dos Defeitos* and *Crítica das Belezas* (Criticism of flaws and Criticism of graceful features)—the former consistently scathing and the latter laudatory—and a third, unfortunately less frequent, more appropriately balanced *Crítica Compreensiva* (Comprehensive Criticism). Assis Duarte gives as examples of unquestioning defense the commentary of the French sociologist of Afro-Brazilian themes, Roger Bastide,[17] and a more conventional literary critic, Eduardo Portella.[18] In a French perspective which mixes references to the heritage of naturalist *engagé* literature and more contemporary existentialist overtones, Bastide attributes to Amado an "innovative contribution in the transformation of the heritage of naturalism" and "a sincretizing of negritude with Marxism and the defense of BEING against POSSESSING." In a similar vein Portella cast Amado in a Balzacian light, which has had considerable currency, as the composer of a Brazilian, or rather Bahian, *Comédie humaine* of Bahian "*pícaros* and vagabonds" with "the commitment of solidarity." He champions Amado's humane and politically conscious cause from the perspective of the grand tradition of French realism, while hailing the Latin American writer as a new chapter, appropriate to the twentieth-century embrace of diverse ethnicities and international solidarity. Assis Duarte notes the populist and potentially unwittingly condescending tendency of each critic to

> (. . .) charge to the account of the common folk whatever may be censurable in the "bard of Bahia", and thereby fall into the critical trap of seeing the text as a true reflection of reality, as well as the sort of populism which idealizes the experience of the oppressed classes. (1991, 239)

Solidarity, right by virtue of political ethics, becomes the aesthetic justification of Amado's artistic project.

3: DOMESTIC AND INTERNATIONAL RECEPTION

The *Crítica dos Defeitos* (negative criticism) is exemplified by Álvaro Lins,[19] probably the dominant literary critic of the 1930s and 1940s and the supreme arbiter of Brazilian talent at the time, and the highly respected contemporary critic, Walnice Galvão.[20] Lins crosses the threshold of unabashed insult; describing Amado as "a primitive of little capability who displayed mush and bad taste as if they were trophies, indulging a poetizing of misery," and whose minimal technical facility amounts to a "stylistic misery" and a "crudeness of techniques and devices." Duarte observes that Galvão's 1976 article has exercised considerable authority in more recent critiques. He reproaches her exclusive focus on the late work, *Tereza Batista Cansada de Guerra* (*Tereza Batista: home from the wars;* 1973) which belongs to Amado's unabashed mainstream period. Galvão's ire centers on Amado's vulgarity in the light of his phenomenal commercial success, which, though substantial from the beginning reached much greater levels from the time of *Gabriela*. Duarte paraphrases Galvão as follows:

> Populist and pornographic postures which would be added to the marketological exigencies of the best-seller: stylistic affectation, flowing prose, suspense, a light politically progressive tone, schematic characters and plot development, Bahian folkloric motifs, sex and violence. . . . Jorge Amado was able to inveigh against the dictatorship only because his adhesion to market tastes afforded him the necessary financial autonomy for this. (Duarte, 240).

Duarte also notes that Galvão's thinking was taken up by a cultural critic, Silviano Santiago, who goes to the extent of postulating a socially conservative, anti-populist *teorema* with a postmodernist slant—that independence in the face of the State implies dependence on public consumption.

The views of Galvão and Santiago must be placed more particularly in the context of the military regime of 1964–1985. Prior to this period there had been a virtual Leftist hegemony in the cultural intelligentsia. During the military regime many artists were prevented from divulging their work, while in a curiously sinister way Dionysian popular celebrations, notably carnaval and soccer, were actively promoted by a nominally Roman Catholic state. The progressive-minded filmmakers of the *Cinema Novo* school were gradually shut out and soft pornography became the mainstay of the film industry with tacit government approval. Amado, whose works were not censored, was seen by a large part of the literary establishment as a hypocrite, ostentatiously waving a banner of defiance in his progressive and populist rhetoric while in fact eliminating the conventional proletarian formula of real class confrontation from his work. The fact that *Gabriela* had been published during the hegemony of Left-leaning futurist populism rather than during the anti-Communist period was unimportant for these critics, as was the long period Amado had spent as a militant enemy of the government. The increasingly predominant element of indulgent sexuality in his work now exposed him to a new version of an old charge, derived essentially from an outrage against (a perceived) vulgarity which was first occasioned by his foregrounding of the ethnic margins of society at the expense of the white elite. The objection to such content is complemented by an objection to the form as being conventional and repetitive. This charge should be understood in terms of the modernist canon of the Eurocentric literary establishment, which emphasizes the difference between high and low art, affirms the prestige of formal innovation and tends to reject as facile and unstimulating literature lacking a minimum degree of intellectual difficulty.

As for Amado's reception within Brazil, there is a clear distinction between the academic literary establishment and Brazilian writers themselves. Amado had close ties with most of the major authors of the second wave of *Modernismo,* the *geração de '30,* (including José Américo de Almeida, Raquel de Queirós, and Graciliano Ramos). This group produced regionalist, socially conscious realist novels, which, while integrating various liberties won by the first avant-garde generation of São Paulo, was directly concerned with the material prospects of progress. In 1961, Amado was voted in by his writing peers, becoming an "immortal" of the Brazilian Academy of Letters, which was at the time dominated by writers from the *Nordeste* residing in Rio.

The real resistance to Amado did not come from this quarter, of which he was an integral element, but from the new university establishment centered in São Paulo. Amado was an obligatory reference for critics undertaking studies of Brazilian letters. In this body of work one finds a curious phenomenon of confusion between a vague, generally accepted truth and the details of original opinion. The general notion is that Amado's work can and should be perceived as divided into phases, the first generally derided as technically inferior, the later phase marked by maturity and achievement. In recent years, the usually suggested division is pre- and post-*Gabriela,* between the structurally scrappy, naïve Marxist ideologue whose brave but ignorant heroes discover the wisdom of conscious class confrontation, and the sophisticated mainstream work of later years where, according to critics, the progressive agenda is diluted by carnal ardor and rhetorical decadence. Marxist-leaning Brazilian critics, with a sharper awareness of the evolution of Soviet aesthetic dogma, have tended to divide the work into three periods: a romantic proletarian realism through the 1930s, a more programmatic and orthodox socialist realism from the 1930s through to *Gabriela,* and a third phase, summarized by Nelson Cerqueira as "de escritor burguês e comercial de após 1958, interessado na confecção de romances 'best-sellers' que narram estereótipos exóticos da classe operária da Bahia" (1988, 7–8). The charge could in fact be hardened, since the focus in the last period is on colorful characters who are often not typical proletarian workers but rather idle bohemians, or members of the petty bourgeoisie, or practicants of quasi-biblical professions such as fishermen, shepherds, and prostitutes.

But if we trace back through the years of criticism, the pattern of describing Amado in Manichaean terms is evident even prior to the above chronological divisions. The critic Álvaro Lins, writing shortly after the release of Amado's generally esteemed work of 1943, *Terras do Sem Fim,* explains that Amado's work should be divided into two phases: before and after *Jubiabá* (1935), since the earlier efforts do not even qualify as literature. Lins is obliged to concede the tremendous success of Amado's work—evidently it is only this circumstance which obliges him to deal with the author at all. But this is quite inconsistent with the 1970s and 1980s perspective of Amado as having sacrificed his political agenda for the sake of commercial success from *Gabriela* on. It seems that the division of Amado's work is really a a recurring rhetorical device by critics, which facilitates vilification of one part of the work by balancing this with concessions to another part.

Amado is curiously indigestible to elite literary critics, who are more sympathetic both to more difficult intellectual writers, by admiration, and, by condescension, to traditional popular texts, often anonymously authored and free from the complications of royalties. The divisions change drastically from one critical perspective to the next, and it is significant that rather than winning unanimous applause from the Left, a large part of Amado's work is condemned by university-trained Marxists, who rejected the folkloric championing of the ethnic underdog as a deviation from the purely economically derived logic of systematic class confrontation. Amado's achievement simply does not fit into the intellectual agenda of the educated elite of either political persuasion.

His work has always been popular. The best known novels are probably *Jubiabá, Terras do Sem Fim, Gabriela,* and *Dona Flor e Seus Dos Maridos*—each from a different decade. With the exception of the 1960s all decades from the 1930s to the 1980s present odd pieces which were relatively unsuccessful. The pattern of Manichaean division between, as it were, white hat and black hat characters, and the attendant moral minimalism and limitations to psychological portraiture are constant, as is the conventional nature of the narrative structure. The exploitation of local color and the championing of the ethnic margins of society are similarly consistent factors. The linguistic abuses or liberties are general. Finally, even the class focus of the different "phases" does not afford a clearly discernible difference. The proletarian cocoa cycle of *Cacau* and *Suor* (1933 and 1934) follows the bourgeois student focus of *O País do Carnaval; Capitães da Areia* (1937) is about street children; *Terras do Sem Fim* (1943) and most later works present major characters from the dominant classes though the protagonists are often petty bourgeois; on the other hand prostitutes are also present, as is the constant of lovable rogue-bohemians. What seems lacking in almost all criticism of Amado is the capacity to drop ideological agendas and consider the work hermeneutically in terms of a steady organic development fired by an original cultural and creative perspective. For good or bad, this is really the core of Amado's lyrical impulse; the ideological theories to which Amado himself subscribed are only superficially related to the singular imagination, and the storytelling talent, without which the work would be as mediocre as a novel written by a social scientist or party member.

Understanding of the reception of Amado can, in fact, be enriched by reversing the critics' politicization of the fiction and considering the cultural circumstances surrounding their own "objective" production. Álvaro Lins, in his critical compendium, *Os mortos de sobrecasaca,* first aims his venom at an alleged abuse of adjectival forms in place of adverbs:

> I ask, then: is it possible that Mr. Jorge Amado does not even have access to a dictionary, in which he will find indicated that "incredible" is an adjective and not an adverb? Is it possible, then, for a writer to be ignorant of what is an adverb and what an adjective?" (1963, 246)

He even harries his victim with a cruelly reductive section title: "Obras Completas de Jorge Amado: um "inacreditável" nas aflições entre adjetivo e advérbio" (The Complete Works of Jorge

Amado: "unbelievable" in adjectival-adverbial afflictions, 1963, 237). His brutal acerbity and the presumption that he has the right to reproach the writer like a schoolmaster reflect his status in the national establishment. The arts in Brazil are still largely reliant upon government funding. But the degree of cultural authority exercised by the establishment was even greater in the 1940s. Curiously, the connection between cultural authority and political status is directly expressed on the jacket of Lin's book:

> Chief of the *Casa Civil,* it was he who articulated . . . a thousand solutions for a thousand political problems which threatened the stability of the Government and the progressive development of the Country. Ambassador to Portugal, it was he, and he alone, who defended national dignity at that inglorious juncture in which all wavered, including the President himself, in a gratuitous and inexplicable subservience to the Portuguese dictator . . . (1963)

Contrary to the Anglo-Saxon convention of obligatory discretion of dual offices, the Brazilian tendency to synthesize distinct authorities is here taken to an unwittingly burlesque extreme. But the same inclination can be seen in a more subtle mode in the previously described tendencies of Amadian criticism generally. His dismissal of Amado as vulgar is not unscientific, but the confidence to do so is derived either from conventional social elitism, or from the university-based circle of High Art which rejects Amado's rather conventional form. The conscious desire on the part of the writer to draw on the resource of the popular imagination and poetry offends socially; the deliberate cultivation of retrograde novelistic formulae, such as the picaresque and the verbose melodramatic announcements of the content of the following chapter, are intellectually offensive because they invoke convention rather than innovation.

Hence Amado's paradoxical situation in relation to the literary establishment: a nominal apotheosis (the title of immortal) in the Brazilian Academy of Letters, but a profound antagonism on the part of literary academia, particularly from aesthetic purists, but also from sociologically oriented critics. The hostile treatment of Amado mentioned above is complemented by a sheer disregard which shows up in the revelations of the University of São Paulo holdings of works by or about, as opposed to theses.[21]

Author	Works by/about	Theses	Approximate Ratio of works by/about to theses
Guimarães Rosa	74	9	8
Mário de Andrade	218	21	10
Drummond	98	5	20
Machado de Assis	262	12	22
Jorge Amado	150	1	150

If the "works about" were transferred to the "theses" category, this pattern would be even more extreme. The relative numbers of theses is proof of the university establishment's spectacular disregard for Amado since this production is shaped by the values and focus of the professors. But the table offers other interesting information. Amado fares very well in terms of library holdings of his own work, whether in the university or in the main municipal library of São Paulo, the Biblioteca Mário de Andrade. Acquisition in the latter institution seems to be a response to consumer taste, reflecting the popularity of his work in diverse sectors of the population. As for the works/theses ratio, it is in fact Guimarães Rosa who emerges as most privileged, despite Mário de Andrade's advantage in absolute terms.[22]

Literature of and for the people. Popular status in contemporary Bahian culture

The flip side to these revelations of domestic reception of Jorge Amado concerns a virtually opposite sector of the population, the mass of the lower classes which represent the overwhelming part of the Brazilian population. For those who do not read, cinema presents an interesting situation. All of the authors have had their work adapted to visual media in some form. A successful *telenovela* (soap opera) was made of *Grande Sertão: Veredas,* drawing on the romance and adventure of the story rather than the project of aesthetic revolution in the work. *Macunaíma* was adapted to the big screen in a 1968 film considered the centerpiece of the *Tropicalismo* phase of the creative *Cinema Novo* school. The film was a success in that it did not lose money and was seen by more

3: DOMESTIC AND INTERNATIONAL RECEPTION 143

than just the cognoscenti. However, in the cinematic domain Amado retains his status as the one really "bankable" storywriter. *Gabriela* and *Dona Flor* were adapted and became two of the biggest films of the history of Brazilian cinema. Both penetrated the American market and are readily available on video, thus joining a tiny group of genuinely successful Brazilian films, domestically and internationally.

The unique popular status of Jorge Amado, however, lies not in these material projects but in the nebulous public consciousness. Brazilian writers are embraced at the popular level with a strong sense of regionalism. Mário de Andrade is known to most São Paulo school children, who sooner or later get a historical tour of the municipal library. The figures of Drummond and Rosa are reinforced in the minds of *mineiros* by their constant evocation in the local press, particularly the *Minas Gerais Suplemento Literário*. This recognition is contingent, however, on bourgeois income and reading habits. There is also a *Grande Sertão: Veredas* national park. Like the mountain peak lying somewhere on the border between Brazil and Paraguay which was named after Guimarães Rosa (occasioned by a combination of his renown and his government post in the cartographic division) this must be seen as intervention from above rather than recognition of a local reality.

The situation of Amado in Bahia presents an altogether different perspective, one absolutely unique in Brazilian letters, and in its own way reminiscent of the status of a handful of writers in France, at least in the past. In a collection of didactic survey works on Brazilian writers, *Literatura Comentada,* the following notes are included on the back cover of the volume dedicated to Amado:

> In few authors is the relation between life and work as intimate as in Jorge Amado. This may be the secret to his enormous success with the people.
> His life has also been a fantastic novel. One of the twelve *Obás* of Bahia, friend of the *pai-de-santo,* Procópio, of Joãozinho da Goméia, of Menininha do Gantois and of the *capoeira* master, Pastinha, to name but a few of many representatives of Bahian culture, a miscegenist culture. Political militant, former member of the Communist Party, form Member of the Constitutive Assembly, former exile, former political prisoner, son of a cocoa planter, a frequenter of brothels during his childhood, a member of the Brazilian Academy of Letters, included on the short list for the Nobel Prize various times. All of this wealth of a "life lived ardently" may be the element which makes his work acquire a degree of realism which goes beyond the narrow limits of conventional reality and enters the marvelous realm of the fantastic, taking

with it millions of Brazilian readers and millions of foreigners who read his novels in 42 different languages. (Gomes 1981)

Political radicalism and the halo afforded by persecution imbue a writer with a larger-than-life aura. This has been the situation of many major writers. But in the case of Amado, what is truly exceptional is rather the genuine link with the folkloric figures who partly inspire many of his characters (particularly those with supporting roles). It is not easy to convey the peculiarity of Amado's Bahian situation. Unlike the writers of the American Beat generation, for example, who took up and made characters of obscure, eccentric real-life figures who for whatever reason assumed an existential significance in their eyes, Amado's friends had a stable existence and maintained a public profile in Salvador. They are incarnations of folkloric traditions with archaic roots and at the same time prominent public citizens in a metropolis which is the third biggest city in Brazil. Amado's contact with them did not stem from an active cultivation or pursuit of a marginal element in society, but rather was the consequence of an organic local cultural citizenship, in its own way perfectly conventional once the writer had made the perceptual breakthrough of realizing what his true cultural values were and where his personal sympathies lay.

The small, historical, and physically decadent Pelourinho area of central Salvador was a gravitational center for various distinct groups: students and bourgeois bohemians seeking revelry, clerics (apart from the local monasteries and convents, cathedral and churches, the Church owned much of the property), various Afro-Bahian cultural groups and, most numerously, very poor people including many thieves and prostitutes. Amado had frequented the area as a student and used as it as the setting for his first novel, *O País do Carnaval*. Thirty years later, in a novella entitled *A Morte e a Morte de Quincas Berro d' Agua* (*The Two Deaths of Quincas Wateryell*), considered be some critics as the high point in his career in terms of structure and control, the setting is the same, though instead of focusing on a group of bourgeois men for whom the Pelourinho characters constitute a sort of local color, the group is now balanced between members of different colors and classes—bourgeois, petty bourgeois, and popular—united by empathy and the Bahian zest for communion. Amado had been forced to withdraw to Salvador after the proscription of the Communist Party, occasioning an ongoing association with these figures. He became virtually the only writer of note to reside in Salvador rather than Rio or São Paulo, and in recent decades has maintained Salvador as his home, with frequent lengthy stays in Europe. As for the other main region in which Amado's stories are set, the cocoa-growing area of southeastern Bahia in the first decades of the century (*Gabriela, Terras do Sem Fim, São Jorge dos Ilhéus*) this is nothing other than the land of his father and Amado himself, who was born on a plantation.

The point of this biographical information is that the charge of exoticism must acknowledge Amado's genuine ties with the folkloric figures who inspired his own characters. He was widely known in the Pelourinho area, that is, by the poorest section of society. According to the book jacket quoted above, the writer is even one of the "doze Obás da Bahia," a Candomblé honorific which recalls the "twelve peers of France," the chivalric heroes preserved in Brazilian *cordel* literature. Amado has considerable status, then, not just as a famous author but also within popular folkloric mythology. It is this status which makes his life stretch beyond conventional reality and into the fantastic. The aura of political persecution and acquaintance with great European minds is not the source of the local veneration, which derives from the familiarity of the figure, the persons he has helped through his connections and influence (the *Obá* is more a patron than an active celebrant of Candomblé) the esteem in which he is held by persons of particular power in Bahian culture and, one presumes, the rumors of his power to fictionally immortalize sundry local personages and institutions. In tandem, the significance of Jorge Amado in the mind of the local masses is enhanced by the same superstructural mechanisms that pertain across Brazil—the school syllabus, State honors, newspaper references and so on. In a word, Amado's institutionalization as a Bahian is a phenomenon of ethnocultural identification rather than literary fame. He has had a penetrating interaction with local popular culture which only appears deeper the more it is examined.

One must see State institutionalization in this light. After years of appreciation by foreign tourists and denigration by the local social elite, the physically crumbling red-light area of the Pelourinho was recently renovated and reappropriated by the State and the local commercial elite. One of the first buildings restored, and one which dominates the central square so that it is the most central edifice of the area, is named the Casa Jorge Amado. It now houses a public display and bookshop, and an archive collection. Just outside, Afro-Bahian music is played in the square in an endless series of celebrations. The tourists, often enthused in advance by an Amadian novel, are drawn by the architectural beauty of the area. It is hard to accept the charge of exoticism, let alone of exploitation, under these circumstances of felicitous communion and economic transformation of an area of desperate poverty. At any rate, the popular reception of Amado was to be gauged in a public celebration at the Pelourinho on his eightieth birthday. Various famous singers, no longer young themselves, joined in the entertainment, most of which was provided by youthful local groups. Though the crowds may have been there for the dancing and singing by pop stars more than the speeches, the performers were there because of Amado, who had even mentioned some of them in his books. With around eighty thousand people, this was one of the largest and most euphoric events ever held in the area. Such a phenomenon is quite an aberration in Brazil, a preponderantly nonliterate society.

North American Critical Perspectives of Brazilian Literature

Valorization of Amado's social testimony and comparative thematic analysis of criticism of Guimarães Rosa, Machado de Assis, Drummond and Mário de Andrade

In terms of critical reception there is a strong contrast between Amado's domestic and international treatment; the latter is more substantial, and more favorable. Quantitatively, the pattern for the other writers is the reverse.

The following observations derive from quantitative analysis of the computerized database of international records of critical articles and books, compiled by the Modern Language Association (M.L.A.), and from the computerized database listing North American university dissertations, Dissertations Abstracts International (D.A.I.). Our concern is with patterns as to the nature of interests of international scholars in the writers studied here, and the volume of research.[23]

In the case of Guimarães Rosa, literary-centric issues predominate (35 of 57 items). His work is fertile ground for the application of theory ("kenosis"; Bakhtin; "reader-response" theory . . .). The author is compared to a rich array of eminent world writers (Conrad, Mann, Melville, E. Bronte, Calvino, Rulfo, Tolstoy, Conrad, Céline, Hesse, Faulkner, García Márquez, Borges, Cortázar, Frisch . . .). Most significantly, Guimarães Rosa is featured in no less than three studies attempting a definition or characterization of the New Novel of Latin America (under various titles). Four studies focus on meta-literary issues. The writer is also recognized as a significant voice on a broad range (15 studies) of metaphysical issues (time, the devil [2], magic, madness, mystery and antithesis, deferral/plurality, self-representation, Taoism, the baroque, predestination and freewill, desire, redemption, and occidental-oriental universalism). The other main area of consideration is the depiction of nature in his work (5). Interestingly, regionalism is barely pursued. Questions of ethnicity, Brazilian identity, sociohistoric testimony and politics are virtually absent.

The pattern is similar for Machado de Assis. Literary technique is most important (35 of 74 items, in addition to 5 items concerned with meta-literary issues, 10 items on literary history, sources, and influences). Critics also pursue extraliterary abstract themes in Machado de Assis (16 items, including matriarchy/patriarchy (2), feminism, ideology/religion; "the double" (2); the love story; skepticism; myth, consciousness/dream, ambiguity, betrayal, jealousy (2), positivism, and time). The writer is, similarly to Guimarães Rosa, honored with a wide range comparisons with members of the international canon (Flaubert, Lispector, Nabokov, Fuentes, Sterne, Barth, Goethe, Cortázar . . .). Discernible differences between the two are the greater number of conventional literary studies of Machado de Assis and consideration of his work in relation to traditional literary stylistic genres (satire, allegory, comedy, and tragedy), and the predominance of psychological portraiture (jealousy, love, betrayal, and so on). Consistent themes are Machadian irony and humor and the role of the narrator. Some consideration has been given to Machado de Assis's attention or lack of attention to sociohistorical questions and even to race relations (together, 4 items). On the other hand articles have been written on his Francophilia and acceptance of the notion of *les tropiques délaissées*, the degeneration of (European) man south of the equator. But in overall terms it is clear that Machado de Assis is not studied as a literary means to a sociological or Brazilian end concern. He is a writers' writer and is celebrated essentially in terms of the universal canon by a limited and disparate congregation of admirers.

In the case of the limited number of articles (13) on Drummond, the *crônicas*, which provide an engaging portrait of daily life for the petty bourgeoisie of Rio, attract virtually no attention. Despite Drummond's domestic status as the national poet, internationally his poetry is not studied in terms of Brazilian identity. Nor is Drummond endowed with the prestige of meta-literary studies, despite the prevalence in his work of the theme of the creative act—presumably because his work in this area is more akin to post-romantic individualism than to the contemporary inclination to the idea of a decentered, community subject. Given his recognition as an accomplished poet, it is not surprising that a number of articles treat his literary technique (use of metaphor, etc.). But the number is somewhat disappointing. The predominant area of international Drummondian study is that of extraliterary abstract themes: love, the self, the individual and society, the confessional mode, irony, compromise, and memory.

In summary, the minimal international impact of Drummond has been in terms of a general humanism, comparable, for example, to that of midcentury Italian writers such as Moravia or Montale. His role on the international stage has almost certainly been compromised by the absence of any radicalism which might have excited enthusiasm in the world audience. In market terms, the third world writer has erred on the side of a conventional, European maturity which diffuses the issue of violence and that conspicuous social or ethnic difference which draws the North Atlantic audience to Latin America.

Mário de Andrade has fared moderately well in international scholarship (27 items). The main interest of the criticism has been in using his nonfictional writings to trace Brazilian literary or intellectual movements. The extraliterary content of his work has not provoked much reaction, with only five studies: myth (2), indolence, exoticism, and memory—themes which can be integrated with the other major area of criticism, Brazilian national identity (6 items). Unlike Guimarães Rosa and Machado de Assis, Mário de Andrade is not a writer's writer. Important as a nonfictional intellectual and the most important literary voice in the unresolved twentieth-century debate over Brazilian identity, Mário de Andrade has warranted a not insubstantial body of scholarly investigation, in which the nationally comparative element is significant.

Except for the issue of Brazilian national identity, most of the categories concerned with sociohistorical matters appear at this stage to be unnecessary. But they acquire significance in the exceptional case of Jorge Amado. Of a total of 55 studies, only six consider literary technique (3 on narrative technique; 2 general explications of a work; and 1 comparison with Steinbeck). Extraliterary themes are prominent (11), notably sexuality (8 of the 11 deal with sexual identity and/or gender roles). A range of specific social themes is found. Five articles study the ethno-urban evocation of Salvador, the Bahian capital. Three more address the ethnic question of negritude (in the French sense). Three sociolinguistic articles use Amadian fiction as documentary material on the popular classes, and five relate it to his radical politics. No studies seek to place Amado in relation to Brazilian literary movements, but one article considers his work in relation to (Spanish American) magical realism. While two studies address his status in the U.S.S.R. and France, none considers his reception within Brazil. Amado is apprehended as a major writer of Latin America rather than of Brazil—which raises the interesting question of the ethnicity of the researchers. Whereas in the case of the other writers a large number of article authors have Iberian names, this proportion is greatly diminished for Amado (4 of 21).

It is clear that international criticism relishes the stimulating Amadian diet of sex, exotic religion, and politics. Beyond this, there is a strong interest in his cultivation of Afrocentric ethnicity; and he is perceived by critics as a significant social witness, providing a window on to the colorful mass of the Brazilian population. This interest is, however, Bahia-centric rather than national. In the previous chapter it was suggested that Amado's work, particularly *Gabriela,* does in fact develop a genuine national ideology in which the Bahian experience, as the most holistic instance of miscegenation, has a privileged but not exclusive role. In this sense the ideological themes woven into the Amadian text have everything to do with the national debate fostered by Mário de Andrade. However the international studies of Amado's *baianismo* are not typically framed from within the literary parameters which trace Mário de Andrade's trajectory through *Modernismo* and the associated phase of political nationalism. Their focus is essentially sociological, alien to the humanistic rhetoric of national identity, and concerned with Amado's depiction of resistance by the poor and/or the dark-skinned to the rich and/or white. It is not even clear that Amado's Utopian message of salvation through miscegenation is generally comprehended, since the international perspective focuses more on resistance to hegemony than on the fusion of cultural realities.

In conclusion: whereas the other writers under discussion tend, even in the international context, to be apprehended from within the conventional discipline of literature by a critical readership dominated by Brazilians and Brazilianists, Amado is embraced in a broad interdisciplinary sweep by an ensemble of critics without any personal association with Latin America. Within this ethnically and intellectually heterogeneous readership, the problem of Amado's minimal reception by the literati of his own country is both invisible and irrelevant. Amado stands as a legitimate literary man of the people, an organic intellectual steadily acquiring stature in the interdisciplinary context which is the real focus of intellectual curiosity about Brazil.

Comparative International Reception of Brazilian and Spanish American Modernisms

The dominance of *Boom* writers: Cortázar, Paz, García Márquez, Fuentes, Vargas Llosa, Carpentier, and Borges

The consistently greater penetration of the international market by modern Spanish American as opposed to Brazilian literary works is a very clear pattern.

The celebrity of Spanish American writers, known as *el Boom*, reached a crescendo in the 1960s. This moment was preceded by steady swelling of literary ambitions through the twentieth century which can be traced back to the *modernismo* of Rubén Darío at the turn of the century and subsequently the *vanguardismo* of the 1920s and 1930s. During the 1940s and early 1950s major prose works appeared sporadically, notably those of Alejo Carpentier and Miguel Angel Asturias. Continuity with Parisian intellectual movements was maintained throughout the course of the century, and a Pan-Latin American credo, ideologically enlightened by Sartrean West European Marxism, exercised intellectual authority over much of the emerging generation of the *Boom*.

The work of perhaps the most universally respected and widely disseminated of Spanish American writers, Jorge Luis Borges, demands particular notice. Although Borges belongs to the *vanguardismo* generation in that it was during this period that he was a conventional literary activist, much of his best work was written later, through the 1940s and 1950s. His international celebrity took off with official recognition by the French literary establishment in the early 1960s. From then on, the obscure Argentinian librarian and scholar of Old English literature and language, living a sedentary existence in Buenos Aires and almost blind, became a sort of mythical institution, a prototypical mandarin of various thematic motifs dear to the postmodernist avant-garde: intertextuality ("Pierre Menard, autor del Quijote"),[24] the world as an imaginative plane irrespective of objective existentiality ("Tlön, Uqbar, Orbis Tertius"), the fractious nature of knowledge and the resourcefulness of illusion and so on. In a manner which quite preempts Roland Barthes, for example, Borges cultivated the implicit notion of the text as a self-referential and terminal reality. Reversing Oscar

Wilde's elevation of everyday living to an art form, Borges reduced objective notions of reality to the level of fiction. In doing so, he became a legend.

In what is the mark of a great writer, Borges appeals across national barriers to quite different agendas. His enthusiasm for fantastic literature ("El Aleph," "El sur," "Las Ruinas circulares" . . .) is shared by a broader and less intellectual audience. In this way, Borges prospers in many locations, from the seminar room to the labyrinthine bookstores of malls which would, no doubt, have intrigued him. Borges gives food for thought in many other domains, notably in the world of conventional literary history (as opposed to avant-garde theories). He published both *An introduction to American literature;* and *An introduction to English literature,* was an early admirer of Faulkner, and dedicated commentary to many nineteenth-century figures such as Browning, Swinburne, Stevenson, and Hawthorne. Lastly, he was concerned with Argentinian themes; in his early years of literary activism he helped found the *vanguardista* journal *Martin Fierro,* named after the great nineteenth-century gaucho literary hero created by Hernández.

Despite Borges's prominence in international criticism, his truly eccentric genius is, in the Spanish American context, the exception to the rule. The ideological path of this apparently apolitical and detached Anglophile has virtually nothing to do with that of the *Boom* writers (despite Borges's influence on Cortázar and García Márquez). The career of Alejo Carpentier, the father of Pan-Americanist *Boom* theory, provides an interesting comparison. Whereas Borges participated in the lively and very specific variety of *vanguardismo* prevalent in Buenos Aires, Carpentier spent a good part of the 1920s in collaborative contact with the avant-garde luminaries of Paris before returning to Cuba and spending the next decades in various Latin American nations. Like Borges, his most important works were written at middle age. In relation to the *Boom* itself, Carpentier is a sort of John the Baptist figure, announcing and delivering the generation to the light of day without really being a peer of the major *Boom* writers, though he was still very active during the 1960s and 1970s. It could be argued that Octavio Paz, old enough to be present at and influenced by the Spanish civil war, is not really a contemporary either, and is a poet rather than a prose writer, whereas the *Boom* was dominated by the novel. However, since Paz's rise to prominence and artistic maturity occurred in the 1950s, 1960s and 1970s, he is generally associated with García Márquez's generation, which can be stretched to include these slightly older writers, as well as the younger Mario Vargas-Llosa.

Finally, Pablo Neruda must be mentioned for his ideological position, though age disqualifies him from consideration as a *Boom* writer. Essentially a *vanguardista,* Neruda's adherence to the Communist cause gave him a tremendous importance over a long period in the 1950s and 1960s, during which time he produced a seminal body of work. At the time of Allende in Chile he was closely associated with the debacle of the Left in Latin America.

The MLA catalog listed 930 items for Borges, the greatest single number for any Latin American writer. Borges is followed by García Márquez (721), Carlos Fuentes (455), Octavio Paz (384) Alejo Carpentier (382), Mario Vargas-Llosa (347), Pablo Neruda (259), and Juan Rulfo (245). In the D.A.I. record of theses, García Márquez ranks first (101 dissertations), followed by Fuentes (91), Paz (89), Borges (85), and Vargas-Llosa (60). García Márquez is more favored in specialized Hispanic literary studies, whereas Borges is a more popular general reference often found grouped with authors in various domains outside the Latin American world. Borges maintains a consistently high level of thesis attention (24 through 1981, 23 from 1982–87, 20 from 1988–92, and 18 from 1993–94[25]), but García Márquez had a tremendous spurt in the 1980s (about 60 theses).

The evidence is difficult to interpret with precision, but does indicate certain tendencies worthy of note. There are actually more listed articles about Carlos Fuentes (220) and García Márquez (329) in English than in Spanish (211 and 328 respectively). For the other *Boom* writers, Paz, Cortázar, and Vargas Llosa, there is a generally consistent ratio of approximately twice as many articles in Spanish as in English. This also holds for the older heralds of Pan-Spanish Americanism, Neruda and Carpentier. Interestingly, this pattern of proportion does not hold for two major writers of the period: Juan Rulfo and José Lezama Lima, the Cuban poet whose novel, *Paradiso,* is in many profound ways comparable to Proust's *A la recherche du temps perdu*. More important than the comparative interest of different language camps is the total number of items. Excluding Borges, of all Spanish American writers the five nominated champions of the *Boom*—García Márquez, Carlos Fuentes, Octavio Paz, Vargas Llosa, and Julio Cortázar—are, according to the M.L.A. records, the most studied writers in the Spanish American world. This underlies the sheer domination of the *Boom* in the history of this literature.

The citation stakes also offer interesting conclusions on the comparative situation of Brazilian and Spanish American literatures, particularly in scholarship in English. The total number of articles in English on Guimarães Rosa, Jorge Amado, Carlos Drummond de Andrade, Machado de Assis, and Mário de Andrade (150) is less than the individual tally for Borges (330), García Márquez, and Carlos Fuentes; and only marginally greater than the figures for Paz (103), Carpentier (103), and Vargas Llosa (119). The preponderance of the domestic language is far greater in the Brazilian case, ranging from the extreme of Carlos Drummond de Andrade (72 items in Portuguese and only 9 in English), through Guimarães Rosa (112 to 34), Mário de Andrade (33 to 17), and Machado de Assis (89 to 56). The exception to this is Jorge Amado, with 29 items in Portuguese against 34 in English, a ratio which actually exceeds that of García Márquez and Carlos Fuentes, though in overall numbers the Brazilian remains spectacularly neglected in comparison to the Spanish Americans.

In regard to publications of the writers' works in translation, another clear pattern emerges.[26] In the Brazilian domain, with the exception of Amado, publication in translation is essentially a scholarly activity, with translations by academics commissioned by university presses or specialized publishing houses. The Spanish American *Boom* writers, by contrast, have all successfully penetrated the commercial publishing market, each having a large number of titles in translation: 11 for Cortázar, 14 for Fuentes, 11 for García Márquez, 30 for Paz, 10 for Vargas Llosa.[27] The scholarly presence, indicated through publication in university presses, is much less conspicuous because the *Boom* writers clearly cross the threshold of marketability. Even more revealing in the Brazilian case is the fact that initial publication through a commercial publisher is often followed by a reprinting and/or retranslation, and re-release by a university press some time later, which suggests commercial failure. Finally, the *Boom* writers each have an impressive portfolio of major publishers on both sides of the Atlantic: Pantheon, Allison & Busby, Collins, Avon, Harvill, Arena, Alfred Knopf for Cortázar; Farrar Straus & Giraux, Collins, Secker & Warburg, Panther, Cape, André Deutsch, Dutton, Penguin, Picador for Carlos Fuentes; Harper & Row, Cape, Picador, Avon, Knopf, and Penguin for García Márquez; Grove Press, Penguin, New Directions, Contact Press, Cape Goliard, Viking, Calder & Boyars, Seaver, Anvil, Harcourt Brace & Janovitch, Carcanet, Bloomsbury, and Faber & Faber for Paz; Grove Press, Penguin, Cape,

Picador, Harper & Row, Faber & Faber, and Farrar Straus & Giroux for Vargas Llosa.

Carlos Fuentes's work is chiefly available in paperback in the United States through Noonday. *The Death of Artemio Cruz,* released in paperback by Noonday in 1991, was already in its third print run in 1993. The same year also saw the sixth printing of the Noonday version of *Terra Nostra,* the eighth of *The Hydra head,* the eighteenth of *Aura.*

A cursory survey of volumes in a modern super bookstore is suggestive of the prolific sales these writers have generated, and the ready availability of the texts in translation. Eleven Fuentian titles in all, in a similarly advanced print or edition number were available. Twelve of García Márquez's works were available, two of them in different editions. Seven titles by Vargas Llosa were to be found, and, impressively, four collections of essays by Octavio Paz were included in the fiction section alone (without counting those in the poetry section). As for the Brazilians, Jorge Amado was strongly represented with twelve items through Avon and another through Bantam. The remaining four Brazilian authors, however, attained a collective sum of only two titles, both by Machado de Assis, one of them through a university press.

The point is that the phenomenal scholarly interest in the Hispanic *Boom* writers is matched by commercial investment and mass consumption. Perhaps the greatest complement, in terms of popular interest, is publication in cheap paperback editions (of which Avon is the outstanding example in the United States for Latin American writers of both languages). All of the *Boom* writers have publications in English of this sort: Avon and Collins for Cortázar; Collins, Penguin, and Picador for Fuentes, Avon and Penguin for García Márquez; Penguin and Viking for Paz; Penguin and Picador for Vargas Llosa. Of the Brazilians, only Jorge Amado's extraordinary sales through Avon match this, though in his case it should also be remembered that the initial publication of *Gabriela* by Alfred Knopf in 1962 actually sold a million copies and was on the United States best-seller list for the better part of a year. Interestingly, the two Spanish American writers who attracted less criticism in English than in Spanish, Lezama Lima and Rulfo, show a translation pattern recalling that of Brazilians other than Amado. Lezama Lima's 1966 masterpiece, *Paradiso,* was released in 1974 by the respectable Farrar, Straus & Giroux in the United States and Secker & Warburg in London. It apparently went out of print and the same translation was subsequently rereleased by University of Texas Press in 1988. The follow-up novel,

Oppiano Licario, has not been translated. Rulfo's seminal *Pedro Páramo* (1955), a favorite of school and university syllabi, has been continuously published in English by Grove Press in the United States since 1959 and was initially coreleased in the U.K. by John Calder. But his other main volume, *El llano en llamas* (1953), translated under the title, *The Burning Plain and Other Stories,* was only released in 1967, again by University of Texas.

The consistent contrasting pattern of international reception of Brazilian and Spanish American literatures

From the previous observations emerges a clear inequivalence between the international dissemination of Brazilian and Spanish American literature of the twentieth century. Domestically esteemed works of Brazilian literature have not penetrated the international market beyond the satellite world of Luso-Brazilian literary scholarship, so that there exists a discernible gap between Brazilian and international reception; Jorge Amado constitutes a conspicuous exception to this rule. A handful of Spanish American literature writers from the first half of the century (Borges, Neruda, Carpentier) achieved a prominence in the international perspective which was subsequently enormously expanded with the work of the 1960s and 1970s in what appropriately came to be known as the *Boom* (Julio Cortázar, Gabriel García Márquez, Carlos Fuentes, Octavio Paz, Vargas Llosa); with the exception of Borges, there is substantial continuity between the work of the pre-*Boom* generation and the *Boom* itself, centering around Pan-Latin American or Pan-Spanish American consciousness. The *Boom* writers were given at least as much attention within scholarly circles as in the commercial market; at least two major writers (Lezama Lima, Juan Rulfo) within the Spanish American world writing about the time of the *Boom* were, however, far less successful and their international reception parallels that of the Brazilians.

How are we to interpret the phenomenon? Various commonsense hypotheses prove inadequate. The greater body of critical scholarship on Spanish language literature is related to its preponderance in university programs—Spanish is the number one second language and/or literature studied in the United States, while Portuguese occupies a lowly position quite out of proportion to the number of speakers worldwide. The same sort of logic might be expected to apply in a looser way to publishing houses: there has traditionally been much more translation to English (and other languages) from Spanish than from Portuguese.

The success of Jorge Amado, who has certainly sold more books than any of the Spanish Americans with the possible exception of García Márquez, disqualifies these circumstantial arguments as necessary reasons preventing Brazilian penetration of the international market. The parallel release by Knopf of Amado's *Gabriela* and Guimarães Rosa's *Devil to Pay in the Backlands* provide a neat comparison. Given that Rosa's work followed Amado's by about a year, during which time the latter had dominated the bestseller list, and that Amado wrote an exceptionally eulatory preface for *The Devil to Pay in the Backlands,* the international failure of Guimarães Rosa cannot be attributed to the circumstances of publication themselves. As for Machado de Assis, thanks to the disparate but enthusiastic support of certain scholars, his work has earned a fair slice of the commercial market on a series of occasions but without great impact; his most popular work, *Dom Casmurro,* has not advanced in the United States beyond the medium-sized commercial editions by Noonday (in 1953, 1960 and 1991) and during this period became so scarce that the same translation had to be reissued by the University of California Press under the custodianship of the translator herself. The remaining Brazilian authors, Mário de Andrade and Carlos Drummond de Andrade are utterly obscure in the United States commercial market.

A qualitative hypothesis can account better for the distinction that must be made between Jorge Amado and the other Brazilians The question thereof is whether the work of Guimarães Rosa, Machado de Assis, Mário de Andrade, and Carlos Drummond de Andrade has some common character reducing its international appeal. But the work of these writers is so heterogeneous that it would seem impossible to find a common characteristic which would unite them, and separate them from Jorge Amado—other than the fact that Amado has been shown to be a pariah of the Brazilian academic literary establishment. Separately, it has been established that there is a curiously inverse relation between, on the one hand, Brazilian literary criticism, whether domestic or international, and, on the other, the interest shown by the international community, which includes both the mass audience and the social science end of the critical spectrum.

Our argument is not that Brazilian literature can be homogeneously characterized with Amado standing out as a radical deviation, but rather that the whole magnificently heterogeneous repertoire of Brazilian writers other than Amado lacks the thematic features which make his work amenable to the international perspective on Brazil, which is not in fact shaped by literature at all, but by other cultural manifestations, and by intellectual investigations which have more to do with a sociological than a literary perspective. The general condition of Brazilian literature is to be condemned to obscurity. Amado's work happily escapes this fate, less through its literary uniqueness than because it is compatible with the international appetite for Brazil, which has nothing to do with the agenda of the Brazilian literary establishment.[28]

4
Socioanthropology and Popular Culture

THE BRAZILIAN SOCIOANTHROPOLOGICAL TRADITION IS CHARACterized by a substantial interaction with literature. Well into the present century, a prevailing norm amongst Brazilian social scientists has been the subjective essay, rather than the empirical study attempting to apply the methodologies of hard science. In return, the literary tradition has been enriched by the contributions of its cultural commentators, some of whom have created fictional works in symbiotic relationship with their social-scientific work: Euclides da Cunha was accepted into the Brazilian Academy of Letters shortly after the publication of his *Os Sertões*. Gilberto Freyre was a respected writer of fiction whose subject matter is close to that of his scientific work.

Such interaction does not necessarily imply a constant sociological imperative in Brazilian literature; on the contrary, later modernist writers moved away from the earlier tendency to synthesize theories of national character. Given the precedent of nationalism in the 1920s and social realism in the 1930s, the detachment of later writers is particularly significant. Further, the later modernist inclination to individualism and philosophy is generally consistent with European intellectual currents rather than with the historical and societal explications which dominate the literatures of developing nations, notably in Spanish America. But the latter approach was not absent from Brazil, for the late modernists did not dominate the nation's cultural discourse. The nationalist imperative remained predominant, but its disciplinary and stylistic locus shifted—from iconoclastic poetry militating against Portuguese cultural colonialism, to politically conscious novels depicting contemporary reality and calling for justice (and in this sense implicitly criticizing the internal Euro-Brazilian elite), to nonfictional socioanthropological apologias for Brazilian identity which rejected the calquing of Eurocentric rationalist models. The consistent literary aspect of socioanthropological writing, notably in Gilberto Freyre, diluted the conventional barriers between fiction and treatise.

There is a continuity, then, between the nationalist essentialism of early modernism, subsequently discarded by the *geração de '45* but sustained by Amado, and social science discourse. The term "essentialism" is here used to mean the attempt to encapsulate the identity of a vast social or cultural mass, or historical experience, in a synthesized description. The writers classified here as essentialist could also be described as determinist, since they presuppose the possibility of identity derived from a stable set of cultural conditions and characteristics. This is less to the point, however, than the tendency to presuppose a sort of essence which can be first intuited by a sensitive and intellectually functional member of the culture, and then verified by conventional scientific or pseudo-scientific inquiry. The concern of these social thinkers is not so much to identify universal variables impacting social relations, but to distill from the infinite set of social relations and activities in a given culture its unique and distinguishing characteristics—to articulate the 'soul' of that culture.

Gilberto Freyre and Brazilian Popular Cultural Identity

Da Cunha and Freyre

The seminal text of the Brazilian socioanthropological tradition is Euclides da Cunha's *Os Sertoes* which examines the extraordinary military campaigns seeking to destroy the Christian, monarchist settlement established in the back lands of the *Nordeste* by the preacher Antonio Conselheiro. Drawing on various scientific and philosophical traditions including Montesquieu's theories of the influence of climate on social structures, Hegelian historical notions, Comptian positivism, social Darwinism, and biophysiological eugenic theories of racial differentiation, da Cunha utilized the ensemble of socioscientific knowledge of the late nineteenth century to explain both the orientation of the rebels and their successful adaptation to local conditions.

The sheer power of da Cunha's explanation of this phenomenon of Brazilian development catapulted the *sertão* to the center of national attention. The scientific soundness of the work, already contested in its time, is dubious. As Wilson Martins notes (1978a, 206) there was more resistance to the writer's admission to the Instituto Histórico than to the Brazilian Academy of Letters. Racially determinist assumptions govern the work. There is no room for circumstantial but vital factors which might have been acknowledged in a more materialistic account. Secondly, there is an underlying implication that because the behavior of the rebels was the most extraordinary manifestation by members of that ethnic group, it must also be the most representative of their deeper social experience and cultural reality.

Da Cunha's work had consolidated the racist theories developed in Brazil towards the end of the nineteenth century by figures such as the folklorist, Sílvio Romero, and the social theorist, Nina Rodrigues. These thinkers mapped out, on the basis of racial heritage, climate, and experience, distinct Brazilian cultural animals: to the coastal mulatto were attributed "neurasthenia" (a disorder of nervosity) and unrestrained sexuality, which contrasted markedly with the rigidity of the *caboclo* (Ibero-Amerindian) of the *sertão,* or with the apathy and cerebral limitations of the languorous Amazonian *mameluco* (a second type of Ibero-Amerindian). The place of honor in this unfortunate hierarchy was assigned to the most European group, the whites of the south and southeast, whose numbers were swelling, owing to a policy based on racial engineering that encouraged European immigration.

In effect, if da Cunha's book is *sui generis,* it created a platform for monumental essentialist explications of Brazilian identity. *Os Sertões* was admired by Gilberto Freyre, whose 1933 work, *Casa Grande e Senzala* is the only sociological work to have had wider repercussions. Freyre locates the genesis of Brazilian civilization in the encounter between the early Portuguese settlers and the local Amerindian cultures, and then with the Afro-Brazilian slave populations which constituted the dominant demographic contingent in what, for him, emerges as the essential formative social matrix—the plantation society of the *Nordeste*. In fact, the interaction with Amerindians is considered less in terms of its concrete influences than as an illustration of the adaptive and interactive qualities of the Portuguese, held to be quite exceptional in the creation of a new civilization.

However Freyre's attitude to Afro-Brazilian culture is qualitatively different. His knowledge of the *nordestino* state of Pernambuco, the quintessential plantation region of Brazil, greatly enriches his description of cultural phenomena both at the material and spiritual level. Freyre is the godfather of *Homo brasiliensis:* "o brasileiro como Luso-tropical," that is, the true New World man constituted by the fusion of three superraces but culturally determined by the prevailing hierarchy: European firstly, African secondly, and thirdly—and much less precisely—Amerindian.

Freyre's analysis of da Cunha's work is revealing on three fronts: the attention to literary and aesthetic rather than anthropological matters; the rejection of the pertinence of both the *sertanejo* and the *paulistano* to the problematics of national identity; finally, in the sheer rhetorical flourish of the critic himself.

> The *sertões* were, in truth, the kingdom of the poet Euclides da Cunha . . .
> In the description of the *sertões*, the scientist would make errors of geography, of geology, of botany, of anthropology; the sociologist, in details of explication and social diagnostics of the *sertanejo* people. But redeeming the technical errors, there was in Euclides da Cunha the poet, the prophet, the artist full of ingenious intuitions. The Euclides that discovered in the landscape and in the human type of the *sertões* values going beyond the right and wrong of the grammar of Science . . .
> The prophet's cry rang out across the *sertões:* he gave them a Brazilian signification alongside the merely pictorial. . . .
> The artist interpreted these backlands in words with the force to pain the ears and trouble the soul of the pallid university graduates of the coast with the sound of a voice which was at once both boyish and at times hard, crying out in favor of the misunderstood desert, the abandoned *sertões,* the forgotten *sertanejos*. . . .
> This was the great message of Euclides: that what was needed was to unite the *sertão* and the coast for the salvation—and not simply the convenience—of Brazil. The *sertão* was the "savior": the savior of Euclides himself, and the savior of Brazil. The message was transmitted to the men of the Republic of 1889 in the words of an artist with a taste for politics. The message was subsequently deformed by those who made of the *sertões* in themselves—and not of their communication with the agrarian coast—a mystique, a sort of Protestant sect, believing Brazil could be saved with water from dams in the *Nordeste*—works which have absorbed an amount of investment funds disproportionate to their social value for the Brazilian nation. For Euclides, in the tropical vegetation and the landscape dominated by the sugar mill there was something repugnant in its abundance, its fat roundness, the mould of its forms; its flesh-like suppleness, the clammy texture of the earth, the sweetness of the fertile soil. He was attracted by sharp angles, the boniness and stiffness of more ascetic visual aspects, or at most, those dryly masculine lines of the '*agreste*' and the '*sertões*'. Among the *sertanejo* types and scenes, he emphasizes the most harshly angular aspects, in words which are also hard, almost without any fluidity and even, as it were, asexual.
> Because he is, in truth, a sort of El Greco or Alonso Berreguete of Brazilian prose: he extracts from words the maximum of their sculptural qualities, though sacrificing not rarely elements of discrimination

and inflection—the great qualities, in the Brazilian masters who were his contemporaries, Machado de Assis, Nabuco and Pompéia himself. These were qualities virtually incompatible with the taste for metal, for the sculptured, the geometric, the stiff, the angular in which Euclides refined himself as if he were under the domination of an almost mystical obsession: to avoid the flesh, its curves, its inconstancy, the passing moment, the banality of everyday life. (1971, 4–5[1])

Other than Mark Anthony's rebuttal of Brutus in *Julius Caesar,* it would be hard to find an equally dexterous repudiation of an acknowledged hero. Freyre casts da Cunha as inspired but eccentric, alienated from the definitive Brazilian genius. He insists on the relative importance of the fertile coast which is his own area of focus. He distances da Cunha from the great fiction writers of the time, Machado de Assis and Raul Pompéia, without acknowledging that their themes—the existence of the Euro-Brazilian elite in Victorian and Belle Époque southeastern Brazil—are equally remote from his own chosen society—the old plantation world of the *nordestino* coastal region. Further, he slips into this grouping of novelists an abolitionist orator from his home state of Pernambuco, Joaquim Nabuco, thus introducing the issue of slavery. Freyre stresses da Cunha's empathy with *sertanejos* caught up in a sort of Jonestown misadventure of rural Ludditism. Elsewhere, he insists on the Lusitanian roots of Brazilian society; for example, the Afro-Brazilian dominated magic practiced for sexual protection is seen as a mere extension of medieval Iberian practices. But da Cunha's asceticism is not considered, as it might be, in terms of patriarchal Iberian Catholicism, though the conflict between this moral ideology and tropical liberality is surely one of the generative tensions in the Brazilian psyche; on the contrary, Freyre embues it with the aura of Protestant fundamentalism, inferred as not being nationally authentic.

Such masterly criticism is important to the topographic determination of the cultural and aesthetic center of gravity of Brazilian identity: da Cunha's insistence on the *sertão* is diametrically opposed to Freyre's preference for the coastal *litoral.* The irony, of course, is that both microcosms are contained within one specific region, the *Nordeste,* within which the traveler passes from one zone to the other simply by going a couple of hundred miles inland. Both societies, plantation and *sertão,* were formed in the distant past, and have been eclipsed economically by the industrial development of the southeast, just as in the U.S., both Southern plantation society and the entrepreneurial Northern rural society were eclipsed by trading in New York, industrial expansion in Chicago, and the tertiary technologies prospering in the southwest. But in the same way that Southern folk traditionalism and Yankee liberal puritanism still constitute a generative tension in American culture, it is possible to read the Ibero-Amerindian tale of the *sertão* and the Afro-Iberian tale of the *nordestino* coast as polarized influences on the development of a national culture. The two expanding religious models in twentieth-century Brazil are Afro-Brazilian cults and Protestant fundamentalism, the latter prospering particularly amongst former devotees of "Folk Catholicism," the characteristic faith of the *sertanejos* (a fact which lends an unintended perspicacity to Freyre's analysis of da Cunha). In popular music, apart from the foreign-influenced rock and pop favored by the established population of the southeast and the steady increase in Afro-Bahian styles, a dominant genre is *música sertaneja*, a commercialized, Americanized form of the improvising pairs of troubadours traditional in the *sertão*.

Though Freyre, diplomatically, does not present his own research as opposing da Cunha's, this is implicit in the metaphors of rigidity and asexuality he uses to characterize the work of his forerunner. For Freyre, the key to the successful imposition of Lusitanian civilization in the massive expanse of Brazil, where the Portuguese settlers were massively outnumbered first by the Amerindian and then by the Afro-Brazilian populations, lies in their prodigious sexual exuberance—leading to procreation and miscegenation—and in their psycho-cultural flexibility which facilitated the assimilation of diverse traditions and the creation of a genuinely new society based on racial and cultural fusion. He rejects both the negation of the flesh ascribed to da Cunha in essays such as "Os Brasileiros como Luso-tropicais (The Brazilians as Luso-Tropical, 1961), and the notion of *Homo brasiliensis* as a model of cultural and climactic fusion.

Freyre further revolutionized sociological interpretations of Brazil by introducing an element of Utopian narcissism—the notion that the cultural fusion has produced a harmonious civil polity in a green and pleasant land, an eden of the twentieth century. The myth of racial democracy in Brazil, which derives from the appearance of racial harmony and the lack of racial resentment, has been disproved whenever conventional socioeconomic criteria have been applied in scientific studies. This does not necessarily compromise the efficacy of the myth however; on the contrary, its widespread acceptance as a subjective truism sustains it as a shaper of objective social reality, reproducing a certain culture within this ideological frame of reference.

Simply denying the myth, then, would miss the point. But it is important to appreciate the Utopian aspects of Freyre's theory, the gap between the reality it supposes and contemporary developments. As Renato Ortiz points out in his *Cultura Brasileira e Identidade Nacional,* Freyre's project is essentially a championing of a particular segment and phase of Brazilian society—*nordestino* plantation society under the Empire. The halcyon years of Pedro II's reign terminated with the abolition of slavery, and the inception of a positivist-minded, military-dominated Republic which saw the decline of the *Nordeste* as a political power base in national affairs and development; economic and political domination by the state of São Paulo also dates from this period. The poignancy of Freyre's discourse lay in its sense of nostalgia for an earlier, simpler society. His theories about the monarchic era were developed during the Republic; by the time of publication of *Casa Grande e Senzala* in 1933, with the rise of Getúlio Vargas, these theories had become, as it were, two societal generations out of synch with contemporary national development. Ortiz observes that Freyre was ideologically opposed to technological modernization, seeing in it a process of social isolation and spiritual alienation. Whereas Vargas borrowed from Eurocentric national socialist programs and platforms, one of the strengths of Freyre's perspective was that it emphasized Brazil's special traditions, not only *nordestino* agrarian society but also the *negro-mestiço* contribution, the Afro-Brazilian heritage.[2] This constituted a Utopian inversion of the traumatic adaptation by Brazilian social thinkers in the late nineteenth century of Eurocentric eugenic and cultural theories which placed whites at the top of the racial hierarchy and Afro-Brazilians and Amerindians at the bottom, but also condemned the whites and the nation as a whole, in relation to Europe and North America. The reality evoked by Freyre belonged to a past which lived on in the *Nordeste* only because of economic stagnation.

Freyre's conception of national identity must be seen, then, in the following terms: its euphoric note was an aggressive defense reaction to the pessimistic self-analyses of the turn of the century; its Utopian element lies in its focus on societal matrices which no longer were central to national development and power; its narcissistic aspects derive from its self-serving value judgments regarding the competition between opposing models of socioeconomic and cultural organization: *nordestino* plantation society versus the burgeoning industrialized society centered in São Paulo.

While da Cunha had pioneered and provided a cornerstone for "Brazilology," the difference between his project and Freyre's is that da Cunha posits his ethnography as a retrogressive aberration in the progressive national fabric, whereas Freyre develops a prescriptive model for national identity. His particular species of *Homo brasiliensis* is, through an act of ideological affirmation, proposed as the possessor and the legitimate vessel of the Brazilian soul, a sort of cultural center to which frenetic *paulista* industrial modernism is tangential and marginal.

Originally commissioned to write for a São Paulo newspaper, da Cunha had undertaken a voyage of cultural discovery which became a radical revelation, by far the most powerful statement up to that point regarding Brazil's non-European identity. There could be no possibility, however, of the lonely, barren *sertanejo* of the *Nordeste* serving as a cultural model for the rest of the country.[3] Freyre proposed the substitution of Afro-Iberian plantation society for the Ibero-Amerindian society of the dry interior.

Freyre's analysis is politically conservative but culturally progressive, particularly in comparison to the almost masochistic resignation to cultural inferiority of Brazilian social thinkers at the turn of the century. Freyre assigned cultural prestige to the *Nordeste* even as the state of São Paulo became the national breadbasket. Despite the court's nineteenth-century residence in Rio, he observed that the regime was based on a patriarchal oligarchy of *latifundiários* (large land estate owners) whose subculture had been spawned in the *Nordeste* and continued to dictate its social relations. The commonly held perception that the Rio-São Paulo axis led the country and approximated most to the ideal of north Atlantic modernity was thus replaced by a model in which the venerable *Nordeste* was perceived as more authentically Brazilian than the dynamic southeast where waves of alien immigrants did not even speak Portuguese.

State appropriation of the Afro-Brazilian aesthetic

Freyre's proposal for social recuperation through the preservation of the heritage of the colonial past, the Empire, and the subliminally Africanized social system of the *Nordeste* works most persuasively in the aesthetic domain. With the relentless advances of capitalism in the newly industrialized southeast generating food, wealth, and employment, masses of starving *nordestinos* would head off there each year to seek a better life. Nostalgia for the bygone era was the privilege of the man of letters with an adequate family fortune. But in the aesthetic domain most of the unique and conspicuous Brazilian practices which can claim to be nationally representative are Afro-Brazilian, or perceived as such. The celebration of negritude in the domain of cultural expression has not translated to either empowerment in civil society or moral authority. Although the influence of African religious practices is readily acknowledged in the abstract, such acknowledgment is less common in concrete instances. There has traditionally been an unwillingness to admit to any personal involvement with Afro-Brazilian cults, often seen as malevolent black magic rather than as legitimate belief systems.

The logic of the aesthetic domain works in an opposite fashion, however; it is precisely the non-European factors which provide—from a Eurocentric perspective—unique aspects of mystery, color, and distinction. This sense of difference is doubly efficacious, from the West looking at Brazil, and from within: the European is interested in African aspects absent from his/her home culture, while the Brazilian enjoys familiarity with cultural emblems and encodings for which he/she is culturally literate and which are associated with a positive mythology of social harmony.

There has always been in Brazilian society a productive axis of tension between patriarchal Eurocentrism and the local praxis. In the colonial period religious tension pertained between a stoical, severe Catholicism on the one hand, and animist Afro-centered cults on the other. These opposing systems are often imagined in literary terms as a sort of Apollonian-Dionysian polarization. Another, more contemporary symbolic duality is that of *carnaval* versus the rest of the year. During the Brazilian carnaval the Afrocentric otherness and the ambiance of a euphoric, indiscriminate social harmony are conspicuous, whereas the social regime which prevails during the rest of the year, to which the carnaval is a palliative, is authoritarian, marked by enormous gulfs between classes and clear racial segmentation. Sociologists have long attempted to resolve a peculiarly Brazilian hermeneutic quandary: the obfuscation, or sheer absence, of social and racial resentment, despite glaring inequities. But the struggle for legitimacy by people of color has clearly advanced further in the aesthetic domain than any other; this disparity contributes to the frustrations of conventional rationalist sociological analyses, which focus on material rather than aesthetic indices.

An eminent example of historic paradox is the costume of lace petticoats and ornaments worn by the *baiana* (an initiate in Candomblé), either in religious ceremony or when they sell food in the street. Even as Candomblé *terreiros* were being suppressed in Bahia, the *baiana* was emerging as the sartorially symbolic priestess of Rio's carnaval, and the outfit has become a virtual national folkloric costume. It is important to recognize the semiotic complexity of such a symbol, that is, how its meaning can differ for different sign readers. The *baiana* dressed in an old European clothing (lace petticoats and gown) constitutes an ambivalent symbol: for the European it is significant in its strangeness, for the Brazilian in its familiarity; for the European in its African aspect, for the Brazilian in its recall of national roots in the *Nordeste,* and also—given that the costume derives directly from slavery and the use of domestic maids—in its suggestion of aesthetic, anticonfrontational solutions to the traumatic subjugation of one race by another. For militant Afro-Brazilians who are materialists, the State's appropriation for touristic purposes of the symbolic repertoire of Candomblé is part of a general process of alienation and exploitation.

Such semiotic complexity ultimately arises from differences of social perspective and ideological position. The general failure of Brazilian society to generate a plurality of legitimate and empowered representative bodies, whether political parties or other organizations, and, more uniquely, the lack of resentment in the face of this situation, is one of its most extraordinary qualities. Freyre's ideology lends itself to nondifferential social representation; concepts such as that of the *metaraça* (metarace)—cultural identity which derives from various racial heritages, but forms a sum greater than its parts—focus on assimilation rather than conflict. Indeed it is implicit in this logic that conflict is, like intolerance, an undesirable aberration on the path to harmonious integration, rather than the natural consequence of the systematic exploitation of a given group. The Freyrian model for harmonious integration is the plantation economy predicated on slavery. For Freyre, the celebration of harmony between mansion and shanty is simultaneously a novel recognition of the African input in the Brazilian melting pot, and an apologia for Portuguese-derived civil organs, despite their often blatant, institutionalized racial distinctions. Such a harmony celebrates Portuguese genius in contrast with other, lesser European colonizers who failed to adapt to the tropical clime of which Amerindians and Africans are the successive natural occupants. In this process the non-European races have served as honorable lieutenants to a Portuguese captaincy. The Afro-Brazilian demographic domination during the formative period of the nation does not dissuade Freyre from denoting Brazilian culture as "principally of Portuguese origin," because the socioeconomic and political infrastructure are European. The African and Amerindian contributions described by Freyre interpose themselves not at the level of institutions controlling society, but simply in the aesthetic domain, or at best in subordinate organizations and noninstitutionalized cultural practices—in food, music, recreation, and so on.

Freyre's stance is little different from that of the governmental authorities. Where these practices do become institutionalized, as in Candomblé, they have been subject to suppression by the State, or, alternately, appropriation. During the colonial period institutions reinforcing Portuguese traditions, such as religious orders, were established especially for non-Euro Brazilians. With the impact of more tolerant regimes and tourism in this century, the State has reversed its policy and begun to interact with non-Euro Brazilian groups for the provision of folkloric spectacles and other manifestations of pacific integration.

Freyre's cultural economy of assimilation and adaptation, and his political economy of harmonious democracy based on the absence of resentment and differentiation was of great utility to subsequent regimes. However, these regimes did not share his belief in the superiority of the patriarchal society of the *Nordeste;* on the contrary the economic and political influence of this region was perceived as a brake on progress, and the dual process of impoverishment of the *Nordeste* and advance of the south and southeast continued. The inferior productive capacity of the *Nordeste* precluded its possibility as a socioeconomic model, reinforcing the utility of Freyrian discourse to liberate aesthetic energy, publicize cultural resources, and to camouflage political discontent and discredit critical dissidence.

Freyrian essentialism in the aesthetic domain

The power of the *Nordeste* as the mythical repository of national identity is similar to the way the Amazon zone dominates the image of the vastness of Brazil, both for Brazilians and others, even though it is merely one of a number of frontier zones. This is reflected in the major fictional writings of the second generation of *Modernismo,* from the late 1920s through the thirties. Conventional Eurocentric leftist progressive ideas imbued writers with a sense of social contract, and it was the *Nordeste* which imposed itself aesthetically and socially as the model. Even though *Modernismo* was essentially a *paulista* initiative, São Paulo—unlike New

York or Paris—was never the mecca of the new aesthetic; the São Paulo *modernistas* always aimed at a national fresco, a portrait which integrated the regional variety of Brazil. In this process, the Amazon, vast and difficult to visit, and pre-Colombian Amerindian society provided exotic locales for mythical personae. Oswald de Andrade adopted Amerindian cannibalism as the key metaphor for Brazil's intellectual devouring of foreign concepts; Mário de Andrade makes his Brazilian superego, Macunaíma, an Amerindian from deep in the jungle. But unlike these figures of fantasy, the *Nordeste* offered a degree of continuity with modern life in the south. A large part of the southern population has consisted of recent internal immigrants from the *Nordeste,* and the *Nordeste* itself underwent modernization in the wake of southern industrialization, providing both a past perceived as authentically Brazilian and an urgent sense of the present. The optimism of *Modernismo* lies in the belief that the non-Eurocentric features of Brazilian civilization somehow give it a head start over homogeneous European cultures in the endless pursuit of aesthetic radicalism and novelty, by virtue of the belief that Brazilian society has already achieved the aesthetic liberation sought in vain by more inhibited societies.

The *Nordeste* is the birthplace not only of national society but also of racial and cultural miscegenation—Ibero-Amerindian, Afro-Iberian, and Afro-Amerindian. It exerted a magnetic power over Brazilian writers as an obligatory reference of the national spiritual voyage. Freyre stands alone in his ability to articulate this sensibility. However, it should not be forgotten that there is a gap between the two cultural zones of the *Nordeste:* the characteristically Ibero-Amerindian *sertão,* on which most of the outstanding novelists of the 1930s focused, and Freyre's Afro-Iberian *litoral.* Freyre was critical of Brazilian identifications in *sertanejo* terms: ". . . The message was subsequently deformed by those who made of the *sertões* in themselves—and not of their communication with the agrarian coast—a mystique . . ." (repeated from the long citation above).

Another important work of the 1930s, *Raízes do Brasil* (1936), by *paulista* Sérgio Buarque de Holanda, also has something to say about the relative status of region. Predictably, Holanda assigns a greater place to the *Nordeste* than Freyre does to the non-*Nordeste,* yet Holanda's ultimate concern is to construct a pathology of Brazil in order to analyze current and future developments, notably the political developments based in the south. He displays the same sort of essentialist thinking as Freyre or their predecessor, Paulo Prado (*Retrato do Brasil,* 1931), substituting his own *homem cordial* for Prado's *homem triste*. As in Freyre, Portuguese lineage is attributed with innate qualities, and a destiny:

> Pioneers of the conquest of the tropics for civilization, the Portuguese achieved with this their greatest historical mission . . . we must recognize that they were the bearers of this mission not merely by circumstance but by predisposition (1956, 19).

Identifying 1889 (the beginning of the Republic and modernization) as the key year in national development, rather than celebrating Luso-Brazilian adaptation, Holanda grapples with the difficulties of progressive positivist assumptions about the eventual advance to democracy in Latin America. Here he is no doubt influenced by the 1926 anti-federal rebellion in São Paulo and the subsequent rise of Vargas, influenced by European fascism. He identifies what has become a key issue for political sociologists of the present era of democratization: on the one hand the heritage of a highly personalized system of political power (identified in the nineteenth century as *caudillismo* by Spanish American and Brazilian writers focusing on the leaders, and in recent times as "clientalism" by sociologists observing the patronage system of social interaction) and on the other hand an overly optimistic confidence in the possibility of reform through the law—the expectation that human problems can be resolved through drafting legislation similar to that of more developed democracies, without an educative transformation of individual civil responsibility. Holanda, like his *paulista* peers, embraces the national spectrum of regions and critically scrutinizes an identity derived from the past in order to inform contemporary issues. São Paulo may be the front door opening onto the twentieth century, but the whole house must be explored; the door from the kitchen to the back garden with its array of precious childhood reminders and its humble domestic staff—for Brazil, the *Nordeste*—must also be included in the psychological picture.

Freyre and his literary *nordestino* peers of 1930s did not feel any reciprocal need to include the south in their portraits. The implicit logic is that the south is less authentically Brazilian, that if it has become the center of the nation it is only through its adoption of modern innovations derived from elsewhere. But all symbols of past and present are complex. The most conspicuous guarantor of a unique Brazilian identity is racial miscegenation, which is concentrated in the *Nordeste*, and non-European cultural practices, again concentrated in *nordestino* folklore. In the psychological economy of national society, the *Nordeste* maintains a greater aesthetic density than the South, compensating for the greater economic density of the latter. The *latifundiário nordestino* is more authentic than the southern factory owner, but the *caboclo* sharecropping peon is also more authentic than his patron, the slave the real bearer of the culture claimed by the master. The economic stagnation from the nineteenth century on has distanced the *Nordeste* from material and political power but enhanced the mythological aura of the region. The exoticist fetishism, a centrifugal *paulistano* energy, materially creative and unconsciously exploitative, is matched by the *nordestino* narcissism which must celebrate archaism as a defense against the imposition of the alien modern.

The locus of Brazilian national identity is thus a volatile issue affected by changes in political reality and ideology. There have been constant shifts in the literary designation of the Brazilian Toscana, the original cultural basin, from the virgin jungle (Atlantic or Amazonian) to the *sertão* and then to the coast of the *Nordeste*. Set in the northeastern state of Ceará, José de Alencar's *Iracema* (1865) which provides a fictional incarnation of the trope of miscegenist national identity in the offspring begotten from the romance of a Portuguese seafarer and a noble Indian maiden, is emblematic of the convenient naïveté of Romantic nationalist Indianism. The pseudo-science of eugenic theory exploded in the national consciousness with the publication of da Cunha's magnum opus in 1902. The *Nordeste,* in the paradoxical position of combining a large area, substantial population and historical pedigree with economic stagnation, acquired a unique significance as the archetypal source of Brazilian identity. But within this zone, two radically distinct cultures exist, the Ibero-Amerindian *sertanejo* culture and the *litoral* Afro-Iberian. Freyre's thesis established a clear hierarchy of geographical and ethnic regional significations, favoring northeast over southeast, tropical over dry, male over female, Portuguese over Amerindian and African—and yet, cautiously, of Brazilian over Portuguese.

The message of Freyre's patriarchal position is that Afro-Brazilian influence has been both aesthetically innovative and social efficacious, managing to influence and penetrate the central protagonist of national history, who is of Portuguese extraction. While Freyre publicizes the talents of the *mulato,* he does not suggest the *mulato* is superior to his Euro-Brazilian overlord in the exercise of power or in a leadership capacity. However, if this Luso-tropical individual, master of a greater and more modern nation than Portugal, is different because he is mixed, his superiority paradoxically derives from the cultural input of his supposed cultural inferior.[4] Here the relative positions in the hierarchy become crucial. The African contribution to national character is central, while the Amerindian and even the Ibero-Amerindian influence simply have not exercised such a power, despite attractive mystic auras. The Afro-Brazilian cultural strand emerges as the key to Brazilian identity, singularity and cultural value, even if Freyre himself has no intention of casting the Afro-Brazilian individual, or even the *mulato,* in place of the Afro-Brazilianized Euro-Brazilian, as the central protagonist of history, and as an appropriate inheritor of political power and not merely a cultural character within the system.

The more Eurocentric southern cultural zone also has a place within the national hierarchy—at its apex even, in terms of material power—but is overlooked by Freyre because of its lesser contribution to cultural uniqueness when compared to the aesthetic enrichment derived from racial miscegenation. Freyre's system is fascinating in its unstated potential paradoxes; it leads to an undesired clash between material and aesthetic capital, between power, maintained by a patriarchal elite determined to maintain racial and cultural purity, and uniqueness, derived precisely from nonpurity.

But the consequences of the argument go beyond what Freyre conceived. With the dissemination of his and others' similar ideas, there is an accumulation of aesthetic prestige in the African corner of the Brazilian racial triangle which does not, however, carry over to the political domain. On the contrary, the aesthetic locus of attention to miscegenation is susceptible to variable ethnic appropriations, its practices assimilable by any individual, notably the luso-tropical Euro-Brazilian.

The long-term power of Freyre's message is impressive. To a large extent, intellectual opinion about Brazil is divided into mainstream progressive apologists who underline Brazil's low-stress racial integration and miscegenation, and militant dissidents, who attempt to empower the urban *negro-mestiço* masses, and whose main capital, in the face of political and social disenfranchisement, has been the undeniable aesthetic prestige and centrality of non-European aspects of national culture.

The Hegemony of Rio de Janeiro

Rio de Janeiro—imperial center, republican capital and, from the international perspective, surrogate capital even since the creation of Brasília—has been conspicuously absent from the preceding discussion of *nordestino* and *paulista* perspectives. Much of the best Brazilian writing of the modern era has come from this city but it did not assume mythological proportions until the twentieth century. In the previous century the works of Machado de Assis made no attempt to affirm a Brazilian, let alone a specifically *carioca* mythological ideology. Aluízio de Azevedo, however, in his naturalist novel, *O Cortiço* ("The Tenement"), consciously attempted a representative social portrait of the lower classes. This reading of Brazilian society predicts the social career of various cultural types, in particular those of immigrants. The two main protagonists are Portuguese-born and follow opposite paths; one successfully applies his European advantage to the task of upward socioeconomic mobility, using the colonist's opportunity to widen the gap between himself and his Brazilian-born peers; the other, the more admirable but less shrewd Gerônimo, falling under the influence of a Carmenlike temptress, gradually looses sight of his intention to work for prosperity and degenerates both professionally and morally. The femme fatale is not native to Rio; Rita Baiana by name, physically vigorous and graceful, energetic but willful, she is an incarnation of all the seductive charms of the Afro-Brazilian *Nordeste*. Rita is basically virtuous, but free of the severe Catholic repressions of her Portuguese rival. After losing a fair fight with Rita's original lover, Gerônimo's pursuit of Rita is abetted by his friends, who gang up and murder the Afro-Brazilian with all the cowardly sadism of a Southern lynch mob in the U.S. Azevedo sees the rapidly expanding Rio of the 1880s as a Darwinian melting pot, a neutral meeting ground where various cultural types square off. The European and indigenous Brazilian poles are represented by the Portuguese and *nordestino* characters. The Amerindian is absent. A "truly Brazilian" cultural type, derived from the Afro-Iberian experience, is conspicuous in specifically Afro-Brazilian traits. In *O Cortiço* Rio has not as yet produced its own native, but as the city at the crossroads of national development and a site of extraordinary growth is occurring, it may give rise to a new Brazilian type.

Lima Barreto's *Triste fim de Policarpo Quaresma* (1915) provides a wonderful glimpse of social mores and emerging cultural practices in the outer suburbs of Rio and in the southeast. The high-minded but naïve Policarpo is marvelously oblivious to the reality of a Eurocentric city with a substantial Afro-Brazilian influence in its popular culture, as suggested by the scenes of musical gatherings where the proto *samba modinha* is developing away from its Iberian roots to integrate African touches. A true idealist, he believes that the indigenous Tupi-Guarani should be adopted as the national language. This quixotic figure moves from the city back to the land, seeking spiritual renewal in the soil. His efforts are frustrated and eventually he perishes ignominiously. Indianist romantic nationalism without a base in social reality is exposed as impotent and irrelevant.

Of these three outstanding *carioca* writers, only Lima Barreto, a social reformer, could be considered an idealist, and even his approach is characteristically negative. Machado and Azevedo, despite their stylistic differences, share a preference for a realism detached from ideological agendas. All three reject conventional myths of identity and origin and make pragmatic, subtly subversive responses to the Darwinian mechanisms driving national development and individual interaction. Unlike the engagé novelists of the *Nordeste* of the 1930s, they do not attempt to aesthetically recuperate human dignity and cultural value in the economically marginalized provinces. Distinctively original, their work is difficult to unite stylistically or thematically. They are products of the era of liberalism, but rather than optimism, present a sophisticated pessimism tempered by humor and acerbic wit. Their ethical perspective borders on amorality, setting them apart from their Spanish American peers, and suggesting a deep assimilation of late-nineteenth-century French cynicism. It is an impressively cosmopolitan outlook which sees through both national ambition and individual pretense, and is typical of the worldliness of the citizens of great cities. These writers experienced the disillusionment of the transition from Empire to Republic, the arrogance and cruelty of the dismissal of the old emperor Pedro II after the liberation of the slaves, the incompetence and careerism of positivist-inspired bureaucrats and military officers, and the general failure to modernize Brazilian civil society in an equitable way. The imperial *ancien régime* had fallen, only to be replaced by coffee barons; *carioca* café society of the Belle Époque was prosperous, but essentially a slavish Southern Hemisphere pastiche of European sensibilities. Curiously, amidst the materialist euphoria of unprecedented development, the most interesting Brazilian writers of the period were skeptical realists but with sensibilities influenced by the Saturnian melancholy of European symbolism.

The city of Rio was however to develop a strong mythology of its own, and now occupies a special place in Brazilian culture. Economically, the state of Rio is dominated by the city, whereas São Paulo State is balanced between the industrial titan of the capital and the world-competitive agrarian zone, which, with the rise of coffee production in the nineteenth century came to provide the backbone of national export development. As an economic reality, then, São Paulo has more in common with the south than with Rio. Rio has always enjoyed a massive derivative wealth, first as the port of export of gold and minerals from landlocked Minas, then as the royal and imperial capital gathering in national revenues, and finally as the premier tourist destination. Both Rio and São Paulo, the two megalopolises of the nation, have had their numbers steadily swelled by immigration. However, Rio received more slaves from Africa during the eighteenth century, and from the *Nordeste* during the nineteenth. In this city of the Court many slaves were assigned domestic functions, and before and after emancipation in 1888 moved into the mainstream urban population (as in Salvador). São Paulo received the greater part of the large European immigration from the 1880s on, and through the employment offered by coffee plantations and later city factories, has continued to draw massive immigration from the *Nordeste,* both from the coastal cities and particularly from the drought-afflicted *sertão.* In appreciating the two cities it is not misleading to draw on local mythologies: São Paulo as represented by the entrepreneurial and materially innovative spirit of the pioneering *bandeirantes* and Rio by the phenomenal beauty of Guanabara Bay, its magic lying in an eternal present rather than a promising future. Rio has always drawn on its political power and prestige, São Paulo on its economic dynamism. Rio maintains a certain legitimacy as surrogate capital of the nation: its population almost rivals that of São Paulo and dwarfs other cities; within the economic context of the southeast it shares in the developmentalism of São Paulo which in turn links it to the south; it has a strong Afro-Brazilian cultural element as evidenced by the carnaval; it is the international gateway and for many foreigners the only known Brazilian city; finally, and perhaps most importantly, as the site of the Court in the nineteenth century, the federal capital for much of this century and presently the headquarters of the entertainment industry, Rio has attracted the cream of the cultural elite. It is the Hollywood, the Manhattan, and the New Orleans of Brazil, and considers itself its Paris. It is also a crossroads, where, as Azevedo suggested, the modern European immigrant interacts with the preindustrial Brazilian legacy, and the exigencies of modern life are tempered by a feast-day mentality going back to medieval times, represented in the Afro-Latin carnaval mix of *samba* and visual flourish. Finally, Rio is a city dependent on patronage rather than material production, from taxes to tourism and from the domestic slaves of the past to the vast masses of underemployed who cannot earn their daily bread and yet must eat.

From this raw cultural material there has emerged a *carioca* ethos, a conviction that Rio is the most beautiful place on earth, its lifestyle uniquely graceful. The prestige of Rio's carnaval, known nationally as "the greatest show on earth," is matched by its international reputation as one of the sociocultural wonders of the modern world. Of equal interest, however, is the emergence in the 1930s of a certain tension between the national-socialist modernizing ideology of the governments lead by Vargas, and the local affection for idle pleasures, or at least the art of artfully employing unemployed hours.

In the popular song (*samba canção*) of the 1930s, disseminated nationwide but dominated by references to Rio, the traditionally well-received rogue figure of the *malandro* becomes the picaresque protagonist of popular lyric. A good example are the following lyrics by an exceptionally gifted composer and lyricist, Noel Rosa:

> "Conversa de botequim"
> Seu garçom, faça o favor
> de me trazer depressa
> uma boa média que não seja requentada,
> um pão bem quente com manteiga à beça,
> um guardanapo
> e um copo d'agua bem gelada
> fecha a porta da direita
> com muito cuidado
> que não estou disposto
> a ficar exposto ao sol
> vá perguntar ao seu freguês do lado
> qual foi o resultado do futebol.
> Se você ficar limpando a mesa,
> não me levanto nem pago a despesa
> vá pedir ao seu patrão
> uma caneta, um tinteiro,
> um envelope e um cartão
> não se esqueça de me dar palitos
> e um cigarro pra espantar mosquitos
> vá dizer ao charuteiro
> que me empreste umas revistas
> um isqueiro e um cinzeiro.
> Telefone ao menos uma vez
> para 34–3333
> e ordene ao seu Osório

que me mande um guarda-chuva
aqui pro nosso escritório
seu garçom me empreste algum dinheiro
que eu deixei o meu com o bicheiro,
vá dizer ao seu gerente
que pendure essa despesa
no cabide ali em frente.

[Café Conversation
Waiter, please be so good
to bring me at once
a café au lait which hasn't been re-heated
a hot bread roll with a lot of butter,
a serviette
and a glass of chilled water;
close the door on the right
carefully, because
I'm not inclined
to be exposed to a hot sun;
and go ask your client over there
who won in the football.
If you should be cleaning the table
I won't get up or pay the bill;
go ask your boss
for a pen and ink,
an envelope and a card;
don't forget to give me toothpicks
and a cigarette to keep the mosquitoes away;
go have the tobacconist
lend me some magazines,
a lighter and an ashtray.
Go call for me
34-3333
and tell Mr. Osório
to send me a umbrella
over here to our office;
waiter, lend me some money
because I left mine with the numbers guy
go tell the manager
to stick my bill
on the coat hanger over there]

(N. Rosa 1992)

In this song the key elements of popular culture are enacted or mentioned: the *samba* rhythm, soccer, cigarettes, the numbers game (*jogo do bicho*), and the aim to get something for nothing.

In another, Rosa's gem concerning the art of the *vida vadia* (the idle life), a window into the psyche of the average fellow is offered:

"João Ninguém"
João Ninguém
que não é velho nem moço,
come bastante no almoço
pra se esquecer do jantar
num vão de escada
fez a sua moradia,
sem pensar na gritaria
que vem do primeiro andar.
João Ninguém
não trabalha e é dos tais
que joga sem ter vintém
e fuma Liberty Ovais
esse João nunca se espôs ao perigo,
nunca teve um inimigo,
nunca teve opinião.
João Ninguém
não tem ideal na vida
além de casa e comida
tem seus amores também
e muita gente que ostenta luxo e vaidade
não goza a felicidade
que goza João Ninguém.
João Ninguém
não trabalha um só minuto
e vive sem ter vintém
e anda a fumar charuto
esse João nunca se espôs ao perigo,
nunca teve um inimigo,
nunca teve opinião.

[Joe Nobody
Joe Nobody
who is neither old nor young
eats enough at lunch
so he can forget dinner;
he makes his dwelling
in a stairwell
without thinking about the yells
that come from the first floor.
Joe Nobody
doesn't work and is the type
to gamble penniless
and smoke Liberty Ovais;

4: SOCIOANTHROPOLOGY AND POPULAR CULTURE 179

> this Joe never exposed himself to peril
> never had an enemy,
> never had an opinion.
>
> Joe Nobody
> has no ideal in life
> other than a home and food;
> he has his love-affairs too
> and a lot of people who boast riches and display
> don't enjoy the happiness
> enjoyed by Joe Nobody.
> Joe Nobody
> doesn't work a single minute
> and lives without a penny
> and goes around smoking a cigar;
> this Joe never exposed himself to peril
> never had an enemy,
> never had an opinion.]
> (Vadico e Noel Rosa, "Conversa de botequim"; N. Rosa
> 1992)

The main point is the protagonist's profound indifference to work, and the absence of any resentment against the system or of any desire to change his condition. Nothing could be further from the government sponsored work ethic; indeed the government attempted to root out the popular *malandro* figure from the average man's psyche. After tomfoolery, the recurring element in the *samba canção* is of course love, expressed as a game of sexual desire aroused by the Venus figure of the *mulata,* the Afro-Iberian woman, sprung from the popular quarters in the hills, which look down over the more refined suburbs onto the legendary beaches and the beautiful bay.

Rio, with its physical exuberance, its sense of festivity and folkloric pageantry, its work-discouraging weather, its many diverting leisure activities, and its unique soaring granite peaks reflected in the narcissistic mirror of the bay, is a legend, an aesthetically self-adequate, self-fulfilling universe, as evidenced by the song composed by the great contemporary composer, Caetano Veloso (a Bahian resident of Rio):

> "Menino do Rio"
> Menino do Rio,
> Calor que provoca arrepio.
> Dragão tatuado no braço,
> Calção, corpo aberto no espaço,

Coração de eterno flerte,
Adoro ver-te.
Menino vadio,
Tensão flutuante do Rio,
Eu canto pra Deus proteger-te.
O Havai
seja aqui,
Tudo o que sonhares,
Todos os lugares,
As ondas dos mares,
Pois quando eu te vejo eu desejo teu desejo.
Menino do Rio,
Calor que provoca arrepio.
Toma esta canção como um beijo.

["Rio boy"
Rio boy,
Warmth that tingles
A dragon tattooed on the arm,
Shorts, open body in space,
Heart of eternal flirtation
I adore seeing you
Idle boy,
The floating tension of Rio,
I sing that God may protect you,
Let Hawaii
Be here
Everything you dream of,
All the places,
The waves of the ocean
Because when I see you I desire your desire.
Rio boy,
Warmth that tingles,
Take this song as a kiss]

(Veloso 1979)

The lines "O Havai / seja aqui" constitute an aesthetic sublimation of the *carioca* ambiance, just as the insistence on the desire of desire is a reminder of the narcissistic aspect of this perfection. Indifference to serious concerns and a blurring of the borders between political ideas, popular art, history, sport, and personal acquaintances also characterizes these lines by Caetano from "Os meninos dançam": "Circo transcendental / (Jorge, Pepeu, bola, Didi) / A história do samba, / A luta de classes, os melhores passes de Pelé / Tudo é filtrado ali . . ." [Transcendental circus (. . .) The History of samba / The class struggle / Pelé's best passes /

Everything is filtered (. . .), 1979]. In the popular art of the 1930s there was none of this sort of self-conscious articulation, although the roots of this disregard for social convention are already evident in the *samba canção*. Composers emerged from other areas of Brazil, but to achieve success they had to come to Rio and follow the lead of established musicians by making the city and its women their muses.

In the *Bossa Nova* of the late fifties and early sixties the dazzling array of musical and lyrical talent—the latter led by the recognized poet, Vinícius de Moraes—was just as closely focused on Rio as in the 1930s. Whereas this new sound was heavily influenced by foreign jazz, the lyrics were more consciously enamored of Rio, as suggested by the most famous song of all, "Garota de Ipanema" (Tom Jobim and Vinícius de Moraes), whose heroine is pictured in the song as strolling along the famous beachfront boulevard, at one with the soul of the city. It is at this point that the evocation of Rio reaches a genuinely Utopian level. Another example is Tom Jobim's "Corcovado" (hunchback, the name of a crooked mountain on which stands the famous statue of *o Redentor*—Christ the Redeemer). The suave romantic intimacy of this gentle celebration of love integrates the quintessential *carioca* spectacle, the silhouette of the *Redentor*, this time seen not from the street as in the film *Black Orpheus,* but from the window of a pleasant apartment, perhaps in the wealthy residential belt around the lagoon between the Corcovado hill and the sea. The noisy, public *alegria* of the city, and its endless spectacle of material misery and playful resilience is effaced by a more intimate sigh of love. The singer has his lover at his side, there is no threat from anywhere, no need to compromise this tranquillity with worldly responsibilities. He has achieved a sort of lyrical nirvana, a complete calm with time to dream of a happiness which will continue till the end of his days: the giant statue is the talisman of a perfected aesthetic redemption.

"Corcovado"
Um cantinho um violão
Este amor, uma canção
Pra fazer feliz a quem se ama
Muita calma pra pensar
E ter tempo pra sonhar
Da janela vê-se o Corcovado
O redentor, que lindo

Quero a vida sempre assim
Com você perto de mim

Até o apagar da velha chama
E eu que era triste
Descrente desse mundo
Ao encontrar você eu conheci
O que é a felicidade meu amor.

[A low voice, a guitar
This love, a song
To make lovers happy
Lots of calm to think
And have time to dream
Corcovado is seen from the window
The Redeemer, how beautiful
I want life to always be like this
With you close to me
Until that old flame finally blows out
And I that was sad
With no faith in this world
In meeting you I found
What happiness is, my love.]
(Antonio Carlos Jobim, in Jobim 1994)

The main *Bossa Nova* composers were almost universally Euro-Brazilians of socially advantaged classes, in marked contrast with the humble socioeconomic origins of many of the *samba canção* composers, many of whom were Afro-Brazilian. The *malandro* figure and his strategies for outwitting the system are virtually absent. The sociological insight has lost its bite and been replaced by a celebration of a pleasant Latin American bourgeois existence, where social class is inherited and not dependent on arduous dedication to one's career; though the dark-skinned muse remains in vogue, there is less insistence on the treacherous caprices of the willful Rita Baiana type or on the sexual *machismo* which is a constant in popular *samba*. The songs tend to focus on intimate scenes between sensitive lovers, in a more courtly, troubadouresque fashion. *Bossa Nova* was directed essentially at a burgeoning middle-class audience, though it achieved universal appeal. Popular *samba* songs continued to sell well amongst lower classes, however, and have come to be more and more unabashedly dominated by Afro-Brazilian performers.

Carnaval and Social Theories

Rio and Roberto da Matta

Along with the city's beauty and its pleasant lifestyle, the single event which most guarantees the uniqueness of Rio is the carnaval.

Popular wisdom in Brazil tends to confirm the Bakhtinian theory of carnaval as a sociopolitical role reversal, whereby for a few days the rich retire and the poor take over the city, reconfirming the social contract and verifying its ultimate equity. The Rio carnaval is, however, more exactly a color and culture code reversal than a real socioeconomic inversion. What makes this carnaval aesthetically extraordinary, beyond the visual splendor of the floats and the costumes, are the Afro-Brazilian traditions of hard-core *samba* dancing and music dominated by percussion and multiple syncopation. These arts are still dominated by Afro-Brazilians or, more accurately, *negro-mestiços;* contrary to popular wisdom most Euro-Brazilians do not know how to dance *samba* or play percussion with the required skill.

The greater part of the performers are of at least partial Afro-Brazilian extraction, in contrast to the relative absence of this segment of the population from the city's central thoroughfares of business and social interaction. The *negro-mestiço* population is markedly underrepresented in the downtown during regular business hours, and overrepresented for the four days of carnaval. The suggestion that carnaval occasions an inversion or temporary disqualification of social stations (as in the medieval scenario) seems dubious. Rather, the inversion is of the primacy of different ethnic praxes: the Euro-Brazilian commerce which normally dominates the city literally cedes ground to an aesthetic euphoria whose motive energies, considered typically Brazilian, are Afro-derived. Significantly, the Afro-Brazilian element is more dominant in the performance than it is in the ethnically eclectic gene pool of the city's poor. If Brazil is brown (*café com leite*), business is disproportionately white, and carnaval performance disproportionately black.

The carnaval spectacle of Rio should not be seen as an organic cultural tradition however. The privilege of a conspicuous place on the float is purchased by various persons of financial weight, including actors and singers wanting publicity, politicians and criminals seeking endorsement by the city or within the urban community centered around the *escola-de-samba,* and others merely desirous of recognition and acclaim. The financial logistics of the massive display have made the *escolas-de-samba* curious entities, poised between neighborhood associations and corporate capitalism, and plagued by the infiltration of organized crime and dirty municipal politics. The capitalization process dates back to the Vargas administration's successful attempts to manipulate the carnaval as a propagandistic ritual affirming social harmony and racial integration and then to promote it as a unique tourist attraction. The high financial stakes involved require powerful players in the form of populist demagogues—politicians, gangsters, and other celebrities. The aesthetic prestige possessed by the *escola-de-samba* is marketed out to these buyers in accordance with their ability to pay, thus integrating the operation into the Euro-Brazilian dominated cash economy, legal or illegal.

And yet this prestige is predicated on the precious commodity of a perceived cultural authenticity, essentially Afro-Brazilian. The element of genuine popular participation is a necessary ingredient in the mix. To be successful and win the grand prize, an *escola-de-samba* must combine the element of hardcore capitalist extravaganza with authentic musical mettle.

The *escola-de-samba* is thus the meeting place of two divergent motivations corresponding to positions in the social hierarchy. Of course, the two elements are each dependent on the catalyzing agency of the other. There is no possibility of complete appropriation of one party by the other—without ever increasing material infrastructure victory is impossible, but just as surely a victory cannot be purchased without the coopter himself being coopted into the originary popular ethos which sustains the performance. Financial rewards for winning composers (beating out other composers to provide the theme song of a given *escola-de-samba* or even winning the competition outright) make the carnaval an opportunity for socioeconomic advancement for a limited number of members of the popular classes, so that they, like the big players, find in the *escola-de-samba* their own chance of material gain. These unlikely bedfellows are joined at the navel in a lascivious social *samba*. Folkloric culture, usually perceived as the static, embedded consciousness of a collective memory reaching back to an archaic cultural code, has here an industrial aspect; it generates serious money and unique sociopolitical opportunities to ascend through specific material gain or, by association with the spectacle, to influence popular opinions of one's civic worthiness. The carnaval is a complex web where the material, the aesthetic and the moral interact, and where each can be seen as a sort of mutually exchangeable capital, to be invested or harvested.

For all the nostalgia for the gentility of the benevolent Dom Pedro's Empire and its graceful capital, the twentieth century—the American century in the broader sense of the term—has seen the flourishing of a unique aesthetic *communitas* in Rio. Two musical generations brought *carioca* expression to extraordinary levels of creative proficiency, the first achieving national domination and the second a modern sophistication and world recognition unprecedented for music from the third world (indeed, the urbane sensibility of *Bossa Nova* makes this term utterly incongruous). This progress was abetted by a deliberate policy of concentrating the communications industry in Rio, then the political capital. Merely one of many carnavals in Brazil, the Rio colossus attained in the 1930s a national hegemony comparable to that of its own *samba canção* (which became the national *sound* because of Rio's domination of radio), and an international celebrity as a spectacle which is probably unequaled by any popular festivity anywhere. Its status has been cultivated by the government for the dual purposes of attracting and impressing foreign visitors and as a demagogic symbolic ritual of social harmony for domestic consumption. The reputation of *carioca* life has achieved the status of mythology through the complementary chemistry of an authentic expressive tradition and the external agency of planned material support. A significant part of this support has come from the development of a conscious rhetorical discourse articulated by various entities, from tourist agencies to government departments to academics. Rio and its carnaval have an army of apologists and ideologues.

One of the most influential intellectuals in this sense has been Roberto da Matta, who has developed an ideology of Rio with the carnaval as a symbol of Brazilian society. For da Matta, as for Bakhtin, the carnaval marks an inversion of prevailing social modes. The social laws pertaining in the rest of the year can thus be deciphered from their opposite, the carnaval code. Brazilian society is essentially hierarchical and personal. In this sense it functions in complete contrast to conventional western nations, particularly the U.S., which are based on principles of equality and anonymity. In the United States, the classic liberal association of citizens in a given interest group gives each member equal status and voting rights. Personal data external to interest in the cause and, theoretically, intimacy with the founders or the central clique of the group, are not relevant to each member's weight in the organization. There are no assumptions that status in one domain of social interaction bestows authority in another, for example that the rich man has greater rights than the poor man in some group of which both are members, or that the priest has more rights than the layman in a moral cause. Rather, the individual has a minimal and maximal quantitative value of one (ultimately, his vote), and the anonymity of no assumed personal data derived from social identity. The vote of each citizen is of equal value, and indeed, any citizen may become president.

For da Matta, Brazilian institutions—spawned in imitation of those of conventional modern Western societies—maintain the external dressings of a democratic ideology. This rhetoric is actually taken to the extreme in the Brazilian suspicion of any officially exclusive grouping—thus preventing the formation of legitimate specific interest groups, normally a hallmark of pluralistic democracy. Despite this rejection of official exclusivity, the institutions do not work democratically; rather they preserve and reflect the importance of personal relations—obtaining advantages through networks of acquaintances.

The carnaval of Rio is compared by da Matta to the Mardi Gras of New Orleans; each is an inversion of prevailing social laws and mentalities, but in opposite ways. The carnaval of New Orleans represents a reaction against the relentless egalitarian spirit maintained and pursued in the legislated social rules of modern American society.

> The carnaval of New Orleans seems to recreate, at the level of ritual, the deepest truths regarding the exclusivity of class, in a society which claimed to banish hierarchy . . . [the king] stands in radical opposition to the President of the Republic . . . A state of individuals is abandoned . . . to enter into a hierarchical world, where nobles and plebeians complement each other not as classes but rather as estates or orders. (1978, 131)

The New Orleans event is thus identified as a throwback to the aristocratic values of the pre-Revolutionary era where distinctions of caste separate persons in a consistent pattern, whatever the social activity concerned, and where marks of superiority are conspicuously and proudly displayed. Thus the emblematic figure of the New Orleans festivity is the Rex, the totem of old world authority. The parade is ordered in accordance with the prevailing social hierarchy, with the place of honor going to the old "krews" made up of the white elite of established families, who condescend to throw coins out to the hopeful and grateful throngs in a ritual reenactment of royal indulgence and aristocratic benevolence. The singularity of the New Orleans carnaval in the North American context derives from the Latin background of the city, an island in a sea of Anglo-Saxon puritanism. But this carnaval is of limited sociopsychological depth. There is no rigid demarcation for the celebrations, rather they occur in a loose association of days prior to the conclusion. On the other hand the carnaval is negatively defined spatially—set aside in a certain area rather than taking over the whole city.[5] In short, it could not be said that society

4: SOCIOANTHROPOLOGY AND POPULAR CULTURE 187

abruptly stops and enters carnaval mode—the reversal of social rules—in a universal communitary observation.

The Rio carnaval stands, in da Matta's perspective, in diametric opposition both in terms of its social sense and in the degree of impact. The carnaval abolishes momentarily the rigid hierarchical order, replacing it with a situation where all are equal, and introduces a unique moment of free social competition where talent is rewarded. The competition comes in the form of vying for the prize of best carnaval group. Da Matta enumerates the various divisions into which carnaval groups are divided. Beyond the leading *escolas-de-samba* there are also secondary divisions; each year the bottom teams drop to the next division down, replaced by upwardly mobile victors. Apart from the *escolas-de-samba* there is a host of different classes of carnaval groups with differing degrees of formality and choreography, from the *blocos de enredo* (who present a story) to *grupos de frevo* (smaller groups dedicated to certain dance forms), right down to *fantasia sem forma definida* and *banhos-de-mar-a-fantasia* (randomly costumed persons and exotic swimsuit bearers). For all these groups there are various prizes and competitions. But the carnavalization process is not limited to this vast assemblage of official participants (numbering in the hundreds of thousands). The whole city becomes carnaval territory. Individuals dress and assume an alternate social persona as their fantasy dictates, crossing gender, socioeconomic and cultural lines. The rules of a minimal safe distance between individuals, so powerful in Anglo society, are not respected; anybody is fair game for the intrusive gregariously minded merrymaker. The verb used to denote participation in carnaval—as a wandering individual in the public space more than as a member of a competing group—is *brincar* (to play), suggesting the sort of freedom of social interaction and recreational invention found in the child's playground, though of course with the inclusion of the adult recreation of sexual discourse.

The emblematic figure of the carnaval, for da Matta, is the *malandro,* the likable trickster weaving his way between social rules, identities, and castes, infinitely malleable and always playing at being something he is not. Though this character appears as one of the stock figures in the parades (visually and gesturally recognizable through various clichéd motifs), the *malandro* spirit is also the social mode emulated by the roving individuals in the crowd—carnaval "players," as it were. As for the female participants, there is a parallel pattern of inversion of totem and taboo during carnaval, with an opposition of spiritual/sexual personae recalling the traditional Mediterranean Madonna/whore motifs. The usual requirements of modesty are spectacularly dropped: woman becomes a hyperbolic statement of sexual capacity and confidence. Both the provocative *samba*-muses—literally, *as mulatas*—and the *malandro* are psycholinguistically associated with the groups at the margins of the racial hierarchy. Significantly, though, it is conventionally the half-cast rather than the full-blooded Afro-Brazilian who assumes this role; the carnaval game of slipping through the usual barriers of identity is facilitated by the half-way status between the two poles of white and black, which in the extra-carnaval hierarchization of Brazilian society constitute another instance of totem and taboo.

As da Matta argues, the Rio carnaval is not simply a moment when the usual social repressions are lifted but also one where assignations of social prestige are inverted. In a culture with a very traditional sense of the import of institutional qualifications, the *malandro* becomes the master, the humble chambermaid becomes the expert for her socially superior but aesthetically inept employers; people from the social margins "teach those of the middle and upper classes about the world of samba, the universe of *malandragem* and resourcefulness; the poor teach about the great paradox of harmonizing inequality." The aesthetic prestige derived from being able to do the essential carnaval dance of Rio, *samba,* mixes freely with the psychological and moral universe of the lower social classes, which also assumes a central position in the game of carnaval.

Da Matta's reading of the carnaval of Rio assigns to it a unique and extraordinary social significance, contrasting its euphorically democratic praxis favorably with the New Orleans festivity, which is seen as revealing the false egalitarian pretensions of American civil society. It would be unfair to take this as mere nationalist enthusiasm, since da Matta sees the Rio carnaval as an inversion of a hierarchically rigid social code pertaining in Brazil during the rest of the year. He points out the cultural gulf between the Brazilian mentality and that of advanced democracies, with the implicit suggestion that contemporary Brazilian society would require radical cultural changes if it is to evolve toward a standard democracy.

In da Matta's embrace of Bakhtinian carnaval theory there is a tendency to overlook the manipulated aspects of the Rio carnaval, both in terms of its internal workings and in its relation to other carnavals in Brazil. Da Matta notes in passing that the more communitarian *blocos* tend to criticize the *escolas-de-samba* as being less authentic, orchestrated more as a grandiose, highly capitalized spectacle for the benefit of wealthy spectators, many of them foreign. This issue is not pursued; rather, it is seen as an acknowledgment of the vitality of the carnaval's various elements, each subsumed in the global carnaval spirit. However, it is possible to analyze these different elements as suggestive of tensions between different visions of carnaval. In fact, the *blocos* are more typical Pan-Brazilian carnaval organizations than the *escolas-de-samba*. The *bloco* is the basic unit of the Bahian carnaval and of that of Recife. The *grupo de frevo* is the basic unit of the carnaval of Olinda (Recife's twin city). Rio is distinguished by the massive visual pageantry of the *escola-de-samba*. This is the only carnaval group whose efforts are almost entirely oriented to the performance aspect as perceived by television cameras, tourists, and judges. In most carnavals, there is less of a line between being in and being out of the club; participation in a particular group is seen as a sort of heightening of the general experience of *brincando carnaval*—going out onto the street during carnaval to look for music and fun. The group participants in fact frequently wear their costume at times other than the actual exhibition of their group, and even during this time they can leave the spaced occupied by their group (at times marked out physically with cords) and move along with the crowd. This situation cannot hold in the Rio festivity, which is the only one held in an arena—the *sambódromo* being an artificial street, far from the commercial center (the usual site of carnaval parades) with concrete stands built along its course—for which tickets must be bought, so that the Rio carnaval is divided into performers and paid spectators.

A decisive element in this singular evolution of the *escola-de-samba,* and one which suggests a reading other than the Bakhtinian interpretation of carnaval as a natural expression of an organic society (that is, cultural rather than political), is the deliberate political manipulation to which the *escolas-de-samba* have been subjected. Brazil has a history of national-socialist type cultural mobilization which has never been overturned as it was in the genuinely fascist states whose regimes were eventually destroyed by military force. The manipulation of carnaval-as-spectacle dates back essentially to the Vargas regime; prior to this the carnaval's assault on the Catholic sense of decency was treated at best as dubious by the authorities. Afrocentric carnaval displays were at various times actively repressed. With the Vargas regime arises the intelligence that popular energies can be harnessed through ludic activities, their culturally alternative expressions reoriented as socially cohesive, patriotic celebrations, their anarchic frenzy—

at times provoked by hunger and material misery—dissipated in ephemeral surfeit and exhaustion. This formula for the ideological appropriation of popular energies by the government elite has been extraordinarily successful, whether at the level of suffusing popular energy in "the great paradox of harmonizing inequality" (da Matta) or at the level of creating a sense of unique national spectacle in the minds of Brazilians and outsiders.

It is natural that in this process of ideological appropriation of popular culture into the national project conceived by the government elite there occurs a parallel spatial centralization. As Brasília would become the intended model Brazilian urb of the future, so Rio—capital during the Vargas years—was made the definitive forum of popular culture, perceived as the cultural Rome to which all Brazilian roads lead. This association does not impose itself either through historical experience—Rio as a cultural center is relatively young in national terms, dating from the early nineteenth century—or in ethnocultural terms, since carnaval celebrations in many areas of Brazil, notably the areas of lesser Afro-Brazilian impact, differ greatly from the *carioca* spectacle. The success of the latter has been predicated on at least three basic elements: the cultural substratum, in the form of the healthy presence in Rio of Afro-Brazilian derived *samba;* a critical demographic mass, Rio and São Paulo being until recently the only really large Brazilian cities, endowed with the human and material infrastructure for such a massive mobilization; and finally, the government sponsorship and promotion which has made the *carioca* carnaval into a conscious visual spectacle beyond the naïve participatory level and which has articulated, in the popular and intellectual consciences, an ideologically ambitious national meaning for the event.

It is worth looking at each of these contributing factors separately in order to appreciate the extent to which Rio and *carioca* mythology, rather than being an original source of national culture, has functioned as a synthesis of cultural and economic input from other areas in Brazil which can be considered more authentic as the original source of national culture. The role of Rio as a consumer rather than producer of national economic production has already been mentioned, from its first growth as outlet for the mineral wealth of Minas Gerais, through the Empire with its court and then the Republic with its *de facto* court of government appointees. Apart from the extraordinary natural beauty of the physical site, the government propagandistic sponsorship of Rio was also a natural outgrowth of the cultural wealth which an authoritarian, homogeneous society concentrates in its capital. Major cultural icons such as the opera, the Academy of Letters, the National Library, the horse races, and so on are created deliberately, as civic projects, with government support rather than growing organically from popular participation. The influence of the French model, with its concentration of cultural resources in Paris, is clear in this respect. Though for the better part of a century there has generally been more cultural activity and creativity in the artistic elite in São Paulo than in Rio, it is the latter city which possesses and endows the seal of official status to an artist, marking the passage from eccentric creativity to cultural hagiography and membership in the club of national history.

The carnaval of Rio, one among many, has atypically become a national institution and possession, and has enjoyed national rather than local government patronage. The originality of the *carioca* carnaval lies precisely in this massive, deliberate transformation from participatory rite to consumable spectacle. The cultural substrata at the root of the celebration, on the other hand, is largely derivative, essentially from the Recôncavo da Bahia region around Salvador. The various *samba* rhythms associated with Rio were developed by internal immigrants from Bahia to Rio at the turn of the century. The popular membership of the *escolas-de-samba* is disproportionally Afro-Brazilian (as opposed to other poor ethnicities), many of whose forefathers arrived in Brazil at Salvador, the major port of the Atlantic trade through to the nineteenth century. Amidst the annually reinvented themes and costumes of the *escolas-de-samba,* a constant and obligatory element are the *baianas,* that is, women dressed in the costume of the Salvador-centered Afro-Brazilian Candomblé cult, even though there are many other Afro-Brazilian cults around Brazil, including Rio's own Umbanda. Finally, the *samba* dance itself, though refined in Rio to the magnificently extroverted form used in the display of the parade, is derived directly from a variety of *samba* dances from Bahia. The difference then, between the *carioca* and the Bahian carnaval lies not so much in the music and dance utilized or in the popular attitude to carnaval participation, but in the mobilization of this energy into an externally observable spectacle and its subsumation into a consciously articulated civic ideology for national and international consumption.

What is the significance of the outside origin of the aesthetic forms? To the degree that aesthetic codes incorporated into social rituals are predicated upon socioeconomic realities and moral-mythological or cosmological conceptions, the significance of the carnaval must be interpreted not only according to official propaganda and its extra-festive agenda (dissipating social tension and contestation, generating tourist dollars, etc.), but also in terms of the sociocultural conditions which generated the carnaval practices eventually transformed or appropriated. Of course, sociocultural conditions are not constant and are difficult to interpret as influences on aesthetic and ludic rituals. Further, social conditions prevailing in Rio are at least as important to its carnaval as those in Bahia, even if the latter originally spawned most of the performative forms utilized in the Rio event. The point is that the carnaval must be seen as a complex crystallization of heterogeneous forces, diachronic and synchronic, some contradictory to each other, some of such different order—aesthetic, material, or moral—that they cannot be directly compared. Carnaval represents a constant reappropriation of inherited cultural modes, a dynamic evolution moving in parallel with the historical development of urban Rio and other cities in the twentieth century. A global perspective of the Rio carnaval must acknowledge the specific ethnic origins of aesthetic and moral codes (notably, the Bahian Afro-Brazilian influence as opposed to other Afro-Brazilian and non-Afro Brazilian ethnic constituencies), their transformation in the urban reality of this particular city (distinguishable from Salvador and all *nordestino* cities by its status as megalopolis), the manipulation and recasting of the event by government agencies with various external agendas, and so on. Despite the perspicacity of Bakhtin's elaboration of a ritual based on a medieval social contract, it is no longer possible to read carnaval as a moment in a stable universe and homogeneous culture. The substantial archaic characteristics of social intercourse in Brazil as a Third World nation are counterweighted by radical mutations in a process of extraordinarily rapid modernization. Along with other sociological and aesthetic data, Brazilian carnaval is politically contestable, industrial in demographic and economic terms, and still evolving.

From this point of view, the feeling of the *carioca blocos* that the *escolas-de-samba* are less authentic is not to be interpreted as some kind of merely fraternal resentment susceptible to an ultimately homogeneous integration, but on the contrary suggests two different conceptions of what carnaval means in the modern context. The very act of presuming that carnaval can be read in terms of a culturally cohesive solidarity despite social difference, as da Matta proposes, is consistent with the authoritarian management of Brazil's cultural identity as practiced through government propaganda and cultural institutions. Da Matta discerns the tendency in Brazilian thinking toward motifs and sentiments of universal conciliation, however much this may conflict with social reality, and his own perspective of the carnaval is a reinforcement of this tendency. It is logical, then, that he accepts and argues for the centrality of the carnaval of Rio, which, as it is successfully promoted, is a ritual of euphoric appeasement, of the dilution of social difference and the denial of resentment: a grandiose, ethnically ecumenical, national secular mass.

However, this centripetal reading can be contested by looking away from Rio to other carnavals which have not been the object of such masterly propagandistic articulation and have not been developed with external observation in mind. After all, the Rio carnaval parade, where tickets are sold for places in the grandstands looking over an artificial thoroughfare, known as the *sambódromo*, is a synthetic simulation of the street and thus the least authentic of popular carnavals. Televised, this festivity is the property of the elite who can purchase tickets, and the national public who watch what is shown to them within their living rooms. The other carnavals of Brazil are generally not televised, nor are they subject to the same propagandistic bombardment of meaning; they incorporate more popular participation and less orchestrated forms, and their sense is less susceptible to manipulation from above. If another major Brazilian carnaval, that of Salvador da Bahia, is brought into consideration, the nationally representative status of various attributes of the Rio event discerned by da Matta must be questioned.

The Bahian counterexample

In Salvador, the basic carnaval group is the *bloco*, or carnaval club. Various *blocos* hire out a band. This band is strategically placed on top of a truck literally covered in an electrostatically impressive battery of loudspeakers; this ensemble, known as a *trio elétrico*, was invented in and is associated specifically with the Bahian carnaval and its characteristic music. The *trio elétrico* has the essential feature of mobility; it moves down the street steadily, accompanied by the dancing and reveling neophytes, thus facilitating a key sensation of the carnaval sensibility and aesthetic: the sensation of moving freely through social and physical space with the intention of movement itself rather than of arrival at a destination. In comparison with the Rio *escolas* (though not necessarily with the Rio *blocos*), the members pay much less for their costume. There is no formal choreography; the members will sometimes be dancing, sometimes walking, sometimes drinking. In fact what they do is not very different to what the people who aren't in the *bloco* do, except that they wear the costume and enjoy freedom of movement within a protected area. This area is a thin long rectangle that extends along the street, and which is marked by a rope that is held up by a crew of up to two hundred security men. The onlookers on the street, or rather on the footpath, can't move along with the band and the *bloco* members as they head up the street because of the tightness of the throng in the public space. Instead they stay put and let the seemingly infinite succession of *blocos* and their bands go past, and dance to each new group as it appears.

Most of the bands share about eighty percent of their repertoire, which comes from the common pool of the current local popular music. The most distinguished bands will be well-known composers and recording artists. But anyone can play anyone else's song, and they do, to please the crowd. In fact the bands will often play theme songs of other *blocos* which have become hits on the local airwaves. The instrumentation of the bands is roughly comparable to that of rock bands—drums, guitars, base, and keyboards are the staple, along with the traditional Brazilian element of extra percussion. The style of the music varies from year to year; *lambada* was the dominant style in the second half of the eighties. In the 1990s, the samba-reggae rhythm developed by Olodum's percussion master, Neguinho do Samba, infused the music of most popular groups, even those with a majority of harmonically oriented instruments. By the mid-1990s, however, Olodum, influenced by the commercial success of the *trio* bands which had previously borrowed heavily from Olodum's repertoire, was tending to move back to more harmonic orchestrations. As opposed to the sounds of the south of Brazil, the flux of musical genres in Salvador tends to suggest a dialog with a variety of Caribbean sounds, themselves in a state of constant evolution. In the carnaval of Salvador the line between member and nonmember is less absolute; ownership of the musical material of a given *bloco* is less exclusive and the greater share of the material is taken from the pool of local popular music.

The fundamental difference between the Rio and Bahian carnavals, at least in their official manifestations, lies in the line between performance and passive observation. In the Rio spectacle the division between these modes is unquestionable. In Bahia the distinction is blurred, and in fact the *bloco*-member often steps out of the security ring and moves through the crowd who are dancing at least as much as the *bloco*-members; the latter essentially buy, along with the kudos of the particular *bloco*, the right to *brincar carnaval* in complete abandon, right in the middle of the affair. This is quite a privilege since the public space is restricted to the footpaths of the main avenues and the occasional squares along the route, and is so crowded that it is often physically impossible to move around. But the members' activity is not qualitatively different from that of the general public. There are no real choreographies for the *blocos,* but there are local dances which take on each year and which can be used for the music of any *bloco.* Dexterity in this form of carnaval performance depends simply on practice acquired in various street fiestas held in the months prior to the carnaval, and the paying members are often out performed by the people on the other side of the cordon.

There are two basic categories of *blocos:* Afro and non-Afro. The *blocos afro* differ from what has been said so far in that they do not hire a band; the percussion outfit is numerous and can take up as much room as do the common members without performative obligations. The percussionists are an integral part of the *bloco.* They generally play without amplification, and this enhances the sense of physical presence. Along with a few dignitaries and hangers-on, the truck is reserved for the singer, who does have a microphone, and several dancers. It is common to see a a male virtuoso dancer performing, or to see the *bloco*'s queen of the year. She will have been selected earlier on the basis of her beauty and dancing ability. The dance performed is a sort of original, endlessly extendible improvisation, using jazz ballet techniques but with a firm grounding in traditional west African dance. The costume is similarly a modern reworking of traditional material, completely unlike the jeweled nudity of the female *sambista carioca* (often referred to simply as *mulatas,* so great is the arbitrary association of ethnicity, gender, and vocation). The performance requires great physical sensibility but is not erotically themed. Since the music is based on percussion, the accompanying dances executed by the members are stylistically different to the non-Afro bands. There is an element of spontaneous choreography—one will often see dance patterns pop up in particular pockets of the crowd. Again, jazz ballet and African dance are significant stylistic resources for these steps. As with the dance, the costumes of the *blocos afro* are loosely based on African fabric designs without being tribally authentic.

The membership of the *trio* (non-Afro) *blocos* is essentially a middle-and upper-class affair. A *bloco* might charge $US 200 for its costume. This is a reasonable expense for someone working in a bank, but excessive for someone on the minimum wage of $100 a month.⁶ In Salvador there is not the Rio mythology of the dedicated acolyte who lives in a shack somewhere up near the famous Christ statue, scrimping and saving religiously to buy the costume for the four magical days of carnaval. Buying the costume and participating in the carnaval with membership privileges in a *blocʋ* is a significant but routine leisure option for the middle class. A certain social kudos is attached to each of these *blocos*. The most exclusive have tended to vigorously discourage black membership. All the *trio blocos,* however, through the socioeconomic rationale of their membership fee, effectively screen out the *negro-mestiço* element. This leads to the paradoxical situation that even though the *blocos afro* dominate the external *imaginaire* of the Bahian carnaval, if one watches the event on television the majority of the paying participants are actually white. In a town like Salvador, where blacks make up eighty percent of the population, this occasions a glaring inequity. Whatever may be said of the suspension of regular social codes in the general public—and it is significant in this respect that the main avenues used for the *blocos*' parade are central commercial streets, normally dominated by the middle classes and now given over entirely to the celebrations and the invading throngs from the popular classes—the real socioeconomic dynamic of carnaval in terms of club membership is very different from the socially horizontal process asserted by da Matta for Rio.

The current *blocos afro* date from around 1975. They could not be called a traditional carnaval group; they were founded in the context of the world movement of Afrocentric aesthetic valorization which found inspiration in the "black is beautiful" message in the U.S. in the 1960s and 1970s. In the *blocos afro* there is an extensive discourse of affirmation of specifically Afrocentric culture and of social protest. The social victims concerned are identified simultaneously as socioeconomically marginalized and black or brown. Local sociologists have developed the term *negro-mestiço* (black mixed-blood) to denote this class in which, culturally speaking, the various ethnic constituents of the disadvantaged (Euro-Brazilian, Amerindian, and Afro-Brazilian) have been subsumed into the Afro-Brazilian identity and cultural reality. The discourse is affirmed in the annual theme of the *bloco,* usually a pedagogically inspired homage to political leaders of the Afro world community (including U.S. figures such as Malcolm X), cultural icons such as Bob Marley, or a specific country with attendant Afrocentric mythology, including the ancient world (such as a reading of Ancient Egypt as black). This discourse, discussed at length by activists clustered around the *bloco,* is available in a literature of limited public dissemination and also in a far more effective forum: the weekly or biweekly festive gatherings which take place through most of the year and which culminate in the selection by popular acclaim of the ten songs from dozens of contenders, which will be included in the official repertoire of the *bloco* for that year. These gatherings are the key recreational forum for a substantial part of the population. They do not require membership and take place in the street, where a temporary but robust stage will have been set up. The degree of intellectual digestion of the politically militant themes is difficult to assess; the gathering is polysemantically tilted between the pedagogical and mobilizational intentions of the planners and the hedonistic appropriation of the festive opportunity by politically indifferent members of the public. However, the sociopolitical and aesthetic discourse of the *bloco* has a long-term importance in shaping cultural sensibility. The substance of the aesthetic discourse is Pan-Africanist rather than Afro-Brazilian. The development of the annual theme typically involves extensive research on other predominantly or wholly Afro-based cultures. The costume, which is a result of both research on specific African designs and also free invention, virtually bypasses the Afro-Brazilian traditions such as that of the *baiana*. The *blocos afro,* in their aesthetic ventures, do not celebrate Afro-Brazilian cultural syncretism so much as the cultural continuity across the African diaspora (the global migration, notably to the Americas, of black Africans beginning with slavery); they pursue an Afrocentric enrichment of the diluted African roots of the *negro-mestiço* population. Politically speaking, the *blocos* steer away from separatist rhetoric; they militate instead for the recognition of the effective denial by mainstream society of the problematic existence of the *negro-mestiço* masses, and for their rights, within the frame of the constitution (racism is legally prohibited) and the rhetoric of populist democracy, to socioeconomic, cultural, and political citizenship. There is certainly a degree of the reticence identified by da Matta in officially excluding any group from potential membership and participation in the *bloco afro*. On the other hand, at the aesthetic level so important to psychological impact in the carnival, there is a radical contestation of mores and a delicate balance of color-politics which shifts each year in accordance with the aesthetic propositions of the *bloco,* its political affirmations, the degree of prestige of a given *bloco afro* amongst liberal Euro-Brazilians and other factors. The existence of the *blocos afro* has lead to great political complexity in the judging of the *blocos'* displays (in Salvador, the judged elements are costume and theme;

there is no show per se as in Rio). In what some considered to be a sort of containment policy, the civic authorities created separate categories for the *blocos afro*. These arrangements were then contested by some *blocos* on the basis that there were no grounds for separation, and with the implicit ambition of competing directly with and defeating the mainstream, Euro-Brazilian dominated (*trio*) *blocos*.

As observed, there is certainly a demographically aberrant presence of the non-*negro-mestiço* elite in the daytime parade and in what can be seen on television. Meanwhile, if the membership of the *blocos afro* is more demographically representative, their aesthetic practices must be acknowledged as a mode of vanguard innovation with limited ties to traditional folkloric forms and with a conscious aspiration to an internationally inspired radicalization. The cultural discourse is Afrocentric. The music is influenced less by traditional secular Afro-Brazilian rhythms such as *samba* than by the rhythms and instruments of the Yoruba-centric Candomblé—which, unlike other syncretist cults is generally authentically African at the musical level (though lyrics in Portuguese are sometimes used)—and by interest and research into contemporary African sounds. One of the many radical innovations by the *blocos afro* was to eliminate regular tonal instruments backing the melody. The exclusive emphasis on percussion in combination with simple vocal melodies has produced innovative music which is then susceptible to orchestration, often with great commercial success, by more conventional pop outfits. As a result the *blocos afro* are the major source of innovation in a local recording industry still dominated by Euro-Brazilians and/or the upwardly mobile *mulato* element (as opposed to the socioeconomically marginalized figure of the *negro-mestiço*). In this sense there has emerged at the national level something approaching the U.S. scenario of black and white genres, though with a greater ethnocultural polarization between the Afrocentric chants with short phrases in non-European languages found in the recordings of Bahian *blocos afro,* and the Eurocentric music industry of the south, whether in the syrupy Latin love songs of teenage heartthrobs or the Anglocentric suburban angst of São Paulo. A final point concerning the *blocos afro* is that they constitute the major cultural icon of the Bahian carnaval, as reflected in advertising and publicity. Just as with the *baianas* of Candomblé before them, the Afrocentric aesthetic innovations of a secular cultural avant-garde have become emblematic of what is most distinct and interesting on the cultural horizon.

Evidently, the Bahian carnaval is moving the Brazilian cultural landscape along at a rapid pace, and its basic ideology is more akin to other socially contestatorial Afrocentric movements around the world than to the unique Brazilian mythology of racial democracy as ritualized in the carnaval of Rio.

In the past, however, the survival of Afrocentric practices in Bahia was generally seen by scholars as a folkloric preservation of archaic roots in the collective memory rather than a progressive social force. The economic stagnation of Bahia and the *Nordeste* from the early nineteenth century on reinforced this impression; the *Nordeste* was and still is seen as a primitive, premodern society destined to follow the lead of the south. The same logic applies in both the cultural and economic domains. Thus, belief systems presenting greater syncretic balance between European and African roots such as Umbanda were considered in a cultural Darwinian sense as better adapted to contemporary Eurocentric socioeconomic structures than, say, Candomblé, the most Afrocentric Afro-Brazilian cult.

Curiously, this has not been the case. Candomblé has grown in relative influence not only in Salvador but also in Rio and other "colonized" areas. It is not inappropriate to question the syncretist formula for carnaval either; the Rio carnaval with its rhetorical insistence on racial indistinction, has steadily been losing momentum in comparison with the re-Africanized Bahian carnaval, which is beginning to rival it in the number of outside visitors attracted. The Bahian carnaval has the advantage of being in synch with the international currents of Pan-Africanism and European receptivity to "world cultures," for example, the innovative Bahian *bloco afro* music qualifies better for the fashionable rubrique of "world music" (music from the West or the Third World which integrates elements from both) than does *carioca* carnaval music, since the latter is, by now, a frozen traditional form.[7] It also has the advantage of less aesthetic constriction and so can freely borrow from whatever aesthetic modes and discursive themes are popular in world youth culture; there is no obligation to stick to nonthreatening chapters from Brazilian, biblical, or world history as is the case in Rio.

One of the most interesting aspects to carnaval history is that, contrary to popular belief, though based on tradition there has in fact been a great deal of change over the years in the conception of what should be displayed and what is being celebrated. The Bahian carnaval has undergone a series of radical mutations. Around the turn of the century the *negro-mestiço* contingent would execute pastiches of pastoral African life. This mode was then repressed through outright proscription of Afrocentric themes, particularly in the 1920s with the rise of eugenically derived intolerance. After World War II, *afoxé* groups such as Filhos-de-Gandhi developed a secular performance repertoire derived directly from Candomblé liturgical music. In the 1960s some attempts were made to introduce Rio-style *escolas-de-samba,* but the cost proved prohibitive. Ever unpredictable, the next chapter of the Bahian carnaval was the heyday of *blocos de índio*—in which the *negro-mestiço* youth would dress up as Hollywood "Red Skins." As with their cinematic icons (as a strictly fictional, stereotypically reductive creation, of course), these *blocos* had a reputation for rebellious behavior and were harshly dealt with by the local constabulary. They fell into gradual decline with the rise of unambiguously Afrocentric avant-garde forms pioneered by the first *bloco afro,* Ilê Ayê from the mid-1970s. In the 1980s the Ilê Ayê format retained its prestige, but not leadership of the *bloco afro* movement, which by the late 1980s was dominated by the more specifically youth-oriented festive milieu, and the militant activism of Olodum.

The Bahian carnaval thus presents a substantial alternative to the Rio carnaval. Its system of clubs is in a sense comparable to the caste-preserving system of New Orleans which de Matta posits in total opposition to the *carioca* event. The pursuit of Afrocentric rather than syncretist and characteristically Brazilian modes of expression is completely at odds with the official sociological and government discourse concerning the cultural reality of the country. In contrast to that discourse's color-blind Utopian doctrine the Bahian carnaval is used to construct ethnic specificity rather than to celebrate the dissipation of ethnic difference in fraternal revelry. The *bloco afro* perspective is essentially consistent with that of reggae ideologues: it perceives a global system of cultural unity and political oppression of black ethnicity for which the artistic and socioethnic solution (or response) is Afrocentrism. The logic of the perspective contradicts two tenets of official Brazilian ideology—that blacks are not oppressed in Brazil as they are elsewhere, and that whites have sufficiently assimilated African cultural elements as to share a common culture with blacks.

Contrary to expectation, the Bahian carnaval, rather than representing cultural relics from the past, has shown itself to be more adapted to the postmodern era than the Rio carnaval, which is essentially stabilized in its form and themes and which expands quantitatively rather than qualitatively, relying on a remarkable formula developed fifty years ago. Paradoxically, owing to its obligations as an international spectacle, the Rio carnaval seems to have less and less to say about contemporary social reality in Brazil. The admirable ambition of assigning national representativity to this event, while achieving a great deal in the radical rehabilitation of the Brazilian phenomenon of ethnic fusion in the aftermath of World War II and the discrediting of eugenic theories of racial superiority, has, with time, lost validity. With the slow but gradual maturation of democratic awareness, the Rio-carnaval ritual of social communion, which is antimaterialist in the sense that it disregards or forgives social inequities and thus facilitates their perpetuation, inevitably gives way to demands for a piece of the socioeconomic pie; these demands are predicated on an acknowledgment of sociocultural differentiation and discrimination between groups, as in the U.S. The basic ideology of family cohesion between different socioracial agents espoused by Freyre in his analysis of the generative *nordestino* plantation society, with its implicit rejection of protest which is contingent upon a sense of differentiation of identity and interests, is being replaced by a more conventional pluralism, that is, the sense of competing social interest groups, and its attendant sensibility of social resentment by a given group of the perceived unfair privileges of another. The interaction of these sensibilities with aesthetic manifestations, shows that the Bahian carnaval is intrinsically consistent with the new agenda of a more substantial democratic order—even though the Bahian carnaval in much of this century has been subjected to greater censorship and police brutality, reflecting the more archaic social order of *nordestino* society. The Rio carnaval is a quintessentially modern extravaganza, a virtual aesthetic revolution which has found pale parallels from Las Vegas to Paris. In essence, the Rio carnaval is a masterpiece of modernism, a mix of technology, cultural exoticism and tolerance; could they see it would surely have seemed more of a dream than reality to the European modernist visionaries of the early twentieth century. The Bahian carnaval, on the other hand, is emerging as a postmodern icon for hundreds of thousands of visitors: a participatory rather than passive spectacle, it emerges more genuinely from the Third World in that its discursive subject is not a rhetorical claim to membership in the world club of modern privilege and power—the oft-dreamed Brazil as prospective superpower—but rather an articulation of the marginalized, culturally denied masses, the *negro-mestiço* as proud and even angry rather than as a humble and agile dancing acrobat. The Bahian carnaval is a more organic institution, managing to integrate folkloric traditions with the avant-garde, and also more performatively dexterous, responding to the incessant need in the consumer age for formal innovation. Lastly and perhaps most importantly, it blurs the boundaries between aesthetic, moral, and political codes. The vital element of competition identified by da Matta is, in the Rio carnaval, actually restricted to a narrow band of aesthetic production—the show as show, as is evidenced by the relatively minimal qualitative development of the parade apart from its endless technological innovations. In the Bahian carnaval the boundaries of competition have spilled open to embrace a range of divergent aesthetic visions and contestatorial social agendas.

A certain mythology of Brazilian culture has been fostered that imposes a centripetal theory of national identity by treating the Rio carnaval as its unique manifestation. It is an arbitrary argument in that it misrepresents the complexity of cultural production in this society, but is useful in two ways. For domestic consumption, the ritual of the *"great paradox of social harmony"* is an aesthetically illustrious and socially exuberant denial or purging of social tension. This incomparable aesthetic display makes Brazil, in its own way, the most exotic society on earth—more so than its European, African, and Amerindian progenitors because whereas alien social mores and social practices are normally inaccessible, the Rio carnaval parade is utterly accessible, and conceived for the purpose of observation by consumers with the means to pay.

Just as Rio's carnaval has rendered other regional carnavals provincial, so it has eclipsed, as a representational discourse of national identity, other genres of artistic expression, particularly from the international perspective. For the outside audience it is possible for Brazil to exist virtually exclusively in carnaval mode: carnaval attracts a major influx of tourists, and is the stereotypical image for those who have never been to Brazil. For the national audience, however, though the Rio carnaval has been successfully presented as a national institution, it cannot actually replace the cultural infrastructure. Carnaval is only 4 days of 365, and on the other days society assumes the order to which carnaval runs counter, as a rigidly hierarchical, Eurocentric society.

Literary culture is, firstly, Eurocentric rather than Afrocentric and, secondly, endowed with its own arbitrary aesthetic hierarchization which will be shown to run contrary to that mainstream of cooperation between socioanthropologists and government social architects who have espoused the conventional wisdom that Brazil can be represented as a happy, racially democratic tropical town during carnaval. The effects on literary culture, however, can only be understood in relation to another artistic medium—music—and the impact of both carnaval and music on the socio-aesthetic topographies of the country.

Music as a National Cultural Forum

The particular centrality of music in cultural identification

Although the Brazilian popular culture of the twentieth century draws on medieval Iberian, African, and Amerindian roots, and on their development over centuries of mutual interaction in Brazil, the recognized cultural cosmos was more or less uniformly Eurocentric and elitist until modernism valorized non-European expressions and foregrounded popular culture. Brazilian *Modernismo* begins with the event of the *Semana de Arte Moderna*. Although this was a multimedia event, the dominant intellectuals were mostly literati. The most representative and encyclopedic of the writers Mário de Andrade—something of a renaissance man of modernist cultural endeavors. His search for an authentic and original Brazilian cultural identity lead him inevitably to the extraordinarily rich field of ethnomusicology; in the 1920s and 1930s he put out a series of major works in this area. His *Dicionário musical brasileiro* is perhaps the richest work of its kind, explicating and commentating terms and genres from the myriad subcultures in the country.

Andrade's procedure derived not so much from a musical sensibility as from an immanent truth: Brazil's elite literary tradition did not distinguish it radically from international literary culture, whereas its music was distinguished not just by its uniqueness but also by its exceptional quality, rivaling and even surpassing, with the exception of jazz, the panorama of musics reflecting cultural fusion in other countries of the New World. As literary currents diverged, a development probably inherent to the individualistic and intellectual nature of the medium, the initial common thrust of the *Semana* was lost, and with it the possibility of a cohesive aesthetic. Musical modernism produced at least one nationalist champion, however, in the person of Heitor Villa-Lobos. This composer had acquired in his upbringing in Rio a working knowledge of European musical theory and a great familiarity with and competence in popular genres. In Paris in the 1920s his exceptional talents were received warmly and he was able both to develop a stronger theoretical knowledge and to integrate the advances of European modernism in compositions such as the *Bachianas brasi-*

leiras. In Brazil in the 1930s, Villa-Lobos allied himself with the national-socialist culture of the Vargas regime. His compositions, while largely informed by the European modernist mainstream on the one hand, and the Iberian instrumental tradition on the other, nominally incorporated the contemporary Brazilian ethnocultural panorama, and were conceived patriotically. As a conductor and domestic cultural ambassador, Villa-Lobos went on to lead vast assemblages of choirs of schoolchildren numbering into the tens of thousands, gathered in the famous Maracaná soccer stadium on patriotic holidays; the performances were broadcast nationally on radio.

Villa-Lobos's brilliant opus and careerism thus reveal an extraordinary conjunction of sensibility to the Brazilian popular musical tradition, erudite European modernism, and finally the emerging mythology of nationalist consolidation. He demonstrated to what extent music provided a unique medium of artistic praxis for consciously Brazilian representations at an internationally impressive level of achievement. Music has consistently been the art which has won international acclaim for Brazil. At the domestic level the lyricism and musicality of Brazilians, in conjunction with widespread illiteracy (which is typically compensated by greater aural retention and capacity for memorizing) have given music a special role in the process of cultural identification through art. Until the advent of the *telenovela,* popular music was clearly the most efficacious artistic medium for the propagation of cultural discourse. It is significant also that music has sufficient appeal to successfully communicate across class barriers. The classical literary tradition, on the other hand, despite its strong influence on the upper classes, is inevitably of less impact given that in a population of over one hundred million, editions are typically of ten thousand or less copies.

The musical arena is therefore important to those vital moments of artistic crystallization and articulation which have marked the development of cultural identity in Brazil. As in the United States with composers such as Gershwin and the jazz musicians, there has been a noticeable propensity for "high" and popular art to influence each other, and for appropriation between socioethnic groups of musical genres. Villa-Lobos's development in the field of erudite music was a consolidation of the development of what might be called genteel popular music—virtuoso instrumental music for light entertainment, itself colored and rhythmically informed by musical genres derived from humbler socioethnic levels. On the other hand, the development of the Rio *samba canção* and its national dissemination from the 1930s on owed much to a fruitful interaction between marginalized Afro-Brazilian composers and artists from a background of greater opportunity, equipped with a more conventional Western musical formation and the sentimental lyricism which has always been the mainstay of mainstream popular music. The *Bossa Nova* revolution of the late 1950s and 1960s was, as has been seen, a distinctly middle-class, Rio-centric phenomenon; however it was predicated on the ingenious integration of harmonic complexities derived from U.S. jazz with traditional Afro-Brazilian *samba* rhythms, the latter slowed down so as to completely alter the inferred sensibility. The lyricists of *Bossa Nova*, from the master composer Carlos Jobim to its lyrical doyen, the gifted poet Vinícius de Moraes, generally enjoyed a solid literary education. The outstanding *carioca* successor to the initial *Bossa Nova* generation was Chico Buarque, of the eminent literary Buarque de Holanda family. Despite its middle-class sensibility, however, *Bossa Nova* achieved great penetration of all social classes, substantiating the legitimacy of music as the forum of cultural identification in Brazil.

The three musical instances mentioned so far coincide in a gradual process of concentration on Rio as spiritual center of the nation. In the case of Villa-Lobos there is essentially a combination of, on the one hand, the early modernist embrace of disparate ethnogeographical zones of Brazil (notably the quintessentially exotic Amazon), if only as motifs rather than substantive themes, and on the other hand the celebration of Rio as the ultimate Brazilian locus, the capital of the national project.

Regional energies

While Rio has remained the center of the recording industry, the residence of the most successful performers and the *de facto* point of lyrical reference, the period from the mid-sixties saw the flourishing of an eclectic ensemble of highly talented composers and performers grouped under the rubrique of *MPB, Música Popular Brasileira,* who came from all over Brazil. Often their work reflected their own points of origin, from *paulista* industrial modernity to the deep, mystical Catholicism of Minas Gerais to the archaic social roots of the barren *sertão* of the *Nordeste*. What marked these performers stylistically was above all the integration of a category of music which despite its international status, could not, unlike jazz, lay claim to any veneer of erudition—rock music. *MPB* marks the integration of the Brazilian younger generation into Western youth culture. However, apart from the general liberal tone questioning the values of the military regime, there is no consistent argument of Brazilian identity which could be synthesized in a manifesto, with the exception of the movement known as *Tropicalismo,* whose most important streams are to be found in cinema and music.

The tropicalist perspective emphasizes the absurdity of the juxtaposition, in a Third World nation such as Brazil, between a sudden, often superficial, alien modernity on the one hand, and on the other, cripplingly backward inherited cultural values; the consequent assemblage of heterogeneous and contradictory signs assumes in the *tropicalista* vision a sort of hyper-baroque unreality, from the overly ambitious Utopian social projection represented in the Brasília plan to sadistic and primitive acts of repressive violence at the hands of the security services. The eccentricity and the extraordinary but short-lived exuberance of tropical vegetation enriched the metaphorical load of the movement's title, as did the association with the steamy equatorial latitudes, and the background of Eurocentric eugenic and social Darwinian theories of the disintegration of Western rationalist intellectual capacity in the tropics. The radicalism of *Tropicalismo* was largely consequent to the conjunction of conflicting historical forces—in the Western world the hedonistic and countercultural youth liberation of the 1960s, and within Brazil the military dictatorship from 1964 on, with its neofascist radicalization of State authoritarianism.

In the manner of punk rock, the more radical *Tropicalistas* assumed a sort of negative aesthetics, depicting themselves as protagonists in an absurd dialectic of modernity and barbarism. This negative aesthetic was taken to the extreme by filmmakers from the socioindustrial wastelands of São Paulo. However the musical lead was taken in a more positive direction by Bahians, notable the composer-performers Caetano Veloso and Gilberto Gil. These two songwriters would both gradually emerge as significant intellectuals on the cutting edge of popular music. Initially their focus was on the adoption of rock innovations, in particular the aggressive electrification of instruments which to *Bossa Nova* traditionalists constituted an anathema—sheer musical vulgarity at the expense of graceful, lyrical tradition. (This openness to the Anglo-dominated world of youth culture was then unwittingly reinforced by the government's exiling the pair, who took up residence in the "swinging" London of the late 1960s.)

The *Tropicalista* dialectic articulated by the Bahians differed fundamentally from that in the south through its powerful Afrocentric tradition. The antithesis to the regime's account of Brazilian reality was not just industrial poverty, but an entire alternative ambiance. The Iberocentric authorities in Bahia had led a meandering campaign over the centuries against Afrocentric religion and thus Afro-Brazilian music and dance. Apart from the Afrocentric concentration in the Recôncavo, the inland of Bahia and its sister regions through the *Nordeste* contained a rich repertoire of traditional musics of various ethnically syncretic moldings, and social values which were also potentially contradictory to the agenda of the military regime. Veloso and Gil show a constant experimentation with the entire spectrum of popular music, from the traditional local varieties, to more recent carnaval genres such as Pernambuco's *frevo,* to *Bossa Nova* and the *MPB* of Rio and São Paulo, to the English-speaking pop music world with its black and white domains of rhythm 'n' blues and rock. Both composers, but particularly Veloso, established a fruitful dialogue with the avant-garde Concretist poets and intellectual theoreticians of the south lead by the *paulista* brothers Haroldo and Augusto de Campos. Veloso's work includes both experimental pieces which seek harmonic structures acting in counterpoint to the minimalist phrasal variations of Concretist lyrics, and also more musically conventional pieces which score lyrics derived from the classical poetic canon (an elegy by John Donne translated by the Campos brothers) with a contemporary pop musical sensibility.

However the single most important cultural and artistic resource for both has remained, or rather has increasingly become, the Afro-Brazilian tradition of Salvador, particularly in the wake of the vitalization of the local musical industry with the advent of the last twenty years of Africanization of the carnaval. This process has seen a maturation of the value of the Afro-Brazilian tradition to a typically postmodern integration and confusion of material, moral and aesthetic signifiers. The Afro-Brazilian community no longer perceives itself as behind the Euro-Brazilian; rather, on the one hand it affirms its own reality and its own appropriate hierarchies, and on the other demands correction of social inequities. For the artist, if there is any connection between social experience and artistic product, this means that the Afro-Brazilian tradition once cosidered by scholars as a relic from collective memory, becomes the Afro-Brazilian communal creative praxis, where new musical products become badges for social statements and possibly encourage political mobilization. The bulk of Afro-Brazilian musicians in the Recôncavo participate as social agents, whether directly through their lyrics, or indirectly through their opinions, or logistically through the preponderance of community organizations as sponsors and beneficiaries of performances.

Gilberto Gil, himself *preto* (black) rather than *moreno* (ambiguously brown), like Veloso, has taken a long-term leadership role in this process of integrating art and social activism. He revived a venerable carnaval group, the *afoxé,* Filhos de Gandhi, which was facing extinction. Originally set up by leftist members of the dockworkers' union and taking the name of a figure from the world stage of democratic conscientization, the group had an appropriate ideological pedigree and was at the time in desperate need of help. Gil has gone on to city politics as a councilman, just failing to win the mayoralty, and in recent years his international reputation has even occasioned his appointment as a sort of honest broker supervisor for United Nation funds assigned for city works. Veloso, who has always been more of a cultural free spirit, has nevertheless celebrated in many different songs particular aspects of the Bahian carnaval, and in the great majority of cases specifically Afro-Brazilian ones. Though residing in Rio, Veloso will always be found in Bahia at carnaval time, usually in the company of Gil, leaving the crowd to climb up on to a *trio elétrico* for an impromptu performance.

The original perspectives of Bahian *Tropicalismo* in the late sixties—intellectual, avant-garde, open to the cultural imperialism of the English-speaking world, informed by the Euro-Brazilian leftist fringe in the south of the country—seem to have virtually nothing in common with the communitarian *Africarnaval* movement which dates from the revolutionary creation in 1975 of the first, and most Afrocentric of *blocos afro,* Ilê Ayê. In fact, there is a clear continuity incarnated in the person of Gilberto Gil. Gil and Veloso have remained composers in the individualist tradition of the West, whereas the musical production for the Afro carnaval is fundamentally communitarian, occasionally throwing up talented individuals seeking a conventional show business career. However there is a central cultural reference for both of these polarized creative modes—the social experience and the aesthetic tradition of the Afro-Brazilian community of the Recôncavo.

For all the psychological discernment and poetic finesse of Veloso's portraits of Bahia, Salvador has acquired its role as an aesthetic center of gravity through the *bloco* composers, whose entire activity and focus is centered on that city. Many of the theme songs of Bahian carnaval music specifically evoke districts, streets or certain squares, and speak of particular experiences associated with those places. The unique euphoria of the Bahian carnaval itself arises not only from parochial loyalty but from its actual format—the most crowded and humanly dense of the Brazilian carnavals, and the most intense as a participatory experience.

In summary, then, there has been a growing awareness of Afro-Bahian identity, from the origins of Bahian *Tropicalismo,* which distinguished itself from its southern cousins by its sense of positive community identity, through to the sociopolitical agenda of the *blocos afro* which stylistically if not quantitatively dominate the contemporary carnaval. Fascinatingly, this has even been described as a sort of narcissism by visitors from Rio and São Paulo, who evidently forget that for many southerners the Brazilian frontier begins on the outskirts of these two metropolises. This suggests that at the local level a process parallel to that in Rio in the 1930s is occurring: the constitution of a hegemonic aesthetic identity. While much of Rio's cultural heritage was in fact derived from Bahian motifs, Bahia was for most of the century conceptually of the provinces—like the old south in the U.S., an acknowledged root but not a contender for cultural leadership.

Bahian music, long regarded as provincial, acquired a new potency during the 1980s. Composers such as Gil and Veloso were highly regarded, but their work, delivered periodically in conventional record albums, was normally recorded in and marketed from the south. The popular music which dominated local airwaves in the months preceding the carnaval was drawn from the large pool of compositions commissioned as theme songs by the numerous carnaval groups; this work was not disseminated outside Bahia and often not even outside the city of Salvador. With the acquisition of sophisticated recording studios, carnaval music grew to occupy a larger and larger portion of local airtime throughout the year; simultaneously some of the songs achieved success nationally, being assimilated in other states into the conventional pop market. This was abetted when Veloso included *bloco afro* carnaval songs in his albums. A pattern emerged whereby the most nationally successful items were songs by *blocos afro* rerecorded by the more instrumentally conventional and ethnically bleached groups who hitherto had worked for the non-Afro groups. This process culminated in the spectacular success of a particular singer, Daniela Mercury. As her material became more and more Afro-sounding, she even appropriated the cast and choreography of the *blocos afro* for her videos. At the national level she surpassed the market penetration of all other performers, probably helped in this by her distinctly Caucasian appearance. On the other hand, Olodum itself, by recording its own material with more conventional orchestration, has come to sell millions of copies of its own records around Brazil and internationally. The percussionists of Olodum recorded with, and were brought to New York's Central Park by Paul Simon, the rock world's doyen of the assimilation of "world music" into mainstream popular music. Overseas tours are now staged at regular intervals.

The compositions begin as chants taught to a crowd on a Tuesday or Sunday evening in the Pelourinho many months before carnaval; if they catch on they may be included in the cache of ten or twelve songs in the official repertoire for the year, and be recorded. At the time of their first exposure, however, they are showcased briefly in a vocal solo which then gives way to the motor of the festivity—the pounding percussion which is the real hallmark of the *bloco* and through which new rhythmic nuances are constantly added while new dances are invented in the crowd. In short, the creative process of Olodum presents an extraordinary conjuncture of, on the one hand, traditional communitarian, self-referential praxis, and on the other the modern, industrialized dissemination of pop music at the national level, and even of world music in the global village.

Gil and Veloso were the precursors of Bahian hyperaestheticization and self-referentiality; as intellectuals and composers their Bahian depictions in fact continue to surpass the subsequent generation in complexity, depth and the conventional values of Western art. At the same time, the direct integration of music and sociability, the ubiquitous Recôncavo thematics, the greater reliance on the local music and dance tradition, and finally the locating of the recording studios in Bahia make the work of the carnaval songwriters a more purely Bahian system of production and a more significant social phenomenon. Gil and Veloso are considered in the history of popular music in Brazil as the Bahian contingent in the national emergence of *Música Popular Brasileira*, and like most *MPB* artists of whatever provenance, their success brought them out of the provinces and on to Rio (though Gil eventually returned to Salvador).

The Bahian incursion on the national recording market has been matched, however, by other regional musics, which, though less conspicuously provincial than the Bahian carnival music, are nevertheless alien to the classic generation of *MPB* composers. In market terms, the most important genres which have emerged are types of rock which not only utilize electrified orchestration but also imitate non-Brazilian music. Young Brazilian performers have adopted as staples at least two streams of overseas rock, Latin romantic ballads in the Italian and Spanish style, and Anglo hard rock. In the meantime the consuming market has matured so that it has become financially feasible to bring not just the superstars of international rock but also cutting-edge alternative groups. However, the production and consumption of Anglo-style rock is restricted to the south, particularly the São Paulo area. Rio, in so many ways a cultural hybrid, with a substantial Euro-Brazilian lower middle class—the demographic core of the rock market—is also a significant market in this area, but the basic pattern by which São Paulo leads the rest of the country in the importation of mainstream Western trends has displayed a remarkable continuity; it is the same pattern as that which introduced and disseminated modernism in the early 1920s.

Record sales reveal a steady trend of approximation of the Brazilian market to the international market, so that a growing proportion of the market has been occupied either by foreign acts (generally American or English) or by Brazilian emulators of international sounds. The clear gap between the popular Brazilian *samba canção* of the 1940s and the international sounds imported at that time, such as Frank Sinatra, is a space which has subsequently become crowded with intermediary forms. This occurs both at the level of receiver and producer—in a Brazilian market consuming a greater variety of international sounds and being closer in its listening habits to other national audiences, and in the ability of Brazilian performers to participate in an international system of musical production based in the U.S. This reflects the sophistication and cosmopolitanism of that segment of the Brazilian population whose tastes are similar to those of young Europeans and Americans. However it also precipitates resentment against cultural imperialism. For many middle-class Brazilians, the seductive cosmopolitan kudos of a luxury European car is difficult to question, whereas thrashing guitars played by apparently demented youngsters are called into question.

On the other hand, it has proven virtually impossible for performers from a non-Anglophone culture to achieve significant penetration outside the domestic market. For whatever reasons, non-Anglophone artists can only confirm by inadequate imitation a neocolonial cultural structure.

The resentment of Americanization has in the last few years shown up in elitist disdain for a recently emerging genre of popular Brazilian music, known as *música sertaneja* (of the *sertão,* or rather, for the people from the *sertão,* often now living in urban areas). The style has ostensible roots in the rural Ibero-Brazilian tradition of pairs of male singers, but ultimately derives the greater part of its thematic, instrumental and stylistic repertoire from the world of U.S. country 'n' western. *Música sertaneja* achieved extraordinary market success, particularly amongst the modest population of workers displaced from their childhood homes in the *Nordeste* and Minas Gerais and eking out an existence in the outer industrial belt of São Paulo. But the genre has always been held in contempt by intellectuals and other artists, even those who themselves have developed their work in genres of foreign origin. *Música sertaneja,* dubbed by intellectual critics as *música breganeja*—a pun on the term *brega,* meaning vulgar in the extreme—is considered as harmonically and rhythmically mediocre and lacking rock's caché of innovative novelty and/or titillating rebellion; as an aesthetic travesty, it betrays the real *sertanejo* tradition of authentic, colorful folk music. Themes of tragedy and social resistance are common in this traditional music of a region marked by physical hardship, great class oppression, and resentment. *Música sertaneja* tends to reproduce the bland romantic themes of the more tepid streams of country 'n' western music, abandoning the motifs of specific local evocation common in traditional music of the *sertão* in favor of a vague space in the heart, somewhere between country and city, between north and south, between the aspiration toward the model nuclear family in an individual-oriented capitalist economy and the power of the extended family clan with a clear place of origin, between the endlessly flexible and redefinable modern consumer-producer and the cultural testimonial witness of archaic collective memory.

Bahian music has been the other major wedge driven in the last decade into the national music market; the two genres could not be more opposed in terms of their cultural pedigrees. To the intellectual, nationalist or leftist, who sees in an empty Coca-Cola bottle the sign of a dangerous cultural pollution, *música sertaneja* is emblematic of a process of alienation and loss of identity in a situation of cultural neocolonialism. Bahian music, on the other hand, is magnificently Anglo-eccentric. It is integrally connected with the national tradition of carnaval. But it is also informed aesthetically by the local Afrocentric religious and musical traditions and ideologically sustained in a rhetoric of empowerment proper to neo-Marxist theories of radical democracy. In short it distinguishes itself as eminently politically and ethnically correct.

São Paulo is the *de facto* capital of the two major musical currents of non-Brazilian provenance—rock and *música sertaneja*. These genres correspond roughly to distinct social strata: rock music is preferred by the urban lower middle class and *música sertaneja* by the disenfranchised immigrant worker population—the latter so numerous that São Paulo has become, paradoxically, the capital of the *sertão* though it is not located in this region. These workers live in the huge outer belt of shantytowns which are slowly being transformed into humble suburbs by the arduous application of bricks and mortar and the installation of utilities. With the southern dominance of the media and the substantial local infrastructure for performance, these genres have been integrated into the modern "culture industry" and successfully marketed. But neither of these foreign-derived genres is perceived as providing a legitimate artistic national representation. They perhaps represent the state of Brazilian culture as it really is, that is, heavily influenced by North Atlantic and, more recently, U.S. cultural models, and, apparently, increasingly compatible with the deep psychological patterns and values upon which these cultural models are predicated. It is a long way from what a cultural nationalist would propose as an appropriate model.

Shifting Aesthetic Fault Lines and Cultural Fortunes

Recasting the ethnic lasso. Essentialism and politics

Despite the general acclaim with which the Bahian carnaval renaissance has been recognized by progressive intellectuals, journalists, and other commentators, it would be an exaggeration to say that its flourishing is nationally representative. Such a representation—the subculture of a small part of a single *nordestino* state representing the whole—would be demographically unsound. Yet there are many factors militating for this as a possible eventuality. Contemporary carnaval culture has its roots in the traditions of Afro-Brazilians, a group which for the greater part of Brazilian history constituted the preponderant ethnicity. In this sense, the liberation motif of the Bahian carnaval has hegemonic historical roots, a situation very different from the corresponding "black is beautiful" theme in the U.S. which is directly pertinent to a much smaller portion of the population. Secondly, the marketing of Brazil to Brazilians as a racial democracy and to foreigners as a site of exotic but accessible negritude has emphasized this ethnic group as the recognized face or standardbearer of the national superethnicity. Brazil's elite may be rigorously Eurocentric, but the human icon used to draw foreign interest is the *mulata,* that is, the racially diluted African woman. Gilberto Freyre's thesis is a celebration of a Utopian racial triangle with a particular declaration of the genius of the Portuguese male for adaptability to the Tropics; nevertheless, the impact of his work for readers lies not so much in the championing of his own patriarchal caste as in the aesthetic rehabilitation of the African influence in Brazilian character, a position which magnificently rebuffed previous theories of a Brazilian cultural inferiority due to the climate and the dilution of European blood. His rewriting of Brazilian history is expressed in his most famous title, *Casa Grande e Senzala*. The official history, of the installation of state and church, represented essentially by two buildings—plantation mansion and church—is now recast as a felicitous cultural marriage between a lascivious Ariel and an ennobled Caliban, the European and the African, represented in the mutually dependent and interactive habitations of plantation mansion and slave hut. In popular wisdom, the great vehicles of national socialist cultural celebration, *carioca* carnaval, *samba* and soccer, are seen as different aspects of a common cultural grace, and are socially associated particularly with Afro-Brazilians. This perspective is clearly stated by Freyre in the following statement:

> The Brazilian style of football is like a dance. This must derive from the influence of Brazilians with African blood, or who are markedly African in their culture: they are the ones who tend to reduce everything to dance—work and play—a tendency which appears to be constantly more generalized in Brazil, instead of remaining merely the characteristic of an ethnic or regional group. (1971, 58[8])

Freyre also alerts us to the need to differentiate between different regional cultural modes:

> But it is only superficially that the carnaval dances appear equal across the whole of Brazil. In certain regions or areas, they are 'Dionysian' . . . in others they are 'Apollonian' or of an intermediary type. (1971, 63[9])

The Dionysian tendency is clearly most strongly manifested in Rio and Salvador, and the Apollonian in other Afro-Brazilian regional traditions such as that of Maranhão or even Freyre's own Pernambuco, and also, frequently, in non-Afro based Brazilian carnaval traditions. But the overlapping of these two most conspicuous regional Afro-Brazilian subcultures (*carioca* and Bahian) is not so much the result of common African ancestry developing parallelly in two locations, but the consequence of the fact that the

Afro-Brazilian subculture celebrated in Rio is largely derived from the Bahian (Recôncavo) tradition. As was seen in the case of Afro-Brazilian cults, where Bahian Candomblé is increasingly popular outside its traditional local sphere of influence, the Bahian subculture has gained some moral authority and a pedigree of authenticity for the many individuals seeking not just the preservation of existing traditions, but also a dynamic development of artistic and spiritual practices.

As with Hollywood and Carmen Miranda, such cultural appropriation by a more capitalized agency naturally involved creative adaptation. Rio's version of Afro-Bahian *alegria* focused on heightening the sheer spectacle and, consciously or unconsciously, extrapolating the ethnocultural roots into the ether of fantasy.

The sensually surreal *mulata* icon used to attract attention is a purely *carioca* creation. But changing tourist taste, which has tended to seek popular culture with the feel of authenticity, goes to Bahia as a source of roots. This is confirmed by the preference of hundreds of thousands of younger European tourists who make the often arduous trip to Bahia, twenty-eight hours by bus from Rio. The international pilgrimage is paralleled by southern Brazilian tourists. But there is reason to believe that the growing interest in the Bahian carnaval is more than just a passing vogue. Whether the everyday Bahian subculture is actually more authentic than the Rio subculture (or any other region's) is another question in itself. But what can be said is that in the respective carnaval dynamics of the two cities, the *carioca* event as it is presented to the public is essentially an apolitical, passive spectacle, whereas the Bahian event is politicized as a forum for nonmilitant but aesthetically radical dissent. Secondly, the Afro-Brazilian phenomenon of carnaval is far more pervasive in the popular culture of Bahia since it provides the context for local popular music and is also the major forum for social intercourse for much of the population, through the year round activities of the carnaval blocks. If traditional Afro-Bahian culture is the archaic, travestied source of much of what is associated with Rio and its mid-twentieth century hegemony, contemporary Afro-Bahian culture has assumed a vanguard position in popular culture—particularly in terms of what is palatable to progressive intellectuals as a legitimate national representation or icon.

The eastward shift in the aesthetic center of gravity, from an Amazon jungle more imagined than experienced, to the *sertão*, inhabited by a more real but still obscure *caboclo*, has finally moved to the sea and to the *mulato* population of the coast. With da Cunha, the nominal cultural protagonist of national identity changed from the noble savage of Indianist literature, with no basis in social reality, to a more socially authentic instance of the Brazilian of mestizo blood, the *sertanejo*. His archaic Iberian roots, exotic Amerindian features, and extraordinary adaptation to local conditions made him a worthy object of cultural appropriation and articulation by intellectuals. But also a safe object: as the inhabitant of vast stretches of the oldest settled areas of the interior, the *sertanejo* enjoyed that prestige of the old countryside's status as heartland and as somehow nationally authentic (a superstition paralleled in the United States, for example, by the notion that the Midwest is more American than other areas). Further, the *sertanejo* figure afforded a convenient tableau for national mythologies since the forms of social resistance which emerged there, from the social margins and against the elite, were not the same as those in the immediate social milieu of the intellectuals, who were generally based in Rio.

Freyre's validation of the Afro-Brazilian tradition addressed this disenfranchised stratum of the metropolitan population, the urban poor, who can be included in the umbrella term of *negro-mestiço*. However Freyre's nomination of this ethnic entity was socially anachronistic in that the cultural heritage identified was not that of contemporary urban Brazil but that of the rural plantation society of earlier centuries. Nor can the Vargas regime's championing of an urban cultural identity in which the *negro-mestiço* played a major role be seen as a genuine embrace of an ethnocultural other, since this cultural articulation was a deliberate construct, manipulated with the primary concern of dissipating tension and resentment through distraction and celebration in a classic example of unite-and-conquer. The development of the Rio carnaval as a euphoric but distinctly nonspontaneous spectacle of racial democracy was the consequence of the political manipulation of the carnaval mechanism by groups other than the carnaval associations themselves; such agents coldly assess the carnaval in terms of its implicit ideological discourse and its subconscious impact on the domestic audience. This is a distinct process from both the moral outrage of the Church, which perceives carnaval icons as directly sinful, and the social message promoted by the carnaval group in its banners and rhetoric. The State's comprehension of carnaval as propaganda, and its intervention in carnaval organizations, like the microscope which interferes with its object of study, were the preconditions of its massive material expansion and the gravitation toward mere spectacle. This situation establishes a distance between the carnaval ideal of benign contentment and the dynamic evolution of social needs. As a result, while the Vargas years brought the preponderant urban *negro-mestiço* masses to the fore of cultural identification for the first time, a safe distance was maintained from real recognition of social needs. Both Freyre and the ideologues of the Vargas regime balanced celebration of a cultural tradition with denial of social oppression. But Freyre emphasized the preeminence of the past, while the Vargas regime attempted with some success to orient popular culture into the new work ethic of the 1930s and a futuristic vision of State expansion.

It is crucial therefore to take into account the social strategies behind the adoption of ethnic types as cultural icons; and the same suspicion must accompany the characterization of carnaval. The *carioca* carnaval emerged as an optimistic modernist masterpiece, which subsumed in euphoric celebration social concerns which it was assumed would steadily dissipate. The Bahian carnaval, in the relative freedom of its provincial isolation, was never converted into a spectacle or an example, or co-opted in the manner of Rio. It remained essentially a participatory event dedicated to pleasure, its ideological content simply the affirmation of regional identity in that the music was largely local and original. Ethnicity and counterhegemonic cultural values were also affirmed, facilitating the eventual appropriation of the carnaval by militants mixing an Afrocentric aesthetic with political agitation. The Bahian carnaval closes the gap between aesthetic and economic dissent; the aesthetic protagonist is for the first time a possible civil subject rather than an abstraction. But the Afro-Bahian carnaval in part owes its potential role in the question of national identity to Freyre's and subsequently to the Vargas regime's emphasis on urban Afro-Brazilian culture. The nomination of "musicarnaval" as the dominant cultural expressive form in Brazil has profound consequences for the ethnic superego of *Homo brasiliensis*.

Evolving representative models in historical perspective

In the postcolonial period the symbolic national model was the noble savage derived from nineteenth-century romantic literature. The European romantic's search for roots was motivated by modernization itself and the alienation it occasioned; in the Americas the problem was rather the lack of local roots and mythologies. A diachronic Utopia was impossible in a historically vacuous landscape; instead a synchronic Utopia was posited in the vast and mysterious expanses of unsettled land inhabited by culturally incomprehensible beings. The romantic image of the Indian of the wilds lacked any sort of social precision; it functioned as a semiotic bridge between a bourgeois society keeping abreast of exotic climes and the Amerindians who guaranteed a human presence in the outlands. The appropriation of the Amerindian as an aesthetic and ideological vehicle was dependent on his distance from the social reality of the artist. In the U.S. this early-nineteenth-century exploitation of the Indian gave way to the contradictory imperative of manifest destiny, whose realization precipitated the ugly spectacle of the social degeneration of the Amerindian populations. They remained an icon of decay until their recreation, a couple of generations later, in Hollywood—a nonthreatening enemy, fascinating but savage, a rehabilitation again dependent on their virtual absence as a social reality.

The shift in focus by da Cunha from the incomprehensible Amazon to the barbaric but materially and spiritually analyzable *sertão* reflects a disciplinary evolution from mythical to social object. But this subject/object of study retained a subsocial status: da Cunha was dealing with exotic barbarians, and the crowning humanism of his still largely literary creation was the surprising demonstration that such creatures were actually human. Freyre's Afro-Brazilian subject is the first to bear any relation to a social entity possibly familiar to urban populations with memories of life on the land, but the model is retrogressive. The racial democracy of the Vargas regime substituted the urban Afro-Brazilian (or rather *negro-mestiço*) for his *nordestino* plantation forebear, but in its denial of the fundamental agency of social resentment it posited a social model which is at best apolitical and at worse a conspiratorial illusion of political expedience in a context of gross injustice. The Afrocentric activism of the Bahian carnaval represents both a determination to engage in a political agenda founded on resentment or social awareness, and an attempt to integrate a fuller spectrum of Afro-Brazilian experience than that found in the sexual and social display of the *carioca* spectacle.

The modernist literary models, notably Oswald de Andrade's Amerindian anthropofagist (cannibal) and Mário de Andrade's Amazonian Macunaíma, are of little relevance to the new agenda. Oswaldo's iconoclastic figure was characterized by his creative desecration of the hierarchical infrastructure of the classical artistic tradition. Despite the innovative sense of aesthetic chic assigned to the Brazilian ethnic other, Oswald was not ethnically progressive in terms of a real social community; at best he attempted to assign an aesthetic meaning and purpose informed by the European avant-garde to the disparate energies produced by ethnic complexity and racial miscegenation in the eclectic Brazilian topography. Though it is probable that Oswald would have lauded the modern Bahian carnaval had he seen it, there is no clear connection between his art and this form of ethnic activism. As for Mário, it has been observed already that his *herói sem nenhum caráter* was an indirect but earnest acknowledgment of the difficulty of establishing a nationally representative cultural persona. Again, though Mário's ethnomusicological encyclopaedism was a crucial first step in the integration of the Afro-Brazilian tradition into the mainstream, and a form of cultural praxis contiguous to the work of the recent articulators of Bahian musicarnaval styles and techniques, there is a refusal in his overall stance to confuse politics and art. The post-1960s context, in which aesthetic codes tend to interweave discrete modes of expression such as fashion, music and politics, is simply not the same as the one from which the modernist energies of the 1920s and 1930s spring. Both Oswald's and Mário's heroes are ostensibly derived from the outland of the Amazon; both writers, armed with the critical faculties of their Eurocentric classical education and avant-garde agenda, set themselves up as interpreters of cultural Brazil. Mário de Andrade also probed the psyche of his native city of São Paulo in later work, but this was a retreat from the Icarian ambition in *Macunaíma* of synthesizing the national cultural expanse in a single protagonist. São Paulo was never destined to be a national symbol of anything other than the progressive modernization of the nation towards equity with other global industrial giants.

In terms of the sociological images which have already been discussed, the first consequence is the eclipsing of da Cunha's *sertanejo* Ibero-Amerindian figure as the substratum of national identity, since the urban musicarnaval and its attendant sociability are absent from this rural milieu. The new archetypal Brazilian is *café com leite'* (milk coffee, i.e., *mulato* rather than Ibero-Amerindian [or Afro-Amerindian]). This development is oriented by Freyre, as is the insistence on the relative importance of the *litoral* area as opposed to the heartlands, whether of jungle or barren *sertão*—of these two, the former is more appropriate, since for Freyre and later generations Brazil and Latin America in general as a trope has become quintessentially tropical rather than dry or cold. But the present century has brought to the stereotype a contradictory, urban figure, thriving in the social complexity and ambiguity of the city. The city's abundance affords the possibility of escape from onerous labor and traditional moral codes; it is also the site of carnaval and social euphoria. In short, the new *Homo brasiliensis* of the mid-century in Rio is Epicurean rather than stoic, musico-lyrical rather than industrious, an optimist rather than a perceiver of tragedy, and socially reconciled rather than resentful of difference.

The focus on Rio's musicarnaval inevitably emphasizes the predominance of the Afro-Brazilian influence in music, thus foregrounding this element of the racial triangle, so that darker-skinned *cariocas* whose forefathers immigrated from the Bahian Recôncavo acquire more typicality than do *caboclo* immigrants from the *sertão* to greater São Paulo. The predominant personae in this identity play are the *malandro* man and the *mulata* woman, the former marked by his amoral attitude and his generally opportunistic but nonmaterialistic outlook, the latter by physical sensuality and racial specificity.

5
Third World Culture on the Market

BRAZIL IS CONSIDERED A THIRD WORLD COUNTRY. THAT TERM has been contested as an absurd generalization, given the heterogeneity of societies grouped under that single rubrique. Brazilian popular culture and literature afford powerful evidence against the generalization, both in terms of their mutual differences and their internal complexities.

Brazil is an enormous state, containing within it a middle-class nation the size of an average Western state, and a much larger mass of disenfranchised persons. That this larger mass is conspicuous to the Western eye is morally appropriate, given the injustice to which it is subjected. In terms of aesthetic issues the sheer vitality of Brazilian popular culture and its alterity from the North Atlantic perspective provoke a different reaction. Yet they are connected, for the aesthetic interest and prestige of Brazilian popular culture is a powerful arm in the task of raising consciousness about bringing justice to its citizens. Their inalienable humanity is manifest in their cultural expression and art.

Separately, an impressive amount of erudite literature has been produced in Brazil, usually from a bourgeois perspective which has everything in common with the realities driving North Atlantic literary currents. The quality of this literature warrants international attention. And yet it has proved unable to sustain an audience. Various circumstantial factors could be mustered to explain this; however, the pattern, or process, is not fortuitous but systematic, and there is no reason to think this will change.

The grand Latin American literary adventure of the century, measured by the size of its international audience, has been the achievement of Spanish American writers evoking popular reality. In Brazil, Jorge Amado has undertaken a comparable project to great effect. But there is no reason why the Latin American writer should restrict him or herself to sociological explications and popular evocations. Given that the Spanish American writers who have enjoyed the success have generally been liberal white bourgeois males writing in Europe, the extent to which they can be said to have been talking about everyday life is problematic. These writers have served as a vital link between a North Atlantic audience and a popular Latin American reality, negotiating between these psychological poles, and astutely balancing their knowledge of local reality and the interest of European audiences in an exotic object. In this circumstance the evocation of that object becomes marketologically interesting and politically ambivalent, regardless of the espoused ideologies of the writers in nonfiction formats. It is in this sense that we await the ideological deconstruction of the *Boom*.

Their success is due to talent, but also to circumstance. It would be naïve to conclude that genius will impose itself on the general consciousness. On the contrary, the differing evolution of Brazilian literature suggests a comparable flourishing, but one destined to obscurity precisely because the greatest Brazilian works declined to think in terms of the international market. The market values the Latin American theme of exotic national representation via a larger-than-life protagonist—in contrast to the North Atlantic denunciation of spiritually emptiness and the emergence of an anti-hero who is not the champion of villainy but of mediocrity.

Brazilian literature is not insensible to metropolitan literary models. Rather, its leading writers have not manipulated the dominant conspicuous axis relating the normative *métropole* (Europe) and the extraordinary *Ameripole* (the hemispheric sense is not inappropriate, since one could well argue that North American anti-classicism is another form of larger-than-life eccentricity, an alternate, materialist Baroque spirit). The paradox is that it is precisely the affinity of Brazilian to European writers that precluded an international audience. To be successful internationally, Latin American writers, regardless of their talents, needed to respond not so much to North Atlantic creators as to North Atlantic consumers. Of course, all writers are subject to the vagaries of public taste. But the Brazilian instance suggests a consistent pattern of restricted channels of access from Latin America to the metropolitan market. The disturbing consideration here is that this appears to confirm in the cultural market the most pessimistic historical visions of economic dependency, that is, that rather than gradually narrowing the gap between the developed and developing worlds, countries on the periphery of the trade system are destined to continue to only provide raw material which is processed and sophisticated at the center, and to have their role restricted to this identity. This book is not so ambitious as to respond to that suggestion. The concern is simply, given the impressive dissemination of a certain popular Brazil, to trace the reception of Brazilian literature, and to explore how, contrary to what one might optimistically anticipate, the popular profile worked against rather than for the external recognition of a remarkable literary heritage.

Brazilian Modernism Versus Socioanthropological Populism

A condensed version of socioanthropological analyses of Brazilian cultural identity would read as follows: the matrix of Brazilian musi-culturalism can be located in the Afro-Iberian popular culture of the Recôncavo da Bahia, reinvented in the *carioca* carnaval.

This however is an intellectual construction, highly subjective from several points of view. Demographically, the subculture of the Recôncavo is not representative of the rest of the *Nordeste,* or even of most of the state of Bahia. Even within the logic of the humanist anthropological tradition, the privileged centrality of this subculture is not a constant. Da Cunha's Brazilian was not mulatto or *cafuz,* but the *caboclo* of the *sertão,* derived from neither the plantation zone nor the coastal capital, of Amerindian rather than African ethnicity, stoic rather than Epicurean or Dionysian, and a religious millenarian fanatic rather than an opportunistic syncretist. However, the international obscurity of the *sertanejo* is not just the product of demographic inconsequence. In sociographic terms the single most salient and problematic pattern of Brazilian social development in the twentieth century has been the cycle of drought in the *sertão* and the movement to urban centers, above all São Paulo. One cultural flower of this traumatic migration has been the musical revolution known as *música sertaneja;* though selling more records domestically than *axé music,* this music is as internationally obscure as its audience. The *sertanejo* remains culturally irrelevant to the articulation of a Brazilian persona.

A more plausible alternative was posited from the 1920s on by Gilberto Freyre, still the single most influential Brazilian anthropologist. Freyre's privileged zone was not the Recôncavo but a more diffuse but still restrictive zone within the *Nordeste*—the vast coastal strips supporting the slave-based plantation economy. Freyre's own city, Recife, in the state of Pernambuco, came to supplant Salvador as commercial capital during the more productive period of plantation economy. Both the Recôncavo and Salvador fell within Freyre's key zone, but Salvador, the longest-standing national capital, developed a cosmopolitan sophistication, sensuality and liberality not dissimilar from the future Rio de Janeiro.[1] Although Rio has in its turn become the privileged cultural space of socioanthropologists such as da Matta, outside the academic cultures of Rio and São Paulo Salvador remains the real fulcrum of these evolving articulations, as was demonstrated in the 1960s when a pivotal role was played by Bahian artists, especially Caetano Veloso and Glauber Rocha, in the *Tropicalismo* movement, and since the late 1970s by the prestige of Salvador's carnaval.

Despite a minimal infrastructure in Bahia, some "organic intellectuals" have begun to articulate essentialist apologias of Bahian cultural identity. In the past, recognition of Bahia as the Brazilian ur-source was restricted to references in recorded *samba carioca* songs, the ritual paraphernalia of the Rio carnaval, and the occasional gesture such as Vinícius de Moraes's extended stay in the former fishing village of Itapoan, the Bahian locale privileged by the singer Dorival Caymmi. Vinícius's oft-quoted claim to be the blackest white man in Brazil suggests that the Bahian milieu is perceived as more authentically Afro-Brazilian. As Florence from the 1200s through the 1500s was both the cradle to Italian national identity and a catalytic locus of creative achievement to a degree disproportionate to its fluctuating political powers, so Salvador and Bahian culture have revealed a surprising vitality and an odd juvenescence. Interestingly, much of the repertoire of characteristic icons and institutions emerged during the 1800s, a period of political and economic decline. Afro-Bahian culture—often in Euro-Brazilian articulations—is not merely symptomatic of the residues of collective memory. Rather it suggests a creatively regenerative and reconstituting community with a capacity far beyond its material resources for interaction with and assimilation of certain postmodern currents.

At the international level, however, the vastness of the Brazilian state and the richness of its culture do not compensate for Latin America's marginal position in relation to the world political order. The telling image remains that of Carmen Miranda, a fascinating case study in cultural appropriation, whose fruity Hollywood headgear was an imaginative, philistine extrapolation from the food and religious offerings borne on the heads of Salvador's *baianas*. Her Brazilian signature tune, "O Que é Que a Baiana Tem," was written by Caymmi in homage to the Afro-Brazilian *baianas* who prepare and sell food in the streets of Bahia and participate in religious ceremonies such as the march to the Bonfim cathedral in Salvador. In Rio it became the theme song of the Portuguese-born brunette, star of the new nationally distributed Rio-based recording industry.

Carmen was eventually discovered by Hollywood scouts. Miranda's appropriation of the *baiana* identity provides an unusually candid illustration of the market mechanism between margin and center, at both the domestic level (appropriation of the soteropolitan motif in Rio) and the international (North American appropriation of the "Brazilian" product found in Rio). But the gap in skin color between Miranda herself and the theoretical persona she adopted is evidence of the pro-white socioaesthetic prejudice within the recording industry in Brazil. Though less disturbing, Miranda's *baiana* parallels Al Jolson's minstrel in the curious logic of racial hierarchies: it is not the objectification which produces resentment so much as the perceived violation of subject status, which is contingent upon the social affirmation of one's own identity. Where affirmation is minimal, there can be no protest of violation; thus Al Jolson is profoundly offensive to African-Americans (whose subjectivity is more assertive than that of Afro-Brazilians), whereas Carmen Miranda is a nonproblematic source of national pride for Brazilians, including Afro-Bahians. The Carmen Miranda syndrome may be defined as the ensemble of cultural appropriations from Afro-Bahian popular culture to the State-sponsored and internationally pandered Rio carnaval version of the same, with the presence of the patriarchal State suggesting a subliminal link to the real ethnopolitical cultural order in Brazil, of which the Eurocentric literary tradition, unlike carnaval, is a direct reflection and not a temporary inversion.

The ascendant focus of ethnic socioanthropology is mulatto-centric, i.e., stressing white-black miscegenation, rather than Afrocentric. Gilberto Freyre posits the term "homem luso-tropical" and stresses the assimilation of the African cultural heritage into a white-dominated mainstream; similarly, the work of Da Matta perceives the *carioca* carnaval not in terms of the unusually conspicuous participation of blacks in the ritual performances but as an integrated social phenomenon reflective of Brazilian society as a whole. Even in the more militantly Afrocentric context of the Bahian carnaval, the ethnoaesthetic radicalism of a group like Ilê Ayê, which in the past excluded whites, is offset not only by the substantial participation of white *blocos,* but also, within the *afro-bloco* fold, by socially militant groups such as Olodum, who have accepted an ever-increasing participation by Europeans and non-black Brazilians. The increasingly Afrocentric orientation of the minority sector of the Bahian carnaval which is most conspicuous aesthetically and psychologically is paralleled in the development of religious cults. Contrary to the anticipations of rationalist sociologists, Candomblé has emerged with a greater robustness based on having a more authentic pedigree than other cults with greater syncretic balance, such as Umbanda. There is no clear correlation, however, to the separatist ethnic mobilization of North America, nor any institutional affirmation of black separatism in government policy or major nongovernmental organizations (equivalents to the NAACP, Nation of Islam, etc.). The argument of racial democracy remains entrenched, so it is difficult to maintain discourses of cultural separatism of either an Afro-or a Eurocentric nature.

Brazilian modernism marks out a different ethnographic space from that of populist socioanthropology. The literary tradition, particularly in the third generation of *Modernismo,* is characterized by an abnegation of the theme of Brazilian ethnicity per se. Of course, it could be argued that in dispelling nationalist essentialism from its agenda and cultivating aesthetic form with implicit deference to the grand European tradition, this generation was by default thoroughly Eurocentric. The greatness and originality of the literary opus, however, suggests a fulfillment unattainable within the bounds of pastiche or adulation, so that the work of Guimarães Rosa, Clarice Lispector, or Carlos Drummond de Andrade must be taken as a critical assimilation of the Western heritage. This work is, in any case, reinserted into Brazilian contexts. None of these writers set their material anywhere but Brazil, and Rosa's evocation of rural Minas Gerais is at the most obvious level radically regional, while Drummond's evocation of his own *mineiro* origins is set against his adult absorption in metropolitan Rio. But the earlier generations of *Modernismo,* while nationalist and/or essentialist, also present a very different ethnic focus to that of Freyre, Da Matta, and Bahian scholars such as Antonio Risério, for whom the Recôncavo da Bahia is a fulcrum.[2] Inaugural *Modernismo* celebrated the dynamic twentieth-century spirit of São Paulo, but also appropriated the imaginative space of provincial Brazil, focusing on the exotic motif of the Amerindian.

The second generation of *Modernismo,* dominated by the social realists of the *Nordeste,* tended to focus on the *sertão* and bear a conscious or unconscious prejudice in favor of the *interior* as opposed to the coast (a prejudice expressed sociolinguistically, incidentally, in the slightly pejorative inference of the term *brejeiro*), as for example in the work of Graciliano Ramos or Raquel de Queirós. The dominant *sertanejo* themes and motifs in the *nordestino* novelists are drought, peasant life, rural outlaws, and intense faith.

Apart from the *sertão*, the main economic and cultural reference was that of the sugar plantation. Lins do Rego, contemporary with the *nordestino* social novelists but not directly identifiable with them, requires separate attention. His early *ciclo do açucar* work (*Menino do Engenho, Doidinho, Bangüê*) is in many ways the perfect literary complement to Freyre's celebration of the legacy of the plantation system, particularly in the evocation of a sensuous rapport between white master and black *mucama*, despite the novelist's rather superstitious Catholic moral scruples. His later work, however, particularly *Fogo Morto*, presents a significant shift to economically autonomous individuals, exposed to the harsh realities of shifting professional and political fortunes. The geographical focus moves from the plantation to the marginal zones between the tropical *litoral* and the harsher *agreste*. In this can be sensed the influence of the tougher Darwinian psychology of the social novelists. Almeida's seminal novel of social description and critique, *A Bagaceira* (1928), is also set in the sugar cane country, but against Freyre's unproblematic celebration of the cultural font, Almeida, a civil servant and politician, focuses on material poverty and the pressures caused by drought. Almeida concentrates even more specifically on the cultural margin, examining the tension between the *retirantes* (drought-fleers) of the *sertão* and the traditional plantation inhabitants.

The emphasis on the movement of populations rather than their roots was central to the *nordestino* novel of the 1930s, whose consideration of problems in the local political economy rather than precious elements of the cultural legacy is implicitly anti-essentialist; it observes unresolved problems and calls for pragmatic changes which might only be found in external models.

Going back to the first, aggressively nationalistic generation of *Modernismo*, the political antagonism of Oswald de Andrade and the *Verde-Amarelo* (and *Anta*) movement reveals the superficiality of the *Semana* despite its magnificent iconoclastic energy. The *Semana* did constitute a revolution—the implosion of a nineteenth-century socioaesthetic order and the liberation of dynamic creative forces—but not a new postrevolutionary order. The *Antropofagia/Verde-Amarelo* conflict was essentially a domestically imperialist, exoticist foray, a conquest by São Paulo intellectuals of the psycho-cultural frontiers of an eclectically archaic nation. This is a something of an artistic *conquista*, a cultural anthropophagy of the masses by the elite, in which the class condescension was colored by issues of race. In a period of civil stress and federalist violence, the first generation *Modernismo* was thus more politically volatile than culturally constructive. The superficial assimilation of domestic but alien cultural practices was the stuff of flamboyant rhetoric, lacking both cultural specificity and the quasi-religious aspect of genuine myths of national cultural identity. Massaud Moisés observes in relation to various conflicting movements within Paulista modernism:

> They were, in short, against the idols of the era, without actually taking into account whether in either case they had created a work compatible with the intended Brazilianization. Consequently their nationalism was essentially aesthetic, even if titles such as Pau Brasil, Verdeamarelo, Terra Roxa, Leite Criôlo, might suggest the contrary; one merely has to read the works and manifestos written during this decade to verify this . . . Aristocrats, they developed a carnavalesque notion of Brazil, and were generally touched by a Macunaíma-like spirit. (1989, 31)

Moisés goes on to quote Mário de Andrade:

> The need for authentic, down-to-earth roots, cried out in doctrines and manifestos, was really nothing more than an accomodating conformism. . . . [We lived] in the greatest intellectual orgy the country has every known. . . . This whole destructive period of the movement was for us a time for partying, for the immoderate cultivation of pleasure. (1989, 33)[3]

In this sense the exoticist essentialism of early *Modernismo* cannot be compared to the euphoric anthropology of the socioanthropological current. Mário de Andrade's revisionist vocation—in the last ten or fifteen years of his life (through to 1945) he was an active critic of *Modernismo*—must be seen as an admirable effort to acknowledge, analyze, and perhaps redress the intellectual fallacies and artistic weaknesses of a movement which subsequently became canonical, with Mário the "pope" of *Modernismo*.

Several more subtle characteristics of *Modernismo* show up in this comparison with populist socioanthropology. The growing sense of Catholic devotion in Mário de Andrade, suggested in the above reference to the "immoderate cult of pleasure" is indicative of the ultimate character of *Modernismo*. The hedonistic spirit of the revolution—Manuel Bandeira's naïve enthusiasm for jazz, Oswald de Andrade's Dionysian or Nietzschean Antropofagia, the compulsive hedonism of Mário's own Macunaíma—was ultimately not sustained in the development of the mature works of either the second or the third generations. Once again the case of Mário is particularly revealing, for even within *Macunaíma* are sown the seeds of the futility of hedonism; the protagonist's compulsion is debilitating, and militates against the firm establishment of identity (*Macunaíma, o herói sem nenhum caráter*).

In the second generation, Graciliano Ramos's searing images of the *sertão* as hell-on-earth, and the evocations by various authors of drought, had little place for the luxury of pleasure. Further, along with mysticism, the *nordestino* writers focused more on stoic Catholic devotion and sheer endurance than on the moral tolerance and euphoric celebration of syncretic religions. To the extent that these writers were interested in social reform, the Catholic Church was evidently part of the real power structure and Catholic faith more pertinent to their social critique. But their lack of interest in the Recôncavo, the one region where it might be argued that Catholicism is a less permeating institutional presence than Candomblé, works against both syncretism and Afro-centrism. The social reforms urged by the second generation reveal a top-down perspective onto a Eurocentric State, except that for the first time the classes at the bottom of the social hierarchy are recognized as legitimately human; thus they dispense with the first generation's claim to invert the social hierarchy, an oddly narcissistic maneuver which was essentially an aesthetic gesture rather than a social intervention.

The third generation appears, by and large, unencumbered by either the puerile bravado of an affected amorality or, on the contrary, the psychological substrata of moral guilt and/or social responsibility.

Jorge Amado: Compatibility of His Project and the Emerging Popular Cultural Ideology

Jorge Amado emerges as the constant exception within *Modernismo,* whether we consider his regionalism, his religious outlook, his rapport with the sociopolitical hierarchy, or the question of essentialism and its relation to the socioanthropological tradition.

He is the one major writer for whom the Recôncavo constitutes the central theater of action. Nevertheless, even Amado began with the earth (in the *ciclo do cacau*) and later returned to it (*Terras do Sem Fim, Gabriela*) in his work on the cacao region of southern Bahia. In *Gabriela,* his masterpiece and a work whose deepest themes is a progressive vision of Brazil, Amado not only chooses to locate the story outside the Recôncavo but makes his heroine a *retirante* (one who flees drought) from the north. She is actually *sertaneja* in origin, and possibly from the distant lands at the border of the *Nordeste* and the *Norte*. But Amado's increasing focus on Salvador in most of the great works of the 1960s (*Pastores da Noite, Dona Flor,* above all *Tenda dos Milagres*), his insistent residence there, and his status as an Obá of Candomblé, indicate a move away from his literary roots as one of the *nordestino* novelists, towards a realization of Afrocentric empathy and soteropolitan loyalty. The fundamental difference lies not in his Leftist political stance, paralleled by Graciliano Ramos and others, but in the opposition of his Dionysian paganism to Catholic piety, the Epicurean disinclination to stoicism, the preference for sensuous romanticism rather than deprivation or fanaticism. It is in this sense that Amado finds his cultural antidote in the port of Salvador, and reveals his distance from the dominant themes of the *nordestino* novelists.

Amado also distances himself from the inauthentic, objectifying celebration of exotic voluptuousness of early *Modernismo* (the *paulistano* accounts of lascivious indigenes) which tends toward fetishism. Amado's sympathy for an Africanized Recôncavo puts him in line with the nonliterary anthropological discourse initiated by Freyre. But his privileging of the *boa terra* de-emphasizes the central demographic fact of the twentieth century—migration from the *Nordeste* to São Paulo (Amado's sole work pertaining to this context, *Seara Vermelha,* is far from his best work).

Amado's intellectual trajectory proceeds from a long battle with orthodox Marxism through to the mature flourishing of the Bahian *Comédie humaine* in which the proletarian heroics are subsumed within the sovereign cultural subject of the people. The domination of Leftist orthodoxy is strongest in the early part of the *ciclo de cacau* (*Cacau, Suor* and, separately, *Terras do Sem Fim* and *São Jorge dos Ilhéus,* of 1933–34 and 1943–44 respectively) and then in the monumental and relatively obscure trilogy of the mid-1950s, *Os Subterrâneos de Liberdade.* The continuity of this cyclical oscillation toward and away from orthodoxy is revealing of how seriously Amado took his charge as a Marxist intellectual. The preface to *Cacau* claims that the novel contains "um mínimo de literatura" and asks, "Será um romance proletário?" The interrogative note is interesting, precisely because Amado ultimately found fulfillment as a champion of the people rather than of political theory, in a highly literary style imbued with romantic indulgence, the metaliterary, and the appeal to the melodramatic sensibility. As for his role as a Party member and winner of the Stalin Prize, he would eventually come to terms with its regrettable influences:

> At certain times I accepted and repeated concepts, rules and theses which were not my own; I saw things through other peoples' eyes.... Mightn't it be the case that ideologies are the blight of our times?... I dream of a revolution without ideology.... We have no greater and more inalienable right than the right to dream, the only one that no dictator can reduce or exterminate. (1981, 107–8)

Although Amado's work of the 1970s strays from the Bahian milieu to the greater Nordeste (*Tereza Batista, Tieta do Agreste*), his greatest works, interspersed throughout his long career, are those which center on two domains: the southern Bahian cacao-growing region of his childhood, and the Salvador of his late teens and adult years—*Terras do Sem Fim, Gabriela Jubiabá, Os Pastores da Noite, Dona Flor e Seus Dois Maridos, Tenda dos Milagres*. Amado's treatment of these locales is highly specific. The places and milieus evoked, though idealized and stylized, are nevertheless transparently identifiable for the local citizenry—particularly those whose practices and tastes correspond to the sympathies of Amado. In this sense a totemic quality is ascribed to certain real places which exist in the literature as motifs: in Salvador, the Pelourinho, the Mercado Modelo, and the fishermen's ramp at its side. The same applies to certain individuals immortalized in Amado's *méthode à clés*. These persons are notorious in the folkloric fabric of Salvador which is nothing less than an informal alternative society to that of the local white elite, itself the intersection between power structures received from the era of slavery and the more recent south-dominated tentacles of the modern Brazilian State. Amado's fiction similarly ascribes to the often Afrocentric cultural practices of the popular soteropolitan classes both a sanctity which rejects the previously hegemonic religious order (as in the treatment of Candomblé) and an indubitable validity—no one has grasped as early and as well as Amado the profundity of the notion of carnaval as resistance. Simply and powerfully, Salvador affords Amado a locus of cultural faith to which political resistance will always be consequent. His work is most persuasive when his faith—or his cynicism—coincides with that of the people, that is, when he identifies with his protagonists. *Jubiabá* remains a fascinating text in its tensions between the discordant rhetorics of politics and culture; the title is a tribute to the old *candomblereiro* at the expense of the protagonist, but at the end of the work the former cannot grasp the salvational significance of the strike, discovered as a cause by the protagonist, and exposed rather clumsily by the narrator. Jubiabá is inconsequential to the intrigue of the novel, but his importance is in his place in the totemic aspect of the Recôncavo, already budding subliminally in the early Amado despite the conscious adherence to political orthodoxy. Places, persons and practices share this quasi-religious halo throughout his work, going against the utilitarian *nordestino* realism of the 1930s where characters were merely representative types. Amado's more complex sense of character is particularly evident in his treatment of figures like the cocoa barons, who according to Amado's own mythology should appear as hollow villains. In fact he often fleshes out these characters with idiosyncratic discourse and dramatic stature. He gives vent to his own lyrical and romantic sentimentality, indulging his love of the literariness of literature while still aiming at a popular readership.

In this way Amado gradually united his various intuitions. His empathy with Afrocentric culture grew as his relation to Marxist orthodoxy diminished—a development which in the end made far better sense of his sentimentalism, in which material want is gloriously deferred through spiritual presence and cultural sustenance. Similarly, Amado's love of popular literature and a literariness which, though self-conscious was not problematically so (compare Boccaccio, Fielding, or Sterne), were more easily contained in this vision than in his earlier attempt at "um mínimo de literatura."

It would be inappropriate however to classify Amado's work as Afrophilia, for his sympathies are with the poor (in Salvador predominantly *negro-mestiços,* for example, the ethnically diverse street urchins he depicts in *Capitães da Areia*). His ideology of miscegenation perceived racial mixing as a means of diluting the sense of racism, and of distilling a new type combining various attributes; his dismissal of the project of a purely African Candomblé (as opposed to a syncretist integration of Catholic and Amerindian elements) is unequivocal in its insistence on miscegenation as a peculiarly felicitous circumstance benefiting and befitting Brazil.

Unlike Freyre, Amado does not emphasize the white man as the assimilator of cultural diversity. The moral in *Gabriela* is rather that the outsider, in this case an Arab, may be admitted to Brazilian society because of its tolerant and assimilative character. His portrait of life in Salvador and southern Bahia tends, nevertheless, to present whites as central players in the *Comédie,* because until recently the nonwhite population was marginalized even from Bohemian life, including domains such as popular music, which draws very directly on Afro-Brazilian sources. Even within Candomblé whites have played a prominent role, notably as scholars, as patrons of a *terreiro* or as high-level clients, but not infrequently also as neophytes. Amado's archetypal carnaval carouser, Vadinho in *Dona Flor,* is blond, but those who enjoy carnaval are inevitably brothers-in-arms to the black population. This bears on a crucial point in Amado's world view: alienation is not to be defined in either raciological or class terms, and the individual is not determined by his or her position in the socioeconomic structure. Amado revolts intellectually and emotionally against the Marxist or Skinnerian abolition of free will. His plots present a web of alliances based on spontaneous sympathy and humane instincts. Alienation, for Amado, might be described as psychological imprisonment within social prejudices which render impossible any apprehension of the beauty abundantly manifest in the people itself—the humbler the people the greater their beauty.

The authenticity of Amado's rapport with the people is important in relation to both the socioanthropological tradition and Spanish American literature. The place he holds in the Bahian popular imagination is extraordinary; there is no such corresponding relation between the popular classes and any other Brazilian intellectual. Amado not only evokes the Bahian *imaginaire,* he genuinely participates in it. While intellectuals such as Freyre and anthropologists such as da Matta cannot be held to account for their lack of popular recognition, it would be difficult to overestimate Amado's unique achievement in writing texts which are actually read by poor Brazilians. He provides the quintessential literary manifestation of essentialist theories of the Recôncavo-Rio axis, compatible with both Freyre's celebration of the *homem lusotropical* and also the contemporary dynamic of Olodum's Pelourinho. The characteristics of this essentialism include social optimism (the emphasis on carnaval as opposed to drought), the preference for the *litoral* and the urban as opposed to the *interior* (seen in *O País do Carnaval* in the narrative's contempt for the bourgeois son who heads off to distant Piauí state to be a lawyer), the focus on the human value of the Afro-Brazilian and its function as a central reference of Brazilianism, the insistence on Brazil as the land of tomorrow, the conviction that Brazil really is uniquely racially democratic, and the surprisingly fertile resource of Bahian narcissism.

Amado also develops Brazilian essentialism within this celebration of miscegenation—surely, the dreamed of "revolution without ideology." His theory has at least two characteristics in common with Spanish American literary intellectuals, and one fundamental difference. The shared elements are the paradoxical union of an essentialist vision of the privileged region—whether Bahia and Brazil or Spanish and Latin America—and an orthodox Leftist politics. Through Amado's gradual self-liberation from the strictures of socialist realism, he retained revolutionary sympathies despite difficulties with first Stalinism, then materialism. His political path for most of his life was that of comrades such as Neruda and younger writers like García Márquez. While not present at the Spanish civil war, he had the opportunity to discuss this event at length with writers like Neruda, who were, and maintained much greater contact with the Portuguese political vanguard and the literary intelligentsia of Lisbon than most Brazilian writers. The marriage of cosmopolitan, Paris-centric Leftist internationalism with intense geopolitical regionalism and cultural essentialism is a coupling which may well appear paradoxical, but its frequence in fact suggests a productive formula based on a Manichaean symbiosis of perspectives and realities. This pattern marks the Hispanic *Boom*.

Still, the essentialism of Amado and the Brazilian socioanthropological tradition post-Freyre is distinct from that of the Spanish American literary tradition. Amado is not a formal innovator, but integrates popular literary genres and classic older models from before the Baudelairean dawn of modern literary consciousness. His work is enjoyed by many readers, but also shunned as vulgar by upper-class Brazilians with high intellectual demands. His work is thus quite different from that of the Spanish American *Boom* writers, such as the Carpentier of *Los pasos perdidos,* the Cortázar of *Rayuela,* the Fuentes of *Terra nostra,* the Vargas Llosa of *La casa verde,* the poetry of Paz, or the essays of any of these writers. Nor is Amado's work open to the charge of perverse elitism leveled by Colás against the *Boom* writers—the disturbing suggestion that the alleged abasement of Latin American popular culture was actually necessary to the Spanish American writers in order to justify their own vanguard position and the formally strange and intellectually demanding qualities characteristic of their seminal works.

In this attempt to locate Amado in relation to the Hispanic Boom, the stylistic motif of magical realism is the key locus of formal overlap; to what extent there is overlap of content is more contentious. Magical realism has come to represent the literary flavor of the Boom to readers whose exposure is limited to *Cien años de soledad.* In fact, beyond Márquez, the other Hispanic Boom writers are not easily encapsulated under the rubric. As a widely consumed style, a key feature of magical realism is that it is, while both real and fantastic, not difficult to digest. This style draws directly on popular modes of discourse and is characteristically as readable as conventional realism. Thus, within the Hispanic world, Fuentes's *Terra Nostra* is magical realism—from a university perspective—but less so than Isabel Allende (considered derivative and not a member of the Boom pantheon) from the consumer viewpoint. If *Cien años de soledad* is the only really orthodox manifestation (from the consumer perspective) of *Boom* magical realism, the other great magical realist is Jorge Amado, in works such as *Dona Flor* where one of the protagonists is a ghost, or *Tenda dos Milagres,* where the Candomblé *orixás* join in the story. One of the reasons for the centrality of García Márquez and *Cien años de soledad* in the popular apprehension of the *Boom* is the sense of narrative authenticity grounded in a storytelling instinct inherited from his *raconteuse* grandmother; the story seems to spiritually belong to the people it represents. This is precisely the virtue which has driven Amado's pragmatic and ideological impulses.

Empirically, the contrast between the literary essentialism of Spanish America, and the anthropological and Amadian essentialism of Brazil is that the former is a dystopian, apocalyptic discourse, and the latter Utopian. The key word for both García Márquez and Paz has been *soledad* which can be taken in the sense of historical isolation from enlightenment or in the sense of alienation from solidarity. The key word for Brazilians is carnaval, with its ideological retinue of *communitas,* of miraculous communitarian solidarity and the possibility of hierarchical inversion which compensates for the regular order and its abuses. It is Amado who seems to have grasped this best; in his first book, *O País do Carnaval,* the protagonist observes, "I only ever felt Brazilian two times in my whole life; once during the carnaval and once when I beat Julieta when she cheated on me." The words suggest a Latin American continuum between Brazil and Spanish America which can be read either way, as celebration or patriarchal abuse. Brazilian essentialism is optimistic—perhaps pathologically so; in good faith it dispenses with the continental trauma of false Utopian projections from Europe, the Spanish American trauma of Babel, and the compulsive comparison with the North Atlantic whether as Ariel (Western European culture) or Caliban (the anglo ogre).

It is legitimate to ask whether Brazilian optimism is not alienation; militant North American race relation analysts insist that it is. Although the case of Amado cannot of itself resolve this issue, it must be said that he grappled constantly with external intellectual currents and continued to refine his own literary vision. His disillusionment with Marxist orthodoxy was, according to Neruda's testimony, particularly painful, but ultimately a blessing, given his sensibilities (Almeida 1979). In relation to patriarchal society, Amado gradually developed from absolute *machismo* and female objectification to a later approach where women were moved into the protagonist role (*Gabriela, Dona Flor, Tereza Batista, Tieta*). And Amado is still exceptional in Brazilian letters in having blacks as central protagonists; one thinks of *Tenda dos Milagres,* but the more radical case is the aggressive Antonio Balduino of 1935's *Jubiabá.* It must be said, then, that Amado has proved highly flexible in matters of sex, race, and politics. The only constant has been his love for his home, which is persuasively presented as center stage as far as the advancement of civilization through miscegenation is concerned. In Gabriela, Jorge Amado created a Beatrice for the new millennium.

João Guimarães Rosa: the Interpretation of His Reception as a Paradigm for Brazilian Modernism

The international and domestic reception of João Guimarães Rosa is symmetrically inverse to that of Amado (positive versus negative response by the domestic critical elite; international obscurity versus popularity). Rosa sits at one extreme of mainstream Brazilian modernism, while Amado, a relatively solitary literary fellow traveler, is at the other, wedded to socioanthropological intellectual populism.

Guimarães Rosa's prestige, contrary to Amado's, works on a trickle-down basis within the Eurocentric Brazilian social hierarchy, and particularly in the university system. The frequent lay suggestion that Rosa's work is more purchased than actually read is a reflection of its curricular imposition. His position is parallel to that of canonical writers in other literary traditions such as Milton. Within the institutional framework, however, Guimarães Rosa is a particularly favorable object because of the general prestige in contemporary literary analysis of the issue of language and the metaphysics of discourse. The top-heavy aestheticism and the arduous philosophy of language in Rosa's work make him a rewarding object of study for the student of literary theory. While sociology may prefer Amado to Rosa, and literary studies the reverse, the growing influence of the social over the aesthetic imperative causes an ideological split within literary studies between the socialists, as it were, and the purists. Those subscribing to the social imperative will emphasize Amado's topicality and forgive his populist appropriation of narrative modes and marketologically savvy, robust sensuality. Literary purists will favor Guimarães Rosa. In Brazil's literary institutions, purism naturally prevails; and given the deference to European models, this must be read as a more conservative act than it would be in the U.S. or Europe. Outside Brazil, a student's selection of Latin American rather than European or North American literature is virtually a choice of the socialist as opposed to the purist imperative. Hence the greater interest in Amado outside Brazil. Inside Brazil, interest in Guimarães Rosa is tantamount to Eurocentrism despite the ruralist pastiche in his work and his complete disregard for nationally or even regionally extraneous elements (there are a minimum of foreigners in his *sertão,* and few Afro-Brazilians). Conversely, external interest in Amado is tantamount to solidarity with the Other, both as a socioeconomic entity and as a cultural object. Given Rosa's international obscurity, it is ironic that he was a diplomat, while the jingoistically Bahian Amado emerges as a cultural statesman of international fame—a recognizable, uniquely flavored Brazilian essence.

The suggestion that literary purism is inherently more conservative than sociology raises far profounder issues than can be discussed here. In relation to the reception of Rosa and Amado, however, it is worth noting that the issue of cultural logic emerges as a natural extension to the observations regarding the predictable or structural aspects of the preferences of sociologically minded literary analysts. Appreciation of Guimarães Rosa rests upon the prestige of the literary object per se. The heritage of the past, still prevalent in institutional topography, is that literature constitutes culture, so that a university department representing a national culture is by definition a literature department, whereas other artistic media, for example music or painting, are taught in departments which must represent the whole world. The pattern is changing, however; interdepartmental programs in area studies are emerging concomitantly with the decline of the literary object as supreme cultural artifact. The most prestigious literary cultures have their own department labeled purely by nation—The Department of French. Traditions of lesser prestige are subject to area expansion, and/or the inclusion of the functional term "language" which implicitly erodes the literariness of the cultural space: The Department of Spanish and Portuguese; The Department of Germanic Languages. Newer traditions (in terms of Western study) incline to labels suggesting culture as opposed to literature: The Department of East Asian Studies. Brazilian literature, purely as literature, is dependent on the universal prestige of literature. But if the new order is represented by interdepartmental programs such as Latin American Studies (which integrate social sciences and humanities), Worlds Arts and Cultures (indifferent to the traditional prestige of literature over folklore and music and the growing nonlinear media), then evidently a writer such as Jorge Amado—compatible with the efficacious, nonliterary *imaginaire* of Brazil—is far fitter in Darwinian terms than Guimarães Rosa.

It cannot be assumed that with time Guimarães Rosa will be recognized and appreciated, as Faulkner was. If the dynamics of artistic perception are as dependent upon the agency of the audience and its external ideocultural agenda as upon the creative power of the author, then it is conceivable that Guimarães Rosa will become more rather than less obscure. A vital element in this equation is the peripherality of the culture concerned. As suggested, the more peripheral the culture, the more simplified and homogenized its projection onto the international screen. The bridge between the periphery and the central world cultural market must often be essentialism, which articulates a recognizable object, often the consolidation of diffuse local products, into a strong, simplified alloy. In this respect Guimarães Rosa's product, couched in an obscure form that does not correspond to the international appetite and bypasses the question of national identity, cannot be expected to prosper.

The earlier comparison to Milton raises a further consideration. It can be confidently asserted that Milton's lack of appeal to contemporary audiences is attributable not so much to inherent literary difficulty as to the irrelevance of his spiritual and political agenda to present-day concerns in the secularized West. On the other hand, in the one hundred and fifty years following his lifetime, Milton was often considered a greater writer than Shakespeare; his receptive fortunes have much to do with the evolution of particular audience concerns. Guimarães Rosa's thematic concerns are universal. The narrative lies poised between an interrogation of knowledge, and a firm sense of landscape. In regard to the first aspect, Rosa's work reveals a subtle resonance with the mainstream of European, bourgeois alienated modernism. The second suggests that his work is as real a portrait of Brazil as that of Amado. Guimarães Rosa, then, responds to both the modernist agenda and to the requirements of authenticity and novelty, and thus should be able to appeal to a wide audience. His stylistic difficulties are in many ways comparable to those of Faulkner, who exercised a great influence on Spanish American writers, or Joyce, particularly important to Brazilian modernists. Rosa can be also compared to Faulkner in his tendency to a meandering, loose somewhat expressionist flow, and to Joyce in the domain of neologisms and strange words.

Why then has the influence between nations not been reciprocal, particularly if we take into consideration Jameson's notion of modernist texts being generated at the margin rather than at the center of the world market? Evidently the intercontinental bridges leading to and from Latin America (as the vertical orientation of standard cartography infers) run downhill from the North Atlantic and steeply uphill in the opposite direction. The case of the Brazilian Amado and the Spanish American *Boom* novelists suggests that the reverse course is still possible, but that the general apprehension of the Latin American subject is restricted to intense but ultimately limited and limited coagulations of ethnocultural identity (though there are, of course, counterexamples including both Borges and Lispector).

In the Brazilian case, it is not inconceivable that the works of Guimarães Rosa should be interpreted externally as a model of national identity. In terms of the theories now in vogue regarding the moral prestige of marginalized social entities and individuals, Rosa's emphasis on liminal beings, human or animal, and on the intuitive powers of these subjects in certain vital tasks of apprehension, makes his work a potentially rich source of extrapolation for victim-analysis, the dominant mode of politically correct criticism. But a series of formal mismatches between the expectations of the international audience and the motifs available in the work militate against such an outcome: Rosa's icons are, as it were, white or light figures projected onto a white screen. His chosen people are ethnically Iberian or *caboclo* rather than *mulato*. They inhabit not the tropical but the arid zone, and are not socially gregarious or easily susceptible to class identification; they rather tend to isolated, introspective individualism. Rosa's perspective is essentially antihistorical or metaphysical whereas the Spanish American *Boom* master narrative is profoundly historical and based, as is Amado's, on the Leftist discourse which has provided the master narrative of the twentieth century, from the Spanish civil War to the Second World War to Cuba and Vietnam. Rosa's account of the rare but extraordinary experiences of humble subjects, particularly in his later short stories, bear the character of parables of an unresolved religion. The marginalized are not used as figures to represent masses of social victims; rather, the experience related in the narrative constitutes a fully adequate existential paradigm. It is to be assumed that there is a subterranean Rosean essentialism, as there must be in any sustained discourse, but Rosa's essentialism is not pertinent to the Rio-Recôncavo axis. On the contrary, it is like a bridge over a cultural chasm, which terminates halfway—awaiting the construction of its other half from the other side. Audience reception is never to be presupposed as generated simply from the greatness of a writer. The translations of three of Rosa works into English were executed by eminent professionals under the auspices of an excellent New York publisher. All these works went out of print quickly. It is difficult, then, to sustain the argument that Guimarães Rosa was the victim of material factors. And while it was argued that the basic problem lay in the translations, Rosa himself saw them as vital conduits, imperfect but essential, for the dissemination of his work. In this sense Guimarães Rosa must be seen as belonging to an older generation which accepted the literary canon unproblematically, without the sense that the apprehension of literary objects is always political, and that the text is at some level created by the receiving audience and/or culture rather than by the writer alone.

Communicable Brazil, that is, the efficacious international Brazilian *imaginaire,* is thus restricted to two cultural poles. The Amazonian Amerindians are the chosen *bons sauvages* of pop anthropology, presumably because of the powerful tropical halo emanating from their vast forest home, the world's ultimate zoological and botanical icon, threatened literally and figuratively by the demoniac fires of modern industrialized consumption. At the other extreme, urbanized coastal Brazil presents a powerful ethnic imagery with its own persuasive frame. This part of Brazil is perceived as endowed with Afro-Brazilian miscegenist magic, the myth of racial harmony standing as a panacea to the North American angst of black-white conflict. The carnival—theorized as a subversion of the conventional ethnopolitical and socioeconomic hierarchy, and successfully appropriated by both the Brazilian state and Brazilian socioanthropology—functions as a living symbol of a host of sanctified motifs: the Baroque energy claimed for Latin America by Carpentier as an antidote to sterile Western rationalism; the Utopian sublimation of a sort of sexual-symbolic cultural intercourse between continents and civilizations, which heals the old dystopian Eurocentric misrecognitions of America; above all, from the North American perspective, the implosion of raciological hierarchy and oppression which, with the emergence of the new "white man's burden" (his identification as the real culprit of racism), have become as oppressive for the master as for the slave. Weaving together the strands of these mythologies, the carnaval—particularly the Bahian carnaval—functions as a modern day passion play. But in a continent known for its colorful faith, Brazilian literary agnosticism, represented in the work of most of its best writers, has failed this new, inverted inquisition.

Notes

Introduction

1. There is no suitable English translation of the Portuguese term *carnaval*. *Mardi gras,* the French term familiar to Americans because of the New Orleans festival, is overly specific in English usage; "festival" would perhaps be a good generic term. "Carnival," a false cognate, is certainly misleading. Given the contemporary world hegemony in the international psyche of the Brazilian instance of carne-vale (the various vulgar Romance versions of the term share this etymology tracing back to the ascetic Lenten "farewell to meat" [or "removal of meat"]; the festival takes place around the world in the days leading up to Ash Wednesday, the first day of Lent) it would seem appropriate to christen the term as a new but legitimate word in English—henceforth it will not be italicized.

2. The *Nordeste* is a cultural and geographic region comprised of the states on the Atlantic seaboard from Bahia to Maranhão; in the text, *Nordeste* and other regional denoters (*Sul*) are italicized when the sense is of a cultural zone; English is used in more objective geographic references. The first phase of Brazilian economic history was dominated by the plantation system in the *Nordeste*. Within this zone there has historically been an economic and cultural difference between the intensive agricultural production through sugar and tobacco plantations in the fertile coastal zone, where a predominant portion of the population was Afro-Brazilian and where there were and are a number of populous cities, and the arid inland, or interior, where agricultural production was more dispersed and sustained by a system of peonage over a peasant class principally comprised ethnically of *caboclos,* that is, a mestizo population with Iberian and Amerindian blood (regarding the term *mulato,* see Chapter 1, note 2, below). Despite the cultural gulf between the two zones, they are subsumed under the rubric of *nordestino* largely because both zones became more and more economically retrograde from the late eighteenth century on when the economic and political center of gravity in Brazil moved south, first to the mineral-rich but landlocked state of Minas Gerais, for which Rio de Janeiro served as a port for export to Portugal, and then to Rio, seat of the Brazilian court in the nineteenth century and national capital through the first half of the twentieth century, and the state of São Paulo, which, through agricultural products such as coffee, and then through industrial expansion, became the undisputed economic center of modern Brazil. In the nineteenth century Rio was a magnet for internal migration of poor *nordestinos* and for the socioeconomic elite from around the country. The single most important phenomenon of internal demographic movement in the twentieth century has been a seemingly endless flow of migration from the *Nordeste,* particularly the drought-afflicted *sertão* (the dry part of the interior) to São Paulo. The culture shock between the archaic collective memory of the *sertanejos* and the economically progressive south, combined with the socio-economic marginalization of the

former, contribute to a psychological dichotomy between the *Nordeste* and the southeast (the states of São Paulo, Rio de Janeiro, Espírito Santo, and the south of Minas Gerais), and, in a looser and more global dialectic of development and underdevelopment between *Sul* (the southeast and the states of predominantly European settlement south of São Paulo—Paraná, Santa Catarina, and Rio Grande do Sul) and *Norte* (embracing two cultural zones—the *Nordeste* and *Norte*, i.e., the vast domain of the Amazonian basin).

3. Brazilian scholarship has, with time, come to resemble more and more that of developed Western nations. However, this development has its foundations in the relatively recent creation of a disciplinarily eclectic and conventional university establishment, from the 1930s on. The Brazilian sociological and anthropological traditions today include representatives of most major European and North American methodological currents. The focus of this study is restricted to a handful of "star" social theorists who have tended to be speculative essayists— thus, in our own terminology, humanists—rather than devoting themselves to objective data gathering within the strict confines of a scientific investigative model, as is typical particularly in the U.S. It is likely that the future tendency will be to more conventional scientific procedures, and the practice of the speculative essay no doubt has much to do with the recency of the establishment of the institutional infrastructure; the work of several of the most important of these figures predates the Brazilian university system. The situation is illustrated best by the case of Euclides da Cunha, an engineer and military analyst, whose seminal work of natural philosophy, *Os Sertões,* is read alternately as geography, sociology, anthropology, and literature. The situation of Brazilian socioanthropologists is more akin to nineteenth century European pseudo-scientific speculative thinkers in its interdisciplinary indiscipline, and to Greek natural philosophers in the sense that a completely new world (a social or cultural civilization in the Brazilian case) is being written about, thus justifying certain liberties pragmatically. I reiterate that this study does not have the ambition of intrascientific judgments, nor does it give a complete portrait of social science in Brazil; the work of da Cunha, Gilberto Freyre, Roberto da Matta, and others is here presented in its aspect as subjective, ideological cultural discourse, that is, as literature.

4. The present study does not have the scope to analyze whether Amado should, uniquely amongst Brazilian writers, be considered a *Boom* writer, or alternately, whether certain Spanish American writers who have won honors within Spanish America without being able to penetrate the international market—such as Lezama Lima—might not present a dilemma comparable to the Brazilians, that is, the disinterest of the métropole in individualistic, nonessentialist, nonideological, and nonhistorical works created at the margins of the world system.

Among the Spanish American writers, Borges is exceptional both in terms of international recognition and themes. Borges eludes any of the generalizations made here about Spanish American literature, which essentially concern the ideological heart and stylistic predisposition of the *Boom* writers: the sense of existing at a historical turning point and participating as intellectuals in a real struggle, and the inclusion of literary motifs defying the usual notions of reality and conventional expectations of realism. Even within this generation, certain writers fit the mold of "revolution via magical realism," as it were; if this is best applied to García Márquez, it must also be noted that in many respects he defines the popular sense of the *Boom,* and that elements of his political consciousness and his style recur in most other notable writers of this period of singular conspicuousness of Latin American literature.

5. Apart from their qualitative aspects, the choice of writers was largely dictated by preeminence. These are considered, *grosso modo,* the greatest Brazilian men of letters. Though mentioned in passing, a conspicuous absence in this study must be Clarice Lispector. The omission is not meant as a slight. On the contrary, her case presents peculiarities which would justify a study on its own. As a sophisticated reader of existentialist philosophical literature and a bourgeois feminist Lispector is a striking example of the direct engagement of Brazilian literature in European themes of the moment, largely free of the filter occasioned by a sense of belonging to another world, the Third World. In this sense she exemplifies, as Machado does and perhaps more than other writers of her century, the differences outlined between Brazilian and Spanish American literatures. The specialness of her European and American reception, however, concerns its extraordinary significance for a specific target audience; Lispector was championed by the influential French feminist writer and theorist, Hélène Cixous.

Chapter 1: The Historical Character of Modern Brazilian Literature

1. I employ a typographic device to distinguish between Brazilian *Modernismo* and Spanish American *modernismo:* the first letter of the latter is typically written in lower case, and the former usually, but less consistently, in upper case.

2. Regarding the use of this term, I use "mulatto" for both genders as in the English usage, and separately, when contextually appropriate (i.e., when the connotation is specifically within Brazilian culture), the Portuguese *mulato* and *mulata*. Regarding the sense of the term in either language the meaning is racially specific, referring to persons of mixed European (Caucasian) and African blood, and thus should not be confused with more general terms such as the Spanish *mestizo,* which indicates mixed racial ancestry of various specific elements.

3. For a dissertation length discussion of this fascinating question, see Daniel 1987.

4. The first edition of *Seraphim Ponte Grande* (1933) gives a list of his previous works and *Seraphim Ponte Grande* itself, written several years prior to the publication according to Oswald, under the title "Obras renegadas."

5. In fact, Moisés divides his *Terceiro Momento Modernista* into three subdivisions: 1945–60, 1960–73 (the latter being the date of Osman Lins's *Avalovara*), and after 1973. Apart from his own categories, Moisés provides an overview of alternate literary historical topographies including that of Ataíde. See Moisés 1989, 382. Regarding the citation procedure for this volume and others of Moisés's *História da Literatura Brasileira*. (São Paulo: Cultrix, 1984–89), note that the volume numbers changed during the course of release of the series, with the first edition's Vol. II. *Romantismo e Realismo* appearing subsequently as Vol. II. *Romantismo* and Vol. III. *Realismo*. The following volume, *Simbolismo,* is thus alternately Vol. III (1st ed., 1985) and Vol. IV (subsequent editions). The final volume, unavailable in the first edition, is consistently Vol. V.

6. Private letter of 11 May to Vicente Guimarães; quoted in Martins (1978b, 247)

7. See, for example, Borges's "Definición del germanófilo" (1985, 166–68)

8. It is certainly not the case, however, that Leftism ceases to be an orthodoxy. Neither the emerging conservatism of Paz nor the middle-ground Democratic stance of Vargas Llosa are radically conservative. Paz's discord with the Mexican government in the late 1960s, for example, can really be seen in a similar light to the dissent against Castro by committed Leftists, consisting essentially of protest against abuses of power rather than direct ideological contestation in terms of the conventional political Left-Right spectrum. Again, Vargas-Llosa's opposition to the Maoist Shining Path is hardly an ideological attack (see *Historia de Mayta* and *Lituma en los Andes*). The master parable of this global experience—the disillusion occasioned by the universal continuity of corruption—is the story of the Mexican revolution, and the inability of its political Goliath, the surreally tautologically entitled Partido Revolucionario Institucional, to change the plutocratic order. This is notably critiqued in Carlos Fuente's *La muerte de Artemio Cruz* as well as in many other novels. While the master motifs of corruption and abuse have proven compatible with regimes of all political positions, a fact discrediting the Left's pretensions, it is also the case that the distaste for these social ills feeds radicalism, thus potentially sustaining the socialist call for a new man.

9. The *Boom* generated a subsequent massive critical meta-discourse, kicked off in part by a book, *Historia Personal del Boom,* by a secondary *Boom* writer, José Donoso. The question of elite construction of popular identity opens onto the proliferating field of theories of the postcolonial condition. See, for example, Santiago Colás's 1995 article, "Of Creole Symptoms, Cuban Fantasies, and Other Latin American Postcolonial Ideologies."

10. This theme is developed explicitly in a mixed essay and fiction format by Eduardo Galeano in *Las venas abiertas de America Latina* and *Memoria del fuego.*

11. It is in this sense, the compulsive indulgence, within a denunciating exposure, of perversion, and not simply in the parallel of Macondo to Yoknapatawpha—that García Márquez's avowal of his debt to Faulkner must be understood.

12. See Carpentier's collection of essays, *Tientos y diferencias* (1964).

13. Significantly, Jorge Amado, alone amongst the Brazilians studied in detail here, does in fact have one text dealing with the theme of continental identity and discovery, *A descoberta da América pelos Turcos,* albeit with a much less grave sense of historical agenda than the *Boom* writers.

14. A study by Fitz and Payne (Payne 1993) verifies the contrasting tendency to ambiguity in the Brazilian as opposed to the Spanish American literary traditions; its focus is on gender relations, however. I would argue that the same pattern holds more broadly.

15. The question of the ideological militating of Amado's fiction has, nevertheless, been hugely controversial. For a complete discussion, see Almeida 1979.

16. It is telling, for instance, that a sociopolitically conscious collection of interviews with leading Latin American writers, focusing on the validity of the term "Latin America," and including discussions with Fuentes, Paz, and fourteen other literary luminaries of the continent, includes only one Brazilian: Amado, interviewed in Paris (Marras 1992).

Chapter 2: The Brazilian Writers and Their Work

1. For a thorough analysis of the relation of Guimarães Rosa's discourse to modes of orality in rural Minas Gerais, see Sperber 1982.

2. Citations of *Grande Sertão: Veredas* are taken throughout from the 20th edition (Rosa 1986). For details of the first, second, and third publications (each different) see 1956b.
3. All citations of Drummond's poetry are from *Obra Completa*. 4th edition. Rio: Aguilar, 1977.
4. First published in Spanish as *Vida de Luís Carlos Prestes, el caballero de la esperanza* (Buenos Aires, 1942), then in Portuguese (São Paulo, 1945).
5. More precisely, Socialist realism required three things, untranslatable into English: narodmnost (nationalism but also folkiness, i.e., the spirit of the people), klassovost (classness; i.e. an acknowledgment of the class-based nature of society) and partiinist (partiness, i.e. due acknowledgment of the role of the party in all things, even literary). Even if Amado's work cultivated the first, and was not incomplete with the second, he was contradicting the third precept.
6. Camus's review was found in a loose folio in the general archives of the Casa Fundação Jorge Amado.

Chapter 3: Domestic and International Reception

1. Original publication in *O Estado de São Paulo,* 28, 28 Aug. 1946.
2. Unless otherwise indicated, those newspaper articles cited in this study for which specified subsequent book publication is not indicated were derived directly from the collection of press clippings held at the Arquivo João Guimarães Rosa at the Instituto de Estudos Brasileiros of the University of São Paulo. Reliable page numbers were not always available. All such items, where cited, are marked (I.E.B. / U.S.P.)
3. See Coutinho (1991, 321–49). Original publication in Revista do Livro, 4 (16), Rio de Janeiro, 1959.
4. See Armstrong (1995) for quantitative analysis of the U.S.P. library holdings regarding the number of books by and about, and the number of theses on Guimarães Rosa, Machado de Assis, Mário de Andrade, Carlos Drummond de Andrade, and Jorge Amado.
5. Unpublished. Taken here from the I.E.B. / U.S.P. archives.
6. *Books Abroad; Library Journal; Virginia Pilot; Atlantic Journal; Hispanic American Report; Cleveland Press; Baltimore Sun; New York Times; New York Times International Edition; Washington Post; Los Angeles Times; Houston Chronicle; Des Moines Sunday Register; Boston Sunday Herald; The Kansas City Star; Herald Tribune; Springfield Republican; Providence Journal; Chicago Sunday Star; Winnipeg Tribune; Publishers Weekly.*
7. In "Köln und Rio gibt es mehr Mystiker, als man ahnt." *Kolner Kulturspiegel* 10 Oct. 1964.
8. Guimarães Rosa to Meyer-Clason, 17 June 1963; archived at I.E.B./U.S.P., and transcribed in Verlanghieri 1993.
9. Guimarães Rosa to Harriet de Onís, 2 May 1959. The letter cited is an early one, prior to *The Devil to Pay in the Backlands* and *Sagarana—A Cycle of Stories;* it concerns her early translation of "O Duelo" ("The Duel").
10. In the original the full phrase is: "A paisagem era triste, e as cigarras tristíssimas, à tarde".
11. This advertisement and the next were taken from I.E.B./U.S.P. The date (in 1963) was not recorded.

12. "Un candidat au Nobel." *Lectures pour tous,* Radio Télévision Belge, 3 Dec. 1962. (transcript at I.E.B./U.S.P.)

13. The first volume, entitled *Buriti* (Guimarães Rosa 1962b), contains three stories from *Corpo de Baile:* "Dão Lalalão"; "O Recado do Morro" ("Le message du morne"); "Uma Estória de Amor" ("La fête à Manuelzão").

14. Undocumented clipping from the I.E.B./ U.S.P.

15. Amado was employed by the age of twenty-two (in 1930) by the carioca newspaper, *O Momento,* and given an amazingly free range in a column which he often signed under the pseudonym, Alberto Borgia. Many of these articles are preserved at the Casa Jorge Amado.

16. See also Assis Duarte's more complete study, *Jorge Amado: romance em tempo de utopia* (Duarte 1996).

17. In an article of 1944, "Jorge Amado e o Romance Poético," and in the preface to the French translation of *Quincas Berro d'Agua* (Assis Duarte's references: Roger Bastide, "Jorge Amado e o Romance Poético", Rio de Janeiro, *O Jornal,* 2 Feb. 1944; "Sobre o Romancista Jorge Amado", prefácio à tradução francesa de *Quincas Berro d'Agua.*).

18. Assis Duarte's reference: Eduardo Portella. "A Fábula em cinco Tempos", in *Jorge Amado: 30 anos de Literatura* (São Paulo: Martins, 1961).

19. Assis Duarte's reference: Álvaro Lins, "Romance do Interior", *Jornal de Crítica,* 4a. série. (Rio de Janeiro: José Olympio, 1946); "As Obras Completas de Jorge Amado", *Jornal de Crítica,* 5a. série. (Rio de Janeiro: José Olympio, 1947).

20. Assis Duarte's reference: Walnice Galvão. *Jornal de Debates,* ano XXX, no. 5, de 23-2-76. Inserido mais tarde em *Saco de Gatos* (São Paulo: Duas Cidades, 1976).

21. The figures were derived from the U.S.P. computer catalog in 1994. The differences between these figures and the actual holdings of the university libraries, not to mention what a national count would reveal, may well be substantial. The figures are used here to indicate a pattern of proportions rather than provide reliable total numerical values.

22. One other writer, excluded from this study for reasons mentioned in the introduction, presents a case almost identical to that of Guimarães Rosa: Clarice Lispector (72 works by/about and 9 theses).

23. The data here was gathered from 1994 to 1995.

24. For all the stories by Borges referred to here see Borges 1985.

25. These chronological categories are simply those of the D.A.I. CDs; though the cut-off points are arbitrary chronologically speaking, each period, with the exception of the last, contains approximately the same amount of material, so that patterns can be derived in terms of a writer's presence as a proportion of the whole.

26. The main source for the following information is Wilson. See also Hulet 1964, Hulet 1965, and Levine 1970.

27. As regards poetry: twenty-three for Borges and thirty-six for Neruda; the number tends to grow in the case of the poets Paz and Neruda, and the short story writer and critic Borges, as opposed to the novelists, because of the greater possibility of creating a new volume arbitrarily, by cutting and pasting between texts.

28. Two last observations should be made. Firstly, although there is some common identity between the work of Jorge Amado and that of the successful writers of the *Boom,* the other four Brazilian writers studied here—and most conspicuously João Guimarães Rosa—fall outside this thematic band. Secondly, the mar-

ginal status of non-North Atlantic literature should not be underestimated because of the success of the *Boom*.

Chapter 4: Socioanthropology and Popular Culture

1. Originally in Freyre (1962).
2. The term *negro-mestiço* is not used by Freyre. It has come into use by some socio-anthropologists more recently, particularly in Bahia. The term is useful because it comprehends persons of various ethnic mixes who have become subsumed into the Afro-Brazilian cultural tradition. In this sense it connotes economic marginalization and a significant Afro-Brazilian cultural aspect, without excluding other cultural input or alternate ethnicity. For example, a racially *caboclo* person who has moved from the *sertão* to Salvador, Rio or elsewhere, and has become socioeconomically and culturally assimilated into the poorer classes where the Afro-Brazilian cultural heritage is preponderant would be considered *negro-mestiço* despite the apparent racial inaccuracy. The term is used here in relation to Freyre—despite the fact that he does not himself use it—because it illustrates that Afrocentric domination of popular cultural identification for which Freyre provided the initial theoretical impulse.
3. Monteiro Lobato's *caboclo,* from São Paulo state rather than the *Nordeste,* is, however, a significant literary entity working in this sense.
4. David Haberly's insightful work, *Three Sad Races* (1983), explores this dilemma and its consequences in the works for notable Brazilian writers of color.
5. Here da Matta appears to be the victim of an erroneous assumption of a cognate relation between the Portuguese *carnaval* and the English "carnival" (a traveling ensemble of side shows).
6. The minimum wage hovered around $US 60 for many years. It is currently (1997) around $US 100.
7. One *bloco,* Timbalada, created and lead by the talented percussionist Carlinhos Brown, rejects the Afrocentrism of the usual *bloco afro* ideology despite the dominance of percussion in its sound. The aesthetic program integrates diverse elements, including musical innovations from around the world not associable with any folkloric tradition, and miscellaneous ethnic paraphernalia including elements ranging from Australian Aboriginal painting of the body with white spots to designer sunglasses.
8. Originally in Freyre 1947.
9. Originally in Freyre 1957.

Chapter 5: Third World Culture on the Market

1. Such non-scientific descriptors could be related to conventional sociodemographic data, such as the greater number of household employed slaves and urban mulattos and freed slaves. Our focus in this literary-based study has deliberately been on subjective realities.
2. See Risério 1993a and 1993b.
3. The critic's quotes of Mário de Andrade are from the latter's "O Movimento Modernista" (Mário de Andrade 1943: 238, 241, 243).

Bibliography

Alencar, José de. 1960. *Obra completa*. 4 vols. ed. Eugênio Gomes. Rio: Aguilar.
Almeida, José América de. 1978. *A Bagaceira*. Rio: José Olympio.
Almeida, Alfredo Wagner Berno de. 1979. *Jorge Amado, política e literatura: um estudo sobre a trajetória intelectual de Jorge Amado*. Contribuições em ciências sociais. 3. Rio: Campus.
Amado, Jorge. 1931 *O País do Carnaval*. Rio: Schmidt.
———. 1933. *Cacau*. Rio: Ariel.
———. 1934. *Suor*. Rio: Ariel.
———. 1935 *Jubiabá*. Rio: José Olympio.
———. 1937. *Capitães da Areia*. Rio: José Olympio.
———. 1942. *Vida de Luís Carlos Prestes: el caballero de la esperanza*. Buenos Aires: Claridad.
———. 1943. *Terras do Sem Fim*. São Paulo: Martins.
———. 1944. *São Jorge dos Ilhéus*. São Paulo: Martins.
———. 1945. *A Vida de Luis Carlos Prestes: O Cavaleiro da Esperança*. São Paulo: Martins.
———. 1946. *Seara Vermelha*. São Paulo: Martins.
———. 1954. *Os Subterrâneos de Liberdade*. São Paulo: Martins.
———. 1958 *Gabriela Cravo e Canela: Crônica de uma Cidade do Interior*. São Paulo: Martins.
———. 1961. *A Morte e a Morte de Quincas Berro D'Agua*. In *Os Velhos Marinheiros*. São Paulo: Martins.
———. 1962 *Gabriela, Cinnamon and Clove*. New York: Knopf.
———. 1964 *Os Pastores da Noite*. São Paulo: Martins.
———. 1966. *Dona Flor e seus dois maridos, historia moral e de amor*. São Paulo: Martins.
———. 1969. *Tenda dos Milagres*. São Paulo: Martins.
———. 1977. *Tieta do Agreste*. Rio: Record.
———. 1978. *Tereza Batista Cansada de Guerra*. São Paulo: Martins.
———. 1981. *O Menino Grapiúna*. Rio: Record.
———. 1992a. *Navegação de Cabotagem*. Rio: Record.
———. 1992b. *A descoberta da América pelos Turcos*. Rio: Record.
Andrade, Carlos Drummond de. 1965 *Carlos Drummond de Andrade. In the Middle of the Road*. Trans. J. Nist. Tucson: University of Arizona Press.
———. 1977 *Obra Completa*. 4th edition. Rio: Aguilar.

———. 1976. *Souvenir of the ancient world*. Trans. Mark Strand. New York: Antaeus Editions.

———. 1980. *The minus sign: a selection from the poetic anthology*. Trans. Virginia de Araujo. Redding Ridge, CT: Black Swan Books. In U.K., Manchester: Carcanet New Press, 1981.

———. 1986. *Traveling in the family: selected poems*. Ed. Thomas Colchie and Mark Strand. Trans. Elizabeth Bishop and Gregory Rabassa. 1st. ed. New York: Random House.

Andrade, Mário de. 1922 *A Paulicéia Desvairada*. São Paulo.

———. 1933. *Fraülein*. Trans. M. Richardson Hollingsworth. New York: Macauley.

———. 1934. *Belazarte*. São Paulo: Piratininga.

———. 1936. *A Música e a Canção Popular no Brasil*. Rio.

———. 1942. *O Movimento Modernista*. Rio: C.E.B.

———. 1943. *Aspectos da literatura brasileira*. São Paulo: Livraria Martins Editora.

———. 1946. *Lira paulistana*. São Paulo: Livraria Martins.

———. 1958. *Cartas de Mário de Andrade a Manuel Bandeira*. Ed. Simões. Rio.

———. 1968. *Hallucinated City*. Trans. J Tomlins. Nashville, TN: Vanderbilt University Press.

———. 1974. *Aspectos da Literatura*. 1943. 5th ed. São Paulo: Martins.

———. 1982. *Amar, verbo intransitivo: idílio*. Ed. Tele Porto Ancona Lopez. 10th ed. Belo Horizonte: Itatiaia Limitada.

———. 1984 *Macunaíma*. Trans. E.A. Goodland. New York: Random House; London: Quartet.

———. 1987. *Poesias Completas*. Belo Horizons: Itatiaia.

———. 1989. *Dicionário musical brasileiro*. São Paulo: I.E.B.-U. São Paulo.

———. 1993 *Macunaíma: o herói sem nenhum caráter*. Belo Horizonte: Villa Rica.

Andrade, Oswald de. 1925 *Pau brasil. Cancioneiro de Oswald de Andrade*. Pref. Paulo Prado. Paris: Sans pareil.

———. 1933. *Seraphim Ponte Grande*. Rio: Ariel.

Armstrong, Piers. 1995. *João Guimarães Rosa, Jorge Amado and the international reception of Brazilian culture*. Ph.D. Dissertation. UCLA.

Azevedo, Aluísio. 1985 *O Cortiço*. Porto Alegre: Mercado Aberto.

Balzac, Honoré de. 1976–1981. *La comédie humaine*. Ed. Pierre-Georges Castex. Paris: Gallimard.

Borges, Jorge Luis (with Esther Zemborain de Torres). 1971. *An introduction to American literature* Trans. and ed. L. Clark Keating and Robert O. Evans. Lexington: University of Kentucky.

Borges, Jorge Luis (with Maria Esther Vazquez). 1974. *An introduction to English literature*. Trans. and ed. L. Clark Keating and Robert O. Evans. Lexington: University of Kentucky.

———. 1985. *Ficcionário*. México City: Fondo de Cultura Económica.

Braga, Julio Santana. 1992 *Ancestralidade afro-brasileira: o culto de baba egum*. Salvador: C.E.A.O. / Ianama.

Campos, Augusto de. 1959. "Um Lance de 'Dês' do Grande Sertão." In Coutinho, 321–49. Original publication in *Revista do Livro*, 4 (16), Rio.
Carpentier, Alejo. 1964. *Tientos y diferencias, ensayos.* Mexico: Universidad Nacional Autónoma de Mexico.
Cerqueira, Nelson. 1988. *A Política do Partido Comunista e a Questão do realismo em Jorge Amado.* Salvador: Fundação Casa de Jorge Amado.
Colás, Santiago. 1995. "Of Creole Symptoms, Cuban Fantasies, and Other Latin American Postcolonial Ideologies." *PMLA* Vol. 110, No. 3 (May): 382–96.
Conroy, Jack. 1963. "Outlaw and the Devil in Brazil's Backlands." *Chicago Sun-Times* 19 May, 55.
Cortázar, Julio. 1963. *Rayuela.* Buenos Aires: Sudamericana.
Coutinho, Eduardo F., ed. 1991. *Guimarães Rosa.* Series: Coleção Fortuna Crítica 6. Rio: Civilização Brasileira.
Curran, Mark J. 1981. *Jorge Amado e a literatura de cordel.* Salvador: Fundação Cultural do Estado da Bahia; Rio: Fundação Casa de Rui Barbosa.
Da Cunha, Euclides. 1985 *Os Sertões.* São Paulo: Brasiliense.
Daniel, Guilherme Reginaldo. 1987. "Machado de Assis and the meta-mulatto." Dissertation. UCLA.
Da Matta, Roberto. 1978. *Carnavais, malandros e heróis: para uma sociologia do dilema brasileiro.* Rio de Janeiro: Zahar Editores.
Dantas, Paulo. 1956. "Posição de Guimarães Rosa." *Para Todos,* 31 Oct: 16.
Donoso, Jose. 1972. *Historia personal del "boom."* Barcelona: Anagrama.
Duarte, Eduardo de Assis. 1991. "Do rodapé à crítica universitária, Jorge Amado, um caso polêmico." *2 Congresso ABRALIC. Literatura e memória cultural. Anais,* Vol.2, 237–42. Belo Horizonte: ABRALIC.
———. 1996. *Jorge Amado. romance em tempo de utopia.* Rio: Record.
Espinheira, Gey. 1984. *Divêrgencia e prostituição: uma análise sociológica da comunidade prostitucional do Maciel.* Rio: Tempo Brasileiro.
Flaubert, Gustave. 1958. *L'' Éducation sentimentale.* Ed. René Dumesnil. Paris: Société Les Belles lettres.
Freyre, Gilberto. 1947. *Interpretação do Brasil.* Rio: José Olympio.
———. 1956. *Casa Grande e Senzala.* 9th ed. 2 vols. Rio: José Olympio.
———. 1957. *Sociologia I.* Rio: José Olympio.
———. 1961. *O Luso e o Trópico.* Lisbon.
———. 1962. *Vida, Forma e Cor.* Rio: José Olímpio.
———. 1971. *Seleta.* Rio: José Olímpio.
Fuentes, Carlos. 1975. *Terra nostra.* Mexico City: J. Mortiz.
———. 1990. *La muerte de Artemio Cruz.* Caracas: Biblioteca Ayacucho.
———. 1991. *The Death of Artemio Cruz.* Trans. Sam Hileman. New York: Noonday.
———. 1993a. *Terra Nostra.* Trans. Margaret Sayers Peden. New York: Farrar, Straus, Giroux. New York: Noonday.
———. 1993b. *Aura.* Trans. Lysander Kemp. New York: Noonday.
———. 1993c. *The Hydra head.* Trans. Margaret Sayers Peden. New York: Farrar, Straus, Giroux. New York: Noonday.
Galeano, Eduardo. 1982–1986. *Memoria del fuego.* Madrid: Siglo Veintiuno.

———. 1983. *Las venas abiertas de America Latina.* Eduardo Galeano. Mexico City: Siglo Veintiuno.

García Márquez, Gabriel. 1968. *Cien anos de soledad.* La Habana: Casa de las Americas.

Gledson, John. 1979. "The Poetry and Poetics of Carlos Drummond de Andrade." Ph.D. Dissertation, Princeton.

———. 1984. *The Deceptive Realism of Machado de Assis: A Dissenting Interpretation of Casmurro.* Liverpool: Cairns.

Gomes, Álvaro Cardoso. 1981. *Jorge Amado.* Series: Literatura Comentada. São Paulo: Abril Educação.

Grego, Adriano. 1956. "La scoperta di un capolavoro letterario che solo i Brasiliani potranno leggere." *Il Tempo:* 27 Nov.

Guimarães, Vicente. 1972. *Joãozito.* Rio: José Olímpio.

Haberly, David. 1983. *Three Sad Races.* Cambridge: Cambridge University Press.

Hernández, Jose. 1988. *Martin Fierro.* Ed. Giovanni Meo Zilio. Barcelona: Ediciones B.

Hitler, Adolf. 1939. *Mein Kampf.* New York, Reynal & Hitchcock.

Holanda, Sérgio Buarque de. 1956. *Raízes do Brasil.* 3rd. ed. Rio: José Olympio.

Holmberg, Ted. 1963. "Brazil's Wild West." *The Providence Journal.* Apr: 49.

Huidobro, Vicente. 1949 "Altazor," *Altazor.* Santiago de Chile: Cruz del Sur.

Hulet, Claude L. 1964. *Latin American prose in English translation; a bibliography.* Washington D.C.: General Secretariat, Organization of American States.

———. 1965. *Latin American poetry in English translation, a bibliography.* Washington D.C.: Pan American Union.

Jobim, Antonio Carlos. 1994. *Chega de Saudade. The Best of Bossa Nova.* Various artists. EMI-Odeon.

Johnson, Harvey L. 1963. "The Evil One Led the Bands," *Library Journal,* 15 April.

Joyce, James. 1922. *Ulysses.* Paris: Shakespeare and company.

Levine, Suzanne Jill. 1970. *Latin America fiction & poetry in translation.* New York: Center for Inter-American Relations.

Lezama Lima, José. 1977. *Oppiano Licario.* Mexico City: Ediciones Era.

———. 1980. *Paradiso.* Ed. Eloisa Lezama Lima. Madrid: Ediciones Catedra.

———. 1988. *Paradiso.* Trans. Gregory Rabassa. New York: Farrar, Straus & Giroux. Austin: University of Texas Press.

Lima Barreto. 1989. *O Triste fim de Policarpo Quaresma.* Rio: Livraria Garnier.

Lins, Osman. 1973. Avalovara. São Paulo: Edições Melhoramentos.

Lins, Alvaro. 1963. *Os mortos de sobrecasaca; obras, autores e problemas da literatura brasileira, ensaios e estudos, 1940–1960.* Rio: Civilização Brasileira.

Machado de Assis, Joaquim. 1952. *Epitaph of a small winner.* Trans. W Grossman, New York: Farrar & Straus. 1952. New York: Noonday. 1956. Hammondsworth, (U.K.): Penguin. 1968.

———. 1953. *Dom Casmurro, a novel.* Trans. H. Caldwell, introd. Waldo Frank. New York: Noonday.

———. 1954. *Philosopher or Dog.* Trans. Clotilde Wilson, (New York: Farrar, Strauss & Giroux.

———. 1955. *Posthumous reminiscences of Bras Cubas.* Trans. E Ellis. RJ: Min. de Ed e Cult, Inst. Nacional do Livro.

———. 1963a. *The psychiatrist and other stories.* Trans. Helen Caldwell. Berkeley: University of California Press. 1963; rpt London: Owen.

———. 1963b. *What went on at the baroness'; a tale with a point.* Trans. H Caldwell. Los Angeles:, Magpie Press.

———. 1966. *Esau and Jacob.* Trans. H. Caldwell. Berkeley: University California Press. 1965; London: Owen.

———. 1970. *The Hand and the Glove.* Trans. A Bagby, intro. H Caldwell. Lexington: University of Kentucky.

———. 1972. *Counselor Ayres' Memorial.* Trans. H. Caldwell. Berkeley: University California Press.

———. 1976. *Yaya Garcia.* Trans. Robert Scott Buccleuch. Owen: London.

———. 1977a. *The Devil's Church and other Stories.* Trans. J Schmitt and L Ishmatsu. Austin: University of Texas Press.

———. 1977b. *Yaya Garcia.* Trans. Albert Bagby Jr. Lexington: University of Kentucky.

———. 1982. *Quincas Borba.* São Paulo: Editora Atica.

———. 1988. *Dom Casmurro.* Rio: Livraria Garnier.

———. 1988a. *Memorial de Aires.* Rio: Expressao e Cultura.

———. 1988b. *Memórias Pósthumas de Brás Cubas.* Rio: Livraria Garnier.

———. 1990. *The wager: Aires' journal.* Trans. and intro. R. Scott-Buccleuch. London: Owens.

———. 1992. *Lord Taciturn.* Trans. and intro. R.L. Scott-Buccleuch. London; Chester Springs, PA: P. Owen.

Marras, Sergio. 1992. *América latina, marca registrada.* Buenos Aires: Zeta.

Martins, Wilson. 1978a. *História da Inteligência Brasileira.* v.5 (1897–1914). São Paulo: Cultrix.

Martins, Wilson. 1978b. *História da Inteligência Brasileira.* v.7 (1933–1960). São Paulo: Cultrix.

Melo Neto, João Cabral de. 1956 *Paisagens com Figuras.* in *Duas Aguas.* Rio: José Olympio.

———. 1966. "A Educação pela pedra," *A Educação pela pedra.* Rio.

———. 1967. *Morte e vida severina.* Rio: Sabia.

———. 1968. *Poesias completas (1940–1965).* Rio: Sabia.

Moisés, Massaud. 1984 *Romantismo e Realismo.* Series: *História da Literatura Brasileira.* Vol. II. São Paulo: Cultrix.

———. 1989. *Modernismo.* Series: *História da Literatura Brasileira.* Vol. V. São Paulo: Cultrix.

Monegal, Emir Rodriguez. "Em Busca de Guimarães Rosa" in Coutinho 1991, 47–61.

More, Thomas, Sir, Saint. 1923. *More's Utopia.* Trans. G. C. Richards. Oxford: B. Blackwell.

Neruda, Pablo. 1944. *Residencia en la tierra. 1925–1935.* Buenos Aires: Losada.

O'Leary, Theodore. 1963. "Ruffians May Have a Certain Majesty." *Kansas City Star,* 12 May, 50.

Ortiz, Renato. 1985. *Cultura brasileira e identidade nacional.* São Paulo: Brasiliense.

Payne, Judith A and Earl E. Fitz. 1993. *Ambiguity and gender in the new novel of Brazil and Spanish America: a comparative assessment.* Iowa City: University of Iowa Press.

Paz, Octavio. 1959. *El laberinto de la soledad.* Mexico City: Fondo de Cultura Economica.

Prado, Paulo. 1931. *Retrato do Brasil; ensaio sobre a tristeza brasileira.* Rio: Briguiet.

Prescott, Orville. 1963. "Living is a very dangerous business." *New York Times* 17 April.

Proust, Marcel. 1968–69. *A la recherche du temps perdu.* Paris: Gallimard.

Ramos, Graciliano. 1962. *Linhas tortas. Crônicas escritas de 1915 a 1952.* São Paulo: Martins.

Rego, José Lins do. 1934. *Bangue.* Rio: José Olympio.

———. 1937. *Doidinho.* Rio: José Olympio.

———. 1939. *Menino de engenho.* Rio: José Olympio.

———. 1943. *Fogo morto.* Rio: José Olympio.

Riserio, Antonio. 1993a. *Caymmi: uma utopia de lugar.* São Paulo: Editora Perspectiva.

———. 1993b. *Textos e tribos: poeticas extraocidentais nos tropicos brasileiros.* Rio de Janeiro: Imago.

Rodo, Jose Enrique. 1900. *Ariel.* Montevideo: Dornaleche y Reyes.

Ronai, Paulo. "Pertil de João Guimarães Rosa" In Rosa (1973): xvii–xxii.

Rosa, João Guimarães. 1946. *Sagarana.* 1st ed. Rio: Universal, 1946. 3rd ed. (revised) Rio: José Olympio, 1951. 5th ed. (definitive) Rio: José Olympio, 1958.

———. 1956a. *Corpo de Baile.* 1st ed. 2 vols. Rio: José Olympio, 1956. 2nd ed. 1 vol. 1960. As of 3rd. edition, issued in 3 separately titled volumes: *Manuelzão e Miguilim* (Vol 1, containing "Uma Estória de Amor" and "Campo Geral") 3rd ed. Rio: José Olympio, 1964; *No Urubùquaquá, no Pinhém* (Vol 2, containing "Lélio e Lina," "O Recado do Morro," and "Cara de Bronze") 3rd ed. Rio: José Olympio, 1965; *Noites do Sertão* (Vol 3, containing "Lão-Dalalão (Dão-Lalalão)" and "Buriti") 3rd ed. Rio: José Olympio, 1965.

———. 1956b. *Grande Sertão: Veredas.* 1st ed. 1956. 2nd ed. (definitive) 1958. 20th ed. Rio: Nova Fronteira, 1986.

———. 1960b. "The Duel." Trans. Harriet de Onís. *Noonday,* n3, 24–52.

———. 1961 *Buriti.* Trans. J.J. Villard, pref. Javier Domingo. Paris: Seuil.

———. 1962a. *Primeiras Estórias.* Rio: José Olympio.

———. 1962b. *Les nuits du sertão.* Trans. J.J. Villard. Paris: Seuil.

———. 1963. *The Devil to Pay in the Backlands.* Trans. Harriet de Onís, pref. Franklin de Oliveira. New York: Knopf.

———. 1964. *Manuelzão e Miguilim.* (See *Corpo de Baile.*) Coleção Sagarana. 3rd ed. Rio: José Olympio.

———. 1964b. *Grande Sertão.* Trans. Curt Meyer-Clason. Cologne/Berlin: Kiepenheuer & Witsch, 1964.

———. 1965a. *No Urubùquaquá, no Pinhém.* (See *Corpo de Baile.*) Coleção Sagarana. 3rd ed. Rio: José Olympio.

———. 1965b. *Noites do Sertão.* (See *Corpo de Baile.*) Coleção Sagarana. 3rd ed. Rio: José Olympio.

———. 1966. *Sagarana—A Cycle of Stories.* Trans. Harriet de Onís. New York: Knopf.

———. 1967. *Gran Sertón: Veredas.* Trans. and glossary Angel Crespo Barcelona: Seix Barral.

———. 1968. *The Third Bank of the River and Other Stories.* Trans. Barbara Shelby. New York: Knopf.

———. 1969. *Tutaméia (Terceiras Estórias).* Rio: José Olympio.

———. 1970. *Grande Sertão—romanzo.* Trans., note, and glossary Edoardo Bizzarri. Milan: Feltrinelli.

———. 1973. *Seleta.* Ed. and org. Paulo Rónai. Series: Brasil Moço. No. 10. Rio: José Olympio.

———. 1986. See 1956b.

Rosa, Noel. 1992. *Songbook.* Lumiar Discos.

Rulfo, Juan. 1953. *El llano en llamas.* Mexico City: Fondo de Cultura Economica.

———. 1959. *Pedro Páramo.* Trans. Lysander Kemp. New York: Grove.

———. 1967. *The Burning Plain and Other Stories.* Trans and intro. George D. Schade. Austin: University of Texas.

———. 1971. Interview with Alberto Cienfuegos. *Jornal do Brasil,* 25 Sep.

———. 1981. *Pedro Paramo.* Mexico City: Fondo de Cultura Economica.

Sarmiento, Domingo Faustino. 1982. *Facundo.* Havana: Casa de las Americas.

Schelling, Vivian. 1988. "Mario de Andrade and Paulo Freire: Two 'Primitive' Intellectuals." *Bulletin of Hispanic Studies.* (Jan), 65, 1: 73–86.

Schlesinger, Tom. 1963. "Brazilian Bandit Reminisces." *The Virginia Pilot.* 19 March.

Sperber, Suzi Frankl. 1982. *Guimarães Rosa, signo e sentimento.* São Paulo: Editora Atica.

Vallejo, Cesar. 1992. *España, aparta de mi este cáliz.* Eds. Juan Larrea, Felipe D. Obarrio, and Juan Manuel Obarrio. Madrid: Ediciones de la Torre.

Vargas Llosa, Mario. 1965. *La casa verde.* Barcelona: Seix Barral.

———. 1984. *Historia de Mayta.* Barcelona: Seix Barral.

———. 1991. *La guerra del fin del mundo.* Ed. Jose Miguel Oviedo. Caracas, Venezuela: Biblioteca Ayacucho.

———. 1993. *Lituma en los Andes.* Chile: Paneta.

Veloso, Caetano. 1979. "Menino do Rio." *Cinema Transcendental.* Polygram/Verve.

Verga, Giovanni. 1920. *Cavalleria rusticana ed altre novelle.* Milan: Treves.

Verlangieri, Valeria Rodriguez. 1993. "João Guimarães Rosa—Correspondência Inédita com a Tradutora Norteamericana Harriet de Onís." Masters thesis, Universidade Estadual de São Paulo, Araraquara.

Vincent, Jon. 1978. *João Guimarães Rosa.* Twayne's World Author Series. Boston: Twayne.

Waterman, A.E. 1963. "Brazilian Novel Reflects Greatness in Awe, Terror." *The Atlanta Journal* 4 April: 44.

Wheildon, Leonard. 1963. "A Sweeping New Wave from Brazil." (Unidentified newspaper source). Archivo João Guimarães Rosa, University of São Paulo.

Wilson, Jason. 1989. *An A to Z of modern Latin American literature in English translation*. London: Institute of Latin American Studies.

Zola, Emile. 1880. *Nana*. Paris: Charpentier.

Index

Academia Brasileira de Letras, 28,42
Afro-Brazilian: 12, 24, 29, 93, 98, 99, 136; in theory of Gilberto Freyre, 160–65, 168–72; in racial democracy, 165–68; and popular culture in Rio, 172–75; and Rio carnaval, 182–84, 190–92; and Bahian carnaval, 196–99; and Tropicalism, 205–8; and subjective national identity, 213–21; 188, 224, 233, 240, 242, 248
Afro-centric, 12, 18, 99, 149, 166, 189, 196–202, 207–8, 212, 217–18, 225, 230–32, 248
Alencar, Jose de, 23–26; Iracema, 23, 171
Amado, Jorge, 16, 17, 18, 21, 22, 28, 43, 44, 117, 118, 121, 126, 130, 148, 153, 154, 155, 156, 221, 238, 245, 246, 247; Overview of life and work, 90–109; earlier works, 'proletarian novel', 90–93; Gabriela (character) and the Utopian vision, 93–98; Gabriela compared to Macunaíma, 93, 95; miscegenation and Gilberto Freyre in Gabriela, 96; mythic symbolism in Gabriela, 96; deviation from orthodox Marxism in later work, 94, 96, 97, 102, 103; solidarity through populism, 103–9 compatability with dominant cultural imagery, 229–36; Tenda dos Milagres and mature theory of miscegenation, 98–103
—Individual Works discussed: ciclo do cacau novels, 90, 230; Cacau, 108; Dona Flor e Seus Dois Maridos, 97, 104–8,140, 143, 230, 233, 235, 236; Gabriela, 90, 93–98,117, 126; Jubiabá, 90, 93, 139, 140, 231, 232, 236; O País do Carnavál, 90, 91, 140, 144, 233, 235; Tenda dos Milagres, 98–103, 230, 231, 235, 236; Tereza Batista. 91, 97, 137, 231, 236; Tieta do Agreste, 107
—Reception, 133–46. international and domestic popularity, 133–36; Brazilian academia, 136–42; status in popular Bahian society, 142–46
Ameripole, 42, 222
Andrade, Carlos Drummond de. See Drummond
Andrade, Mário de. See Mário de Andrade
Andrade, Oswald de. See Oswald de Andrade
Anglo-Saxon, 23, 39, 115, 141, 186; philistinism, 23
anthropophagy: reverse anthropophagy in Amado's Tenda dos Milagres, 102, 227
anxiety of influence, 17
axé music, 223
Azevedo, Aluízio, 24, 42; O Cortiço, 173–75

Bahia, 12, 16, 18, 22, 43, 135, 136, 139, 149, 167, 191, 192, 215, 220, 223, 224, 226, 229, 230, 232, 233, 234, 240, 242, 248; evoked in work of Jorge Amado, 90–110; place of Jorge Amado in Bahian culture, 142–46; carnaval of Salvador, 193–203; musical production, 207–11.
baiana, 24; semiotic complexity, 166–67, 173, 191, 197, 198; appopriation and Carmen Miranda, 224–25
Bakhtin, 146, 183, 185, 188, 189, 192
Balzac, 44
Bastide, Roger, 136, 247
Black Orpheus, 181
blocos afro, in Bahian carnaval, 195–200, 208–9, 248
Boom (Spanish American), 15, 17, 18, 21, 22; character compared to Brazil-

257

ian literature, 34–40, 43, 115, 117, 128, 133–34; international dissemination, 150–55; 222, 234–35, 239, 243, 245, 247, 248
Borges, Jorge Luis, 32, 71, 116, 146, 150, 151, 152, 153, 155, 239, 243, 244, 247
Bossa Nova, 126, 181–82, 185, 205, 206, 207
brasileiridade, 35
Brazilian Academy of Letters. *See* Academia Brasileira de Letras
Brazilian Literature, enigma of minimal international dissemination, 11–21; historical development, 21–44; before Modernismo, 23–27; geracao de '45, 29–33; political variations in Brazilian Modernism, 28–29; international academic reception and MLA database, 146–50; international reception compared to Spanish American literature, 150–57; incompatible with dominant imagery, 223–29, 240–41
brincar, 187, 194
Buarque, Chico. *See* Chico Buarque
Buñuel, Luis, 35

caboclo, 24, 160, 171, 215, 220, 223, 239, 248
Cabral—João Cabral de Melo Neto, 29, 30; Morte e Vida Severina, 31–32
Caetano Veloso, 179, 206–10, 224; "Menino do Rio," 179–81
café society (Rio de Janeiro), 26, 174
cafuz, 223
Caldwell, Prof. Helen, 130, 131
Caliban, 23, 39, 214, 235
Campos, Augusto and/or Haroldo de, 47, 49, 57, 113, 207
Candomblé, 93, 98, 99, 135, 145, 166, 167, 168, 191, 198, 199, 200, 215, 226; prominence in dominant cultural identity, 229–33, 235
Carmen Miranda, 17, 215, 224, 225
Carnaval, 11, 12, 14, 16, 17, 18, 81, 99, 106, 137, 140, 166, 167, 175, 176, 231, 233, 235, 240, 241, 242, 248; of Rio, 182–93; of Salvador (Bahia), 193–203; and Tropicalism, 207–9; 210, 212; intimate link with Afro-Brazilian ethnicity, 213–15; and racial democracy and black aesthetic inflection, 216–25.
Carpentier, Alejo, 21, 35, 39, 41, 117, 150, 151, 152, 153, 155, 234, 240, 245
Casa de las Américas (journal), 37, 38, 133
Cassiano Ricardo, 28
Catholicism, 28, 89, 98, 162, 163, 166, 205, 229
Cervantes, 128
Chico Buarque, 205
communism, communist(s), 28, 33, 35, 37, 44, 89, 134, 135, 138, 143, 144, 152
Cortázar, Julio, 37, 38, 115, 116, 146, 147, 150, 151, 152, 153, 154, 155, 234
Cruz e Souza, Joao de, 27
Cuban Revolution, 36

Da Cunha, Euclides, 18, 43; critique by Gilberto Freyre, 158–65; 171; Os Sertões, 43, 158, 159, 160; incompatability with dominant cultural imagery, 216–19, 223, 243
Da Matta, Roberto, 18, 197, 202, 224, 225, 226, 233, 242, 243, 248; theorization of Rio carnaval, 182–93; Rio carnaval compared to Mardi Gras of New Orleans, 186–88; testing his theory on Salvador carnaval, 196–202
Darío, Ruben, 22, 23, 27, 39, 40, 41, 43, 150
Darwinian, 24, 173, 174, 199, 206, 227, 238
Dissertations Abstracts International, 146, 152, 247
Dostoyevsky, 32
Drummond—Carlos Drummond de Andrade, 16, 17, 21, 34, 43, 71, 77, 128, 134, 142, 143, 146, 147, 148, 153, 156, 226, 246; overview of life and work, 82–90
—Themes: scepticism, 83; theme of anti-hero, 85; existentialism over nationalism, 86–88; political engagement, 88–89.
—Works discussed: "Segredo," 83; "José," 85; Lição de Coisas, 86; "A máquina do mundo," 86; "A Palavra

INDEX 259

e a terra", 87; "Brasão," 88–9. International reception, 132–33.
Duarte, Eduardo Assis, 136

escolas-de-samba, 183, 184, 187, 188, 189, 191, 192, 200
essentialism, essentialist, 15, 17, 21, 22, 32, 34, 35, 39, 40, 41, 43, 44, 82, 89, 102, 159, 160, 168, 169, 213, 224, 226, 227, 228, 229, 233, 234, 235, 238, 240, 243
eurocentrism, eurocentric, 12, 14, 16, 18, 22, 26, 29, 33, 77, 92, 98, 102, 129, 138, 158, 164, 166, 168, 169, 172, 173, 198, 199, 202, 203, 206, 213, 219, 225, 226, 229, 236, 241

fascism, fascist, 17, 28, 34, 42, 170, 189, 206
Faulkner, William, 42, 146, 151, 238, 239, 245
Flaubert, Gustave, 73, 147
folklore, 12, 29, 49, 51, 52, 53, 60, 77, 170, 238
football (soccer), 137, 177, 204, 214
frevo, 187, 189, 207
Freyre, Gilberto, 17, 18, 81, 96, 114, 117, 158, 201, 214, 216–19, 223, 225, 226, 227, 230, 232, 233, 234, 243, 248; account of miscegenation and Brazilian cultural identity, 159–72; analysis of Euclides da Cunha, 159–65; and racial democracy, 165–68; regional ethnocentrism, 168–72
Fuentes, Carlos, 37, 39, 41, 114, 115, 147, 150, 152, 153, 154, 155, 234, 235, 245

Galvão, Walnice Nogueira, 137, 247
García Márquez, Gabriel, 17, 25, 37, 38, 41, 115, 134, 146, 150, 151, 152, 153, 154, 155, 156, 234, 235, 243, 245; Cien años de soledad 37, 38, 234, 235
geracao de '45, 29–33; 34, 40, 41, 42, 159
Gil, Gilberto, 206, 207, 208, 209, 210
Gledson, Prof. John: on Machado de Assis, 74
Graciliano Ramos, 28, 49, 72, 138, 226, 229, 230

Guimarães Rosa, Joao. *See* Rosa, João Guimarães
hispanidad, 40

Holanda, Sérgio Buarque de, 18, 169
Homo brasiliensis, 43, 78, 101, 160, 163, 165, 217, 220
Hopkins, Gerald Manley, 30
Huidobro, Vicente, 27, 41
Hulet, Prof. Claude, 120, 247

Ilê Ayê, 200, 208, 225
imaginaire, 102, 196, 233, 238, 240
indianism, 26, 171
Itapoan, 224

Jobim, Antonio Carlos "Corcovado," 181–82; 205

Knopf, Alfred A., 116, 117, 119, 122, 125, 127, 153, 154, 156

Lima, Jorge de, 29
Lima Barreto, 26–27, 173, 174; *O triste fim de Policarpo Quaresma*, 27, 173
Lins, Álvaro, 112, 137, 139, 140, 247
Lins do Rego, Jose, 227
Lispector, Clarice, 15, 29, 30, 31, 72, 147, 226, 239, 244, 247; *A hora da estrela*, 31
litoral, 162, 169, 171, 219, 227, 233
London, 36, 79, 154, 206
Longfellow, Henry Wadsworth, 14

Machado de Assis, Joaquim Maria, 16, 17, 21, 25, 26, 32, 42, 48, 114, 133, 134, 142, 146, 147, 148, 153, 154, 156, 162, 173, 246; life and work, 71–76; comparisons with non-Brazilian writers, 75–76; international reception, 128–31; compared to Chekhov, 76.
—Works discussed: *Quincas Borba*, 72; *Dom Casmurro*, 42, 73–75, 130, 156; *Memorial de Aires*, 73, 130
malandro, 176, 179, 182, 187, 188, 220
Mallarmé, Stephane, 76, 113
Mário de Andrade, 16, 17, 21, 40, 42, 43, 71, 72, 128, 134, 142, 143, 146, 148, 149, 153, 156, 169, 203, 218, 219, 228, 246, 248; changing views of

Modernismo, 33–34; life and work, 76–82: as an intellectual leader, 76–78; evocations of São Paulo, 78–79; international reception, 131–32.
—Works discussed: *Macunaíma*, 80–82; *A Paulicéia Desvairada*, 78
Martins, Prof. Wilson: on Sagarana, 110
Marxism, Marxist, 17, 28, 35, 38, 103, 136, 138, 139, 150, 212, 230, 232, 233, 236
Menotti del Picchia, 28
métropole, 42, 115, 222, 243
Meyer-Clason, Kurt, 121, 246
Milton, John, 14, 236, 238
Minas Gerais, 23, 31, 45, 46, 47, 48, 49, 51, 52, 61, 62, 82, 83, 85, 86, 88, 112, 127, 143, 175, 190, 205, 212, 226, 242, 243, 245
Miranda, Carmen. *See* Carmen Miranda
miscegenation, 17, 43, 149, 163, 169, 170, 172, 219, 225, 232, 233, 236. *See also* Freyre and Amado
Modern Language Association (article database), 146, 152
modernism, 111, 132, 137, 138, 149, 150, 158, 159, 165, 168, 169, 201, 203, 204, 205, 211, 217, 218, 219, 229, 230, 236, 238, 239, 244; Brazilian Modernismo vs. Spanish American vanguardismo, 21–45; 66, 71, 75; and Mário de Andrade, 76–81; and Drummond, 82–88
Moisés, Prof. Massaud, 29, 60, 71, 72, 228, 244
Monegal, Prof. Emir Rodríguez, 116, 127
MPB (Música Popular Brasileira), 205, 207, 210
mulata, 101, 179, 213, 215, 220, 244
mulato, 24, 171, 172, 198, 215, 219, 239, 242, 244
Music: as central in Brazilian cultural identity, 203–5; differences of cultural identification according to region and genre, 205–13; modernism and Villa-Lobos, 203–4; and Tropicalism, 206–7; Bahian, 207–10; música sertaneja, 163, 211–13, 223
musicarnaval, 217, 219, 220

nativismo (Spanish American), 41
naturalism, 25, 129, 136
Nazi, 15
negritude, 136, 148, 166, 213
negro-mestiço, 164, 172, 183, 196, 197, 198, 199, 200, 201, 216, 217, 218, 248
Neruda, Pablo, 35, 44, 88, 127, 152, 155, 234, 236, 247
Nobel Prize, 38, 115, 127, 143
Noel Rosa. 176–79. "João Ninguém," 176–77; "Conversa de Botequim," 178–79

Olinda, 189
Olodum, 194, 200, 209, 210, 225, 233
Onís, Harriet de, 117, 118, 119, 122, 246
Oswald de Andrade, 27, 28, 35, 41, 42, 43, 77, 114, 169, 218, 219, 227, 228, 244

Paraguayan War, 25
Paris, Parisian, 22, 23, 25, 27, 32, 34, 35, 36, 37, 39, 40, 41, 42, 44, 47, 92, 103, 135, 115, 127, 150, 151, 169, 175, 191, 201, 203, 234, 245; "Paris-centric," 23, 34, 40, 234
Paz, Octavio, 21, 35, 36, 133, 151, 152, 154, 155; "El laberinto de la soledad," 39; "La búsqueda del presente", 39
Pelourinho, 144, 145, 146, 210, 231, 233
Poe, Edgar Allan, 14
Ponge, Francis, 30
Popul-Vuh, 13
popular culture, 15, 21, 22, 77, 104, 108, 134, 145, 158, 173, 177, 190, 203, 215, 217, 221, 223, 225, 234
populism, 18, 136, 138, 223, 236
Portella, Eduardo, 136, 247
Portugal, 42, 45, 97, 141, 171, 242
Prado, Paulo, 81, 169, 170
Proust, Proustian, 26, 60, 71, 152

racial democracy, 163, 199, 213, 216, 218, 226
Recife, 31, 189, 223
Recôncavo (da Bahia), 12, 191, 207, 208, 210, 215, 220, 223, 226, 229, 230, 232, 233, 240
Rio de Janeiro, 11, 12, 14, 16, 17, 18, 22, 23, 26, 28, 42, 45, 46, 47, 48, 68,

69, 71, 72, 74, 75, 78, 82, 86, 91, 104, 115, 121, 127, 129, 135, 138, 144, 147, 165, 167, 193, 194, 196, 198, 199, 200, 201, 202, 203, 204, 205, 207, 208, 209, 210, 211, 214, 215, 216, 217, 220, 223, 224, 225, 226, 233, 240, 242, 243, 246, 247, 248; singularity in nineteenth century, 24–25; as dominant aesthetic reference, 172–82; evocation by Caetano Veloso, 179–81; evocation in Bossa Nova, 181–82; evocation in samba of 1930s, 176–79; history of Rio carnaval, 182–85; social symbolism of carnaval by Roberto Da Matta, 185–93

Rodó, Jose Enrique, 23, 27, 39, 40, 43
Romanticism, 25, 128, 230
Rosa, João Guimarães, 15, 16, 17, 18, 21, 29, 30, 31, 32, 41, 42, 43, 72, 86, 131, 134, 142, 143, 146, 147, 148, 153, 156, 226, 236, 237, 238, 239, 240, 245, 246, 247; Overview, 48–49; Sagarana, 49–51; Corpo de Baile, 51–61; Early works—Stylistic analysis, 57–61; Grande Sertão: Veredas, 61–71. Sagarana: "O Burrinho Pedrês," 49; "São Marcos", 50; 'A Hora e a Vez de Augusto Matraga', 50; other references: 47, 48, 61, 110, 111, 112, 117, 119, 122, 127, 246. Corpo de Baile: structure of "romances" and "contos", 52; "Campo Geral", 52; "Cara-de-Bronze", "Cara-de-Bronze", 55–57; Corpo de Baile re-named in later editions, 52; Manuelzão e Miguilim, 52; No Urubùquaquà, no Pinhém, 52; Noites do Sertão, 52; other references 47, 62, 66, 70, 112, 127, 247. Grande Sertão: Veredas: plot, 61–65; narrative analysis, 65–71; ; other references 18, 43, 48, 50, 142, 143, 246; English translation (The Devil to Pay in the Backlands), 116–28, 156, 246. Other works: "Com o Vaqueiro Mariano", 47; Magma. 49, 110; Primeiras Estórias, 48; Terceiras Estórias, 48; Tutaméia, 48

—Themes and specific issues: overview of life and work, 45–71; Biography, 45–48; flora and fauna, 47, 49, 51, 53; linguistic and stylistic analysis 57–61

—Domestic reception; translation and international reception, 110–28; Domestic acclaim as of Grande Sertão: Veredas, 114; International academic, 114–16; broader international audience, 116–28. Translation into English and American reception, 116–21; english version of Grande Sertão: Veredas, 116–20; interaction of Rosa and American translator, 122–24; involvment of U.S. publisher Alfred Knopf, 119; marketing support, 126; French reception, 128; German translation and reception, 122

Rosa, Noel. *See* Noel Rosa

Salgado, Plínio, 28
samba, 188, 194, 205, 214
samba canção, 176, 179, 181, 182, 185, 204, 211
samba carioca, 224
Santiago, Silviano, 137
São Paulo, 25, 31, 42, 45, 46, 48, 76, 77, 78, 79, 80, 82, 90, 99, 104, 113, 131, 132, 135, 138, 142, 143, 144, 164, 165, 168, 169, 170, 174, 175, 190, 191, 198, 206, 207, 209, 211, 212, 213, 219, 220, 223, 224, 226, 227, 230, 242, 243, 244, 246, 247, 248. *See also* Mário de Andrade.
Sarduy, Severo, 133
Sarmiento, Domingo Faustino, 23, 43
Sartre, Jean-Paul, 77, 85, 92, 135
Semana de Arte Moderna, 27, 76, 82, 203
sertanejo, 23, 161, 165, 169, 171, 212, 216, 219, 223, 226
sertão, 18, 43, 48, 50, 52, 58, 61, 64, 66, 68, 70, 71, 142, 143, 159, 160, 161, 162, 163, 169, 171, 175, 205, 211, 212, 213, 215, 218, 219, 220, 223, 226, 227, 229, 237, 242, 246, 248
soccer. *See* football
socioanthropology, 15, 17, 18, 21, 22, 38, 43, 158, 159, 202, 223, 224, 225, 226, 228, 229, 233, 234, 236, 240, 243, 248

Socialist realism under soviet doctrine, 103, 246
Spain, 23, 31, 40, 115
Spanish America(n), 11, 13, 15, 16, 17, 18, 21, 22, 23, 25, 26, 27, 28, 34, 35, 36, 37, 38, 39, 40, 41, 42, 43, 44, 114, 115, 116, 117, 127, 128, 133, 134, 149, 158, 170, 174, 221, 222, 233, 234, 235, 239, 243, 244, 245, 247, 248
Spanish American literature: modernismo, 22–23; vanguardismo 27, 34, 39, 150, 151; vanguardismo as parallel to Brazilian Modernismo, 27; political Leftist orthodoxy in Twentieth Century, 35–36; unity of Boom writers, 36–38; theme of Dystopia in Boom, 38–40; international reception (el Boom), 150–55
Spanish Civil War, 17, 35, 42, 88, 151, 234, 239
Spanish-American War, 17, 23
Steinbeck, John, 32, 148
surrealism, 27, 35

Taylor, Prof. James L., 117, 118, 119
theses, 11, 124, 132, 152, 231, 246, 247; distribution of theses at U.S.P. on Brazilian writers, 141–42
Tolstoy, 32, 128, 146
Tristão de Ataíde, 29

Tropicalism(o), 18, 81, 142, 206, 208, 209, 224

Umbanda, 191, 199, 226
Utopia(n), 15, 17, 18, 42, 43, 93, 95, 96, 149, 163, 164, 181, 200, 206, 214, 217, 235, 240, 241, 247
Utopia-Dystopia: as contrasting tendencies in Brazilian and Spanish American literatures, 38–40

Vallejo, Cesar: *España, aparte de mi este cáliz*, 36
vanguardism(o). *See* Spanish American literature
Vargas, Getúlio. Vargas, 31, 164, 170, 176, 183, 189, 190, 204, 216, 217, 218
Vargas Llosa, Mario, 150, 152, 153, 154, 155, 234, 245
Veloso, Caetano. *See* Caetano Veloso
Verde-Amarelo movement, 28, 33, 227, 228
Verga, Giovanni, 49
Verlaine, 22
Villa-Lobos, 203, 204, 205
Vincent, Prof. Jon., 52, 58, 114
Vinícius de Moraes, 181, 205, 224

World War I, 23, 26, 27, 34, 71
World War II, 36, 42, 88, 127, 200, 201